Thinking with Soils

Also available from Bloomsbury:

Anthropologies and Futures, edited by Juan Francisco Salazar, Sarah Pink,
Andrew Irving, Johannes Sjöberg
Organic Food, Farming and Culture, edited by Janet Chrzan, Jacqueline Ricotta
Italian Food Activism in Urban Sardinia, Carole Counihan

Thinking with Soils

Material Politics and Social Theory

Edited by
Juan Francisco Salazar, Céline Granjou, Matthew Kearnes,
Anna Krzywoszynska, and Manuel Tironi

BLOOMSBURY ACADEMIC
LONDON • NEW YORK • OXFORD • NEW DELHI • SYDNEY

BLOOMSBURY ACADEMIC
Bloomsbury Publishing Plc
50 Bedford Square, London, WC1B 3DP, UK
1385 Broadway, New York, NY 10018, USA
29 Earlsfort Terrace, Dublin 2, Ireland

BLOOMSBURY, BLOOMSBURY ACADEMIC and the Diana logo are trademarks of
Bloomsbury Publishing Plc

First published in Great Britain 2020
This paperback edition published in 2022

Copyright © Juan Francisco Salazar, Céline Granjou,
Matthew Kearnes, Anna Krzywoszynska and Manuel Tironi and contributors, 2020

Juan Francisco Salazar, Céline Granjou, Matthew Kearnes, Anna Krzywoszynska and
Manuel Tironi have asserted their rights under the Copyright, Designs and Patents Act,
1988, to be identified as Editors of this work.

Cover Design by Ben Anslow
Cover image: The curb erosion from storms showing the layers of
soil and rock © NOPPHARAT689/Shutterstock

Bloomsbury Publishing Plc does not have any control over, or responsibility for, any
third-party websites referred to or in this book. All internet addresses given in this book
were correct at the time of going to press. The author and publisher regret any
inconvenience caused if addresses have changed or sites have ceased to exist, but can
accept no responsibility for any such changes.

A catalog record for this book is available from the Library of Congress.

Library of Congress Control Number: 2020939746

ISBN: HB: 978-1-3501-0957-5
         PB: 978-0-5677-0652-2
         ePDF: 978-1-3501-0958-2
         eBook: 978-1-3501-0959-9

Typeset by RefineCatch Limited, Bungay, Suffolk

To find out more about our authors and books visit www.bloomsbury.com
and sign up for our newsletters.

Contents

List of Figures

Notes on Contributors

Steve Banwart is the Director of the Global Food and Environment Institute, University of Leeds. His core science expertise is basic chemistry that is also applied to the study of soil systems and natural waters. He champions integrating research into Earth's Critical Zone, the surface layer of the planet from bedrock to atmospheric boundary layer that provides humans with most of their life-sustaining resources. He has published extensively on soil functions within the Critical Zone.

Filippo Bertoni obtained his PhD from Amsterdam University, focusing on earthworms and their scientists. Currently, he is a researcher at the Museum fur Naturkunde, in Berlin, where he investigates the transformation of animals into objects and data across the city's natural history collections and zoological gardens. Embracing an undisciplined approach, the stories he gathers play with genres, styles, and media at the edges of imaginative fiction and various forms of academic writing. Animating the tension between reality, science, and (science) fiction, these stories resist the universalizing push of Western modernity, opening up to the multiplicity of worlds already around us.

David Blacker is a third-generation arable farmer and contractor working in the Vale of York in England. Since 2013, he has been experimenting with using strip-tillage methods. He has become a spokesman for sustainable soil management, and has discussed his experiences in multiple press articles and at farming conferences.

Klaus Dodds is Professor of Geopolitics and Director of Research for the School of Life Sciences and Environment at Royal Holloway University of London. He researches in the areas of geopolitics and security, media/popular culture, ice studies and the international governance of the Antarctic and the Arctic. He has worked for the UK Parliament as specialist adviser to a House of Lords Select Committee on the Arctic and the House of Commons Environment Audit Committee. He is co-author with Mark Nuttall of *The Arctic: What Everyone Needs to Know* (Oxford University Press, 2019). He has been a recipient of a Major Research Fellowship from the Leverhulme Trust 2017–2020 for a project on the Global Arctic. He is a Fellow of the Academy of Social Sciences in the UK.

Salvatore Engel-Di Mauro is Professor at the Geography Department of SUNY New Paltz, He works on soil degradation, urban soils, trace element contamination, ideologies on soils, and socialism and environment. He has also published on critical geographies, the European Union, ethnopedology, Indigenous Peoples' struggles, and pedagogy. He is chief editor of *Capitalism Nature Socialism*. His recent teaching subjects include physical geography, gender and environment, people–environment relations, and soils.

Céline Granjou is a Senior Researcher in Environmental Sociology at the French Research Institute for Environment and Agriculture (IRSTEA), University of Grenoble Alps, and research fellow at the Interdisciplinary Laboratory on Science Innovation and Society (LSIS) in Paris. She has a background in Science and Technology Studies, Political Sociology, and Environmental Sociology. Her current research interests include health and environmental risks, nature conservation policies, biodiversity politics, climate governance, anticipation studies, environmental humanities, soil and human–soil relationships.

Nicholas C. Kawa is an Assistant Professor of Anthropology and a core faculty member of the Initiative for Food and Agricultural Transformation (InFACT) at The Ohio State University (USA). His research centers on questions of human–environment interaction with specific emphasis on human relationships to plants and soils, particularly in the Amazon region. Currently, he is developing a new project that investigates the production, application, and management of "biosolids" (treated sanitation sludge) in American agriculture. He is the former President of the Culture and Agriculture Section of the American Anthropological Association (AAA).

Matthew Kearnes is an Associate Professor and member of the Environment and Society Research Group at the School of Humanities and Languages, University of New South Wales. He also currently services as a CI with the ARC Centre of Excellence in Convergent Bio-Nano Science & Technology (CBNS, 2014–2021) and was an ARC Future Fellow between 2014 and 2018. Matthew's research is focused on the social and political dimensions of technological and environmental change, with current projects exploring regenerative agriculture and carbon farming, and is situated between the fields of Science and Technology Studies (STS) and Human Geography. His most recent book is the co-edited volume with Jason Chilvers, *Remaking Participation: Science, Environment and Emergent Publics* (Routledge, 2016). Matthew is an associate editor for *Science as Culture* (Taylor & Francis) and serves on the editorial board of *Science, Technology and Society* (Sage).

Lindsay Kelley is Senior Lecturer at UNSW Sydney in the Faculty of Art & Design as well as Honorary Research Fellow, Department of Gender and Cultural Studies, the School of Philosophical and Historical Enquiry, the Faculty of Arts and Social Sciences, in association with Sydney Environment Institute, the University of Sydney. Working in the kitchen, her art practice and scholarship explore how the experience of eating changes when technologies are being eaten. Her published work can be found in journals including *parallax*, *Transgender Studies Quarterly*, *Angelaki*, and *Environmental Humanities*. Her first book is *Bioart Kitchen: Art, Feminism and Technoscience* (IB Tauris, 2016). She is the recipient of an Australian Research Council Discovery Early Career Researcher Award.

Juliette Kon Kam King is a PhD candidate in Human Geography at the French National Research Institute for Sustainable Development and at the Leibniz Centre for Tropical Marine Research. Having a background in Science and Technology Studies, she has worked on soil–society relationships in the French context and currently focuses on ocean governance and marine conservation issues in the South Pacific.

Anna Krzywoszynska is a Faculty Research Fellow at the Department of Geography, the University of Sheffield, and an Associate Director at the University of Sheffield Institute for Sustainable Food. Her work investigates how environmental knowledges and ethics are made, communicated, and contested in spaces of food production. She is currently fascinated by soils and their publics, and she has published on soil ethics, sustainable soil management communities of practice, and soil non-human labor. She is the founder and coordinator of the Soil Care Network (soilcarenetwork.com), which brings scholars and practitioners from across disciplines and geographies together around soil issues.

Germain Meulemans is an anthropologist interested in the environment, creativity, and perception. After receiving his PhD from the Universities of Aberdeen and Liège in 2017, he joined the Centre Alexandre Koyré (EHESS, CNRS, MNHN) in Paris as an IFRIS postdoctoral fellow. His current research focuses on the increasing concerns for urban soils in the soil sciences and urban planning, and on the ontological implications of working with anthropogenic environments for the natural and social sciences. He has collaborated with artists on several art-research projects bearing on soils and sustainability, and is a founding member of the Chaoïds collective.

Maria Puig de la Bellacasa is an Associate Professor at the Centre for Interdisciplinary Methodologies, University of Warwick. She works at the crossing of science and technology studies, feminist theory and the environmental humanities. Her most recent book *Matters of Care: Speculative Ethics in More than Human Worlds* (University of Minnesota Press, 2017) connects a feminist materialist tradition of critical thinking on care with debates on more than human ontologies and ecological practices. She is currently researching the formations of novel ecological cultures around human–soil relations, looking at how connections between scientific knowing, social and community movements, as well as art interventions are contributing to transformative ethics, politics, and justice in troubled naturecultural worlds.

Lauren Rickards is an Associate Professor in the School of Global, Urban, and Social Studies at RMIT University in Melbourne, Australia. A human geographer with a science background, her research is situated at the interface of climate change and agriculture. Lauren is a Lead Author with the forthcoming Sixth Assessment Report of the Intergovernmental Panel on Climate Change, an Earth Systems Governance Senior Fellow of Future Earth, and convener of the Institute of Australian Geographers' Nature, Risk and Resilience study group.

Juan Francisco Salazar is Professor at the School of Humanities and Communication Arts and at the Institute for Culture and Society (ICS), Western Sydney University. He is an anthropologist and documentary filmmaker with interests in Indigenous media, community-based adaptation to climate change, social-ecological transitions, futures, and art–science collaborations. His recent work focuses on Antarctica and outer space. His latest book is the co-edited volume with Sarah Pink, Andrew Irving, and Johannes Sjøberg, *Anthropologies and Futures* (Bloomsbury, 2017). His most recent films are *Nightfall on Gaia* (2015) and *The Bamboo Bridge* (2019), a collaboration with economic geographer Katherine Gibson.

Manuel Tironi is an Associate Professor and co-convener of the Critical Studies on the Anthropocene group (antropoceno.co) at Universidad Católica de Chile. He is a principal investigator at the Center for Integrated Research on Disaster Risk Reduction (CIGIDEN). His work leverages the environmental humanities, cultural anthropology, and science studies to investigate how environmental justice, more-than-human ethics, and the politics of the non-living are imagined and articulated in the context of climate change. Working with Indigenous communities in northern Chile, his current project examines alternative theories and practices for ecological reparation at the intersection of extractivism and geo-climatic disruptions.

Levi Van Sant is a human geographer and Assistant Professor in the School of Integrative Studies at George Mason University. His work examines US environmental politics, particularly issues surrounding food, agriculture, and land conservation. He is currently developing a collaborative research project that examines the politics of soil surveys, asking: What assumptions inform them, and how are these technologies used to shape our social and ecological landscapes? Ultimately, this project aims to democratize knowledge about soils and develop soil surveys that are useful for the needs of food sovereignty and environmental justice movements.

Acknowledgments

This book was inspired by the confluence of many people across a number of sites in Australia, Chile, France, and the UK and through many conversations over several years which coalesced around the Knowledge/Culture/Ecologies International Conference held in Santiago, Chile, in November 2017.

In this book, we have aimed to bridge a gap that we think continues to characterize debates about soils today. While the changing nature of our relationship with soils starts to affect multiple arenas, there is still little dialogue between academics and practitioners, and between those in the humanities, social sciences, and the natural sciences. To secure a future for us and for soils, more conversations and encounters are needed. This book aims to open a space for such meetings.

We wish to thank Maria Puig de la Bellacasa for providing an inspiring preamble to the book. Our deep gratitude also goes to all the contributors who worked with us in the development of this collective volume and for their generous time and thought-provoking chapters.

Our sincere thanks also go to our academic editor Mona-Lynn Courteau for her expert and caring editing, copyediting and proofreading services for all the chapters. We also acknowledge the research funders who diversely contributed to the genesis of the book. These include: Labex ITEM in France; the Institute for Culture and Society at Western Sydney University, the Australian Research Council, and the Faculty of Arts and Social Sciences at the University of New South Wales; and the Research Center for Integrated Disaster Risk Management and the Millennium Research Nucleus on Energy and Society in Chile. Lastly, we wish to thank Bloomsbury's editorial team for their support of our project, especially Miriam Cantwell, Commissioning Editor at the time of Anthropology and Food Studies, and Lucy Carroll, Assistant Editor, Anthropology, Food Studies, and Religious Studies.

Foreword

When Soils Liven Up: The Renewal of Human–Soil Imaginaries

I don't know about you, but I have spent most of my life without giving a thought to the soil I walk upon. As such, I am humbled to be invited to write this Foreword. If you are like me, a relative newcomer to the worlds of soil, I suspect that by the end of reading the rich and inspiring material gathered in this book, you will become much more attentive to the intricacies of soil matters. If you already love soils, there is much in this book that could intensify your commitment, even if it makes it a little more complicated.

I didn't think of the soils below when strolling in the countryside or walking through meadows, on the soft forest ground, looking at the trees and flowers that grew there. Not even the sight of denuded and eroded mountains in the lands of my childhood in central Spain made me aware of the plight of soils. Soil was not in my mind even when eating "*Soil* Association"-approved organic foods. And I definitely never considered the soil sealed under the pavement. It was only during activist training on permaculture systems of ecological design that included elements of soil science and soil care that I came to realize how vital soils are and became interested in learning more about them. I became fascinated by their material and living properties, by both their mystery and how soil scientists study them, as well as the relations humans have historically had with them including the diverse cultural and spiritual meanings different peoples give to them.

As this interest came to be a research adventure around ten years ago, I quickly realized that I was joining a broad movement of people for whom the soil had passed from being a passive background easy to neglect to a matter of collective care. The research and interventions collected in this book manifest how this increased interest in soils is permeating further the realms of the social sciences and the humanities, helping to generate new avenues for engagement, re-actualizing human–soil relations with new challenges.

Crucial for the emergence and formation of this eco-social movement are the people for whom soil is no news. Traditional experts and practitioners, such as soil scientists, growers and farmers, agricultural policy-makers, activist soil educators, and alternative practitioners have been calling for more and better attention to the soil. Their efforts have helped to make the soil more visible to different audiences—such as the UN declaring 2015 International Year of Soils. Yet, what has interested me in particular are the specific transformations in human–soil relations as this constituency of soil advocates has grown to include a range of people not considered soil's primary "stakeholders." A variety of individuals and collectives have become soil enthusiasts. Among this eco-social movement of soil advocates, stories of soil discovery abound. A new ecological culture around soils is in the making, blending old and new material concepts, aesthetics, affections, and ethical signification of soils, nurturing soil stories that both rely on, and exceed, traditional meanings such as those intertwined with agriculture.

In this context, I have found it helpful to think of soil as a living infrastructure—a *bioinfrastructure*. Susan Leigh Star told us that when infrastructure works well, it is only perceptible to professionals and maintainers: it becomes a matter for others when it doesn't work well. And indeed, the background story of this surge of care for soils is a global soil crisis with dire consequences for the survival of humanity and other life inhabiting ecosystems affected by soil degradation and pollution. The news has reached mainstream media, with headlines declaring that "We are Treating Soil Like Dirt," or that "Humanity is Eating Itself." Unsustainable soil practices are not new, but they have attained devastating planetary proportions.

It is now the case that soils not only have their experts and practitioners, but a "people" that speaks *for* them. An implicit assumption of soil advocacy is that making soils more appealing and more interesting will motivate people to want to understand and thus care more. There is also an emphasis on highlighting soil's ecological significance *beyond human use* – whether this is agricultural or other. Many examples of changes in soil practices and imaginaries attest to this. Soils are captivating too. A wonderful world to think about, to inspire eco-poetic meanings and wordings. And so soil advocates have concentrated much effort in communicating our "mud love" by sharing lively stories about this natural medium, attempting to counter its use as a resource and encourage ways of caring that cultivate affectionate and ethical forms of more than human kinship. An important part of this work has been to reveal that soil is alive; more, an animated matrix of relations that challenges the biophysical distinction between inert passive matter and living organism. In the past 15 years, the living soil— or living dirt—has become a primary signifier of soil materiality, as well as its conceptual, aesthetic, and ethical representation, passing from marginal eco-social soil advocacy to a central public and cultural perception. Another correlated vision is the integration of human practices as a participant in the making and maintenance of a flourishing more-than-human soil community, rather than as users or exploiters of its produce or services.

And yet, if it were simply the case that knowing that something that is alive is suffering would protect it from abuse, our world would be a very different place. Soil's visibility today is not only something soil advocates and enthusiasts need to encourage, we also need to scrutinize with care, in situated ways, what happens as soil becomes more visible.

At the very beginning of my own personal journey of soil discovery, I came across a piece by artist Claire Pentecost that marked me, and that poses a beautiful challenge for soil advocates. Pentecost's piece seems simple. She molded large blocks of soil into the recognizable shape that is gold ingots, a strong symbol of wealth and investment value, and piled them up on a table in an exhibition space. This exhibit immediately made visible the ambivalence shown toward soil's material and cultural value in these times. Yet, this is not so simple. On the one hand, as Pentecost provocatively argued, soil ingots are a vision of "a new system of value based on living soil, a form of currency that anyone can create by composting"; on the other hand, they also crudely expose what can happen when soil comes to be seen as precious, a new gold. As soils are becoming poorer, more exhausted, scarcer, their status as a coveted resource exposes and increases their vulnerability.

There is nothing new, however, about this. Since the beginnings of agriculture, maybe before, humans have understood their dependence on and connection to the ground they stood upon. Attesting to this today are the many languages in which the word for ground/soil is both homonymous to, yet distinct from, earth with a capital "E." Soils are both inseparable from their environment and a special manifestation of matter. Humans have seen themselves as both entangled with (i.e. grounded in) and separate from (i.e. transcending) the ground they stand upon. Soil is both a resource and a worshipped entity. Origin and end—and origin again. Not surprisingly, there is a strong lure in soil imaginaries to generate conciliatory stories of human (re)grounding, *down to earth*. Because as many worlds as there are on Earth, most depend, in some way, for their nurture on this thin layer of earth.

So, what kinds of people of the soil is this wave of soil interest nurturing in different places, and what fertile or damaging (or both) ambivalences might new ways of inhabiting soils be reproducing? These are questions that our stories need to answer both critically and speculatively. Critically, because this entails becoming involved with how, in specific times and locales, soil keeps becoming visible and claimed as a "thing." That is, ontologically a distinctive entity, to be cherished, but also re-colonized and exploited. And speculatively, because our alternative stories are only as powerful as they recognize impure connections to trends that we might not endorse. How could we affect the worlds we want to change if we consider ourselves untouched by them?

It seems to me that this is what the interdisciplinary interventions in this book are inviting us to do, combining and deepening research thinking with, from, and *for* soils. At the meeting of the social sciences and humanities, they bring to bear on the reinvention of soil imaginaries and practices insights from fields that are radically revisiting human relations with non-human entities—such as critical animal studies, feminist science, technology studies and the environmental humanities—while remaining in tune with radical political analysis (e.g. from political ecology and critical geography). Calling for new ways to address soil's troubles and ambivalences, the interdisciplinary work presented in this book re-actualizes human–soil relations, exploring how we can think and live in radically diverse, but interconnected more-than-human present and future worlds.

This book nurtures (my) hopes that, as soil imaginaries are returning to nurture stories of *more than human material* belonging to earth-as-ground as much as to Earth-as-Planet, meanings of soil can be configured otherwise. Today's return to soil is no *return to Nature*. It is vital to encourage more than human ethico-political involvement in healing the troubled grounds of a *naturecultural* earth in disarray. And while it is clear that scientific and technological knowledge and practices are crucial in contemporary re-configurations of human–soil relations, traditional techno-scientific conceptions of soils are not driving these transformations. It is to the extent that they are mobilized and transformed within new conceptual, aesthetic, ethical, and indeed spiritual re-tellings of soil that human–soil relations across fields contribute to renewed ecological imaginaries. Reading the thinking with, from, and for soils in this volume, I feel the vital companionship of a diverse community committed to re-telling stories that not only critically expand the imagination of possible human–soil relations, but do so in a supportive and caring way, nurturing the collective making of more hopeful ecological imaginaries and practices.

Maria Puig de la Bellacasa

1

Thinking-with Soils: An Introduction

Juan Francisco Salazar, Céline Granjou, Anna Krzywoszynska,
Manuel Tironi, and Matthew Kearnes

Origins

The geneses of this book go back to two parallel encounters. First, the international workshop "Going to Ground," convened in October 2016 in Sydney by Matthew Kearnes, with Céline Granjou and Juan Francisco Salazar, which was designed as an opportunity to think both creatively and earnestly about the dirt we live on and off. The workshop brought together many of the contributors in this book to discuss how soil conservation and improvement practices are being marshaled in response to concerns over climate change, food security, and rural livelihoods, and how these might be indicative of the deep connections between soil and social processes. Second, the book also has its beginnings in a series of panels at the Knowledge/Culture/Ecologies International Conference held in Santiago, Chile, in November 2017, convened by Juan Francisco Salazar and Céline Granjou, where all five co-editors outlined the initial analytical coordinates for this book. These panels also served as a catalyst to start a broader interdisciplinary discussion that had been brewing, and which we see as having been largely initiated by Maria Puig de la Bellacasa through her pioneering work in recent years. This discussion aimed to engage scholars from not only the humanities and social sciences but also the ecological and soil sciences, as well as soil practitioners, particularly those proponents of integrative science frameworks and social-ecological systems thinking. A premise of these conference panels was that, despite notable contemporary reconceptualizations of soil as a matter of care and concern, it is striking to observe how soil, and its manifold entanglements with plants, fungi, bacteria, and other forms of life, remains largely undertheorized or ignored in contemporary social theory. Despite soil's vital ecological importance, its significance as a belowground three-dimensional living world remains elusive in social and cultural research. This book is about developing work that is attuned and attentive to generating more ethical relations with nonhumans who both pervade and create livable environments, such as soil biota (Krzywoszynska 2019).

Figure 1.1 Coonawarra, Australia. Image: Charles G [https://unsplash.com/photos/WO7rUJFaJwQ].

Crisis in the Critical Zone

Historically, critical attention from the social sciences to soils had been predominantly limited to understanding and explaining their role as resources underpinning food production under systems of intensive agriculture in contexts of ongoing capitalist expansion and colonialism. As the vast majority of human food is still derived directly from soils, it is arresting to think that as much as several tons of topsoil are lost for every ton of grain produced. The scale and severity of soil degradation has been highlighted by the natural science community for decades and is indicative of a much broader breakdown of soils as "bioinfrastructures" (Puig de la Bellacasa 2014). Soils are that vital layer, the so-called "critical zone" (Ashley 1998) that involves all the complex interactions connecting rock, soil, water, air, and living organisms that regulate life-sustaining resources. The critical zone enables all the processes that make the terrestrial surface of the globe habitable for humans, plants, animals, fungi and their millions of diverse life forms. That soils are a non-renewable resource in human timescales makes the degradation of this "life support system" even more alarming. Pedogenesis (soil creation) usually occurs at timescales well beyond many human generations.

With this new integrative critical zone paradigm, the natural sciences are positioning soils on the front line of global environmental change and a final frontier of environmental research. Scientists insist on a very critical matter of concern: soil security during what is considered to be a global soil crisis (Koch et al. 2013). As Koch et al. put it, "soil security is a new concept that has arisen during a time of emerging international response to the increasingly urgent problems that face the global soil stock" (2013: 434).

Nearly all terrestrial life, including humans, depends on this critical zone underpinned by geosocial formations linking the Earth's surface processes and geosystems with human practices both ancient and contemporary. Changes in the planet's biogeochemical flows (phosphorus and nitrogen cycles) point to the important role played by soils as a key planetary boundary and for thinking-with about what Will Steffen and others have termed "safe operating zones for humanity" (Steffen et al. 2015). The natural science community has in many ways taken the lead in and set the tone for the urgency of what is frequently referred to as the "global soil crisis." Natural scientists have been leading the charge in raising the alarm about the degradation of soils worldwide and in attempting to address this problem, primarily by seeking to influence policymakers. Their efforts have in recent years led to the publishing of influential reports, the most cited of which is the United Nations' Food and Agricultural Organization's (FAO) 2015 *Status of the World's Soil Resources Report* (SWSR), prepared by the Intergovernmental Technical Panel on Soils (ITPS). The report, which included the assessment of more than 200 environmental scientists of the state of knowledge on soil resources and soil change, was launched in December 2015, simultaneously with the opening for signatures of the Paris Agreement, which entered into force on November 4, 2016. The report's overwhelming conclusion was that most of the world's soil resources are in only fair, poor, or very poor condition. Since then, a series of new reports have shown that since the 1970s nearly two billion hectares of soil—equivalent to 15% of the Earth's land area (an area almost twice the size of Australia)—have been degraded through human activities (FAO 2015).

In this increasingly heard narrative, the running out of topsoil is one of the most serious global threats facing humanity this century, with some scientists estimating that at current rates of soil degradation there could be no more than 60 years of topsoil left (Crawford 2012). Global soil degradation is being linked to "human pressures" on soils, which are said to have reached a pace and intensity that is unprecedented, particularly since the "Great Acceleration" in the 1950s (Steffen et al. 2015). The specter of soil collapse becomes a haunting narrative that "raises concerns marked by fears of gloomy environmental futures, prompting scientists and soil practitioners urgently to develop better ways of taking care of soils" (Puig de la Bellacasa 2015: 691). As Puig de la Bellacasa notes, "in contrast with visions of exhausted soils prey to a voracious humanity eating its nest, transformative involvements with soil's aliveness assert the ecological significance of human–soil interdependency and disrupt persistent binaries between living and inert, species and belonging, the earthly and the spiritual, endurance and breakdown, the cosmic and the domestic, knowledge and mystery" (2017: 63). This is important to point out. In conversations with farmers, for example, Anna Krzywoszynska explains how this "alarmist" narrative about soils is seen very much as "a scientific thing," not connected with the lived experience of farm managers.

While the symptoms are being increasingly better described, diagnosing the causes of the crisis, and imagining ways forward, is proving challenging. The aforementioned FAO report identifies increases in human population, urbanization, education, and social equity, changes in cultural values, as well as "land market failure," unsustainable consumption, war and civil strife, and climate change as some of the key human drivers of soil degradation. Policies, research, and education are seen in the report as the primary mechanisms for acting on these drivers. Existing policy approaches to the management of soils are proving to be inadequate in dealing with the double "nature" of soils as both public goods and private property (Bartkowski et al. 2018). This is leading increasingly to arguments for a greater valuation of soils as natural capital (Davies 2017) and/or environmental services (Bouma 2014), in line with the predominant market-led and technocratic logics of environmental governance in the Global North.

On the other hand, the rise of soil ecology has been relying on the development of soil DNA analysis techniques since the mid 2000s—leading to rising hopes for deciphering soil's genetic "text" (as for instance through the TerraGenome consortium implemented in 2009, modeled on the Human Genome Project), as well as for post-Pasteurian perspectives of prospecting and enhancing underground microbial activities, including using microbes as new lively models for understanding, controlling, and improving global environmental resilience in an era of climate change (Granjou and Phillips 2018; Cavicchioli et al. 2019). Soil biota are not only reimagined as a new site of promissory bio-economical hopes; they are also enrolled in emergent technoscientific expectations of reforming society through fostering "bio-literacy"—i.e., the awareness of the critical and multifarious roles played by microbes, including soil microbes, in the environment—including through a recent call by a panel of microbial ecologists to introduce microbiology fundamentals at preschool (Timmis et al. 2019).

The Dithering: Soils, Humanities, the Anthropocene

Characterizations of the Anthropocene as a human-inflicted distinct geological epoch proliferate: the Anthropocene as aftermath (of capitalism and late liberalism); the Anthropocene as the disaster to end all disasters; the Anthropocene as transition. As these multiple interpretations suggest, it is difficult to theorize an epoch of this magnitude while it is still unfolding. As "the crease of time" (Dibley 2012) and an instance of transition, the Anthropocene has also been described in an original way. In the novel *2312* (2012), US science fiction writer and cultural theorist Kim Stanley Robinson develops a fictional character, Charlotte, a historian who establishes a periodization from the early twenty-first to the early twenty-fourth centuries. She terms the period from 2005 to 2060 "the Dithering." To dither is to be unable to decide about doing something. Robinson mobilizes this concept as a way of accounting for our current epoch as "a state of indecisive agitation" over climate change, and the failure to preempt what came next: the 2060 to 2130 period known as the Crisis (Robinson 2012: 144–45; see also Haraway 2015).

We invoke Robinson's term here to qualify these times of perplexity, where humanity —or rather, its political leaders and economic elites—find themselves dithering, but also to illustrate what Bruno Latour (2018: 40) terms a "reorientation of the site of politics" toward the terrestrial. In part, Latour's argument in *Down to Earth: Politics in the New Climatic Regime* (2018) is that we need a new term for this new "attractor" that might be able to encompass "the stupefying originality (the stupefying longevity) of this agent." For Latour, "the Terrestrial, with a capital T" is emphasized "as a new political actor" (2018: 40).

Soils are a perfect companion to recognize the complex blend of sociopolitical predicaments and physico-material negotiations of planetary "boundary conditions" and "safe operating spaces," which are not only indicative of the need for new ethical engagements but also suggestive of a new kind of "geologic politics."

This book is an attempt to shake up shared assumptions about what it may mean to be "grounded." In it, we seek to burrow into the ground and get our ideas dirtied by soil's multiplicity, complexity, and uncertainty. By contemplating down under our feet, we note the connectivities that exist and emerge between the above- and belowground, and we chart the consequences of this connecting (rather than connection) for the changing understanding of both soils and humans. This is best captured by Latour, who summed it up in his fervent call for an urgent down-to-earth politics: "the very notion of soil is changing" (2018: 4). As Latour observes, "we are beginning to feel the ground slip away beneath our feet [and we] are discovering, more or less obscurely, that we are all in migration toward territories yet to be rediscovered and reoccupied" (2018: 5).

Latour's is yet another call for a shift, not upwards or downwards, but sideways; within and athwart a broader ecology that outlines politics as that which leads toward the earth, which grounds us and gives us a place to land somewhere beyond the master modernist narratives of the global or the national. Vandana Shiva (2009) has enlightened this position in a convincing way in calling for a sustained transition "from oil to soil" as a fundamental question of environmental justice in a time of climate crisis where agroecology principles underpin, as Arturo Escobar (2018) argues, a rejuvenation of biodiversity-based organic food and energy systems operating on the basis of grassroots democracy, local economies, and the preservation of soils and ecological integrity.

The aim running through this book is to illustrate the value and significance of thinking with soil, through its material politics, its practices of care, its recalcitrant ontopolitics. As Maria Puig de la Bellacasa observes: "thinking Earth as soil involves more ordinary aspects of human relations with earthly forces" (2017: 63). The book offers a range of perspectives from a diversity of disciplines and inter-disciplines that are reconsidering both the engagement with and outlook of soils as animate and not as inert. This reassessing is crucial to offer a shift in understandings of soils and ways for reorienting an ethics of caring for soil and its life forms. The volume therefore represents a comprehensive effort to contribute to a more systematic and materially sensitive social theory of soil, which we outline more schematically in Chapter 2. Bringing into dialogue theoretical and empirical contributions and case studies across several regions and disciplines, it aims to unsettle ongoing ingrained perceptions of soil as inert to cultivate novel understandings and assessments of how beings—human and otherwise—engage with soils and are affected by soil in everyday practices. Ultimately, the book is designed as an opportunity to think both creatively and earnestly, not only about the dirt we live on but the soil we are part of and the liveliness of belowground worlds.

As we attempted to signal in the previous section, soil science scholars are not the only ones of course who have taken a lead in setting the tone of a climate emergency and increasingly dangerous tipping points regarding the breakpoint of soils. As a diverse scholarship in feminist theory and science and technology studies has shown, scientific practices affect and are affected by questions of ethics, politics, and justice in the formation of those sociotechnical imaginaries (Mol 2002; Jasanoff 2004) enacted by technoscientific intervention. Critical attention to soil is still scarce in the humanities and social sciences compared with work by soil scientists and Indigenous and rural social movements. This is a significant and surprising gap, considering that all terrestrial life on Earth depends upon soil, from microorganisms to plants and animals. Soil ecologists put it bluntly: "Many, if not most, of the ecosystems on Earth are dependent on, or substantially influenced by, interactions and processes occurring within and among the planet's soils" (Eisenhauer et al. 2017: 2). And yet, until very recently, looking under our feet was a truly niche occupation in the social sciences, associated almost exclusively with certain facets of political ecology and rural studies. While there is a significant body of literature concerned with understanding and improving human–soil interactions so as to maximize the use of soils as productive resources or to better protect them as objects of conservation, "the ontological status of soils as a 'natural thing' remains a relatively settled matter in the social sciences" (Krzywoszynska 2019: 3). Indeed, as we argue in the following chapter, this curious *un-theorization* of soil might be understood as an outcome of the ontological politics of soil, whereby soil is presented as essential for the life of *other* (normally human) beings whilst being figured as a kind of residue produced by, or left behind after, both human and nonhuman use.

This is an exciting time to consider soil and soil futures, a time when humans are being recognized as a central force in global environmental change whilst also being subject to overwhelming socio-natural challenges. Soils are crucial living systems, fundamental to the functioning of the biosphere and to all terrestrial life: they filter water, store carbon, and are the foundation of the food system. Soils host a diversity of microbial communities that provide key functions for environmental resilience. A healthy soil is a living soil: a dynamic belowground ecosystem that is crucial for plant, animal, and human wellbeing. The significance of the problems we address in this book is stark: no soil, no life.

In this volume, we build on emerging work in the social sciences, humanities, and arts to invite scholars across disciplines to think-with soils, and not only to think about them. Through this program of thinking-with, we argue that the concerns and hopes around soils today call for more than an extension of conservation and care into the belowground. Rather, we engage with soils not as preexistent but as emergent, not as static and separate but as dynamic and connected with human action in a multiplicity of ways.

What, then, do we understand by "thinking-with soils"? To some extent, this book responds to the stark predicament identified in the natural sciences: no soil, no life. Animated by the distress call from the natural sciences, we see caring for soil as an animate force of life becoming a global imperative. While recognizing the urgency of the situation, we also, however, wish to recognize the equally urgent need to slow down the reasoning about the future shape of human–soil relations, and to make space, time, and power for different awareness of the problems and situations mobilizing us (Stengers 2005). Thinking-with here means both critically examining the current framings, discourses, and practices that make soils think-able for individuals and organizations, and making time and space for alternative ways of thinking soils and for soil-related action to emerge. While we are fully supportive of the fantastic work being done by our natural science colleagues, we wish to assert with equal authority the need to resist the urge to leap to solutions to problems which are, we show in this volume, often ill-defined and fluid. As Latour argues, the paralysis of action in the face of the most fundamental and existential challenge humanity has experienced—the climate breakdown (which is intimately connected with the soil crisis in more ways than one)—is not caused by a lack of connectivity between those in charge of the diagnosis (scientists) and those in charge of the healing (policymakers). Rather, what this paralysis indicates is that the assumptions that we share about a common world can no longer be upheld; there is no universal Human, no universal Science, and no universal World that we all share. Stengers (2017) proposes that we think of this upheaval as the arrival of Gaia, whose intrusion into our seemingly stable realities is shaking the epistemological and ontological foundations of what it means to be human, and of what it means to inhabit the Earth. As Blok and Jensen write: "Contrary to theatres of political adjudication, where people have a chance to justify their actions, accepting the reality of Gaia means accepting that we are now living in a realm of non-negotiable yet largely indeterminate demands, and that if we fail to respond adequately, our cries will not be heard" (2019: 12). What does this lack of a common world and Gaia's intrusion mean for the futures of human–soil relations? It means that their future shape is yet to be discovered—and not dictated. It means that the futures of humans and soils are yet to be built, and to be built by many communities who seek to orient themselves in a world of both social and ecological change. It is in this process of rethinking and rebuilding that we wish to participate through this volume.

Our project of thinking-with is also based on an assumption about a deep connectivity between humans and soils. While deeply depleted and degraded through a range of industrial and agricultural practices that have become prevalent for several decades, soils are also being remade, manufactured, and healed through myriads of mundane practices of gardening and composting that strive to recreate the conditions for plant growth and life flourishing in the ruins of capitalist ways of life. Whereas many enquiries into soils continue to unfold without exploring this connectivity, there has been a shift in soil sciences toward a recognition of humans as soil-forming and soil-destroying agents. Indeed, humans have been recognized as the sixth element in soil formation (Dudal 2005). Soil scientists are now far more likely to acknowledge the existence of "anthropogenic soils" and a medley of ways in which human forces and actions intersect with soil creation and destruction (Meulemans 2020). These might include farming practices such as terracing, soil manipulation such as the addition of organic matter, the introduction of new parent materials, soil disturbance such as deep ploughing and digging activities, terrain manipulation, and surface change such as forest clearance and deliberate drainage.

Whereas these perspectives maintain the traditional separation between humans and soils as "society" and "nature" respectively, the emerging literature around soils in the social sciences and humanities shares a dedication to blurring these boundaries and exploring different forms of human–soil relationality. We thus align ourselves here with the relational materiality approach to soils proposed by Krzywoszynska and Marchesi, who call for soil researchers to "acknowledge symmetrically the emergent biophysical agency of soil ecosystems, their sociocultural constitution, and the dynamic interactions between those factors" (Krzywoszynska and Marchesi 2020). The relational materiality approach to soils requires an attentiveness to the relations from within which particular conceptualizations and practices of soils emerge—soils' ontological politics (Mol 1999). Without hampering the acknowldgment of the differentiated distribution of powers between humans and soils, including the recognition of a specific sociohistorical responsibility in matters of soil depletion and degradation (Malm 2018), we see this collection as contributing to the important unmaking of soils as a "natural matter," to the description and valorization of existing multiple soil relational materialities and their entanglements with humans and nonhumans, and to the critical, postcolonial, speculative, and participatory remaking of soils to support the "ongoingness" of terrestrial life.

In the project of thinking-with soils, we welcome the recognition within the natural sciences of the interdisciplinary nature of soils, and the need for collaboration between epistemic and practice communities in creating better soil futures (Bouma 2015; Brevik et al. 2015). At the same time, we see the role of soils scholars and practitioners in the social sciences, arts, and humanities as much more than commentators on the societal importance of the "soil facts" established within the natural sciences, or the communicators of science-derived messages. Indeed, we agree with Engel-Di Mauro (2014) that better soil futures require attending to relations of power, and not infrequently to their relations with capital accumulation, as inherent to both soil research and soil action. We want to propose grounded insights into recent advances of soil research and technologies considered as unique forms of engagement with the living soil and the characteristics and activities of underground living communities. As we seek to literally find our feet in the new realities of a climate-broken world, soil research in all disciplines needs to take seriously the social context of scientific work, strive for political awareness, and become explicit about political commitments (Engel-Di Mauro 2020).

Contributions

This book includes contributions from a range of scholars in anthropology, human geography, environmental sociology, and cultural theory, which together develop an account of the conflicting regimes of anticipation of the futures of living and lived soils and issues of the material politics of soil. The chapters in this edited volume challenge us to attend more carefully to the ways in which we think-with soil, both materially and theoretically. While some of the chapters call for new ways of thinking about the politics of caring for soils as crucial living systems fundamental to the functioning of the biosphere and to all terrestrial life, others render visible the ecological and symbiotic relations between soils and their mineral, animal, and vegetable companions. The book invites practices for cultivating the arts of attention and attunement to belowground worlds teeming with microbial life and phytogenetic vitality, and to speculative ethics of care to understand how landscapes work and how species, including the human, come into ways of life through soils. It opens debates on how the productive capacities and contested governance of soils are deployed as matters of political concern across different knowledge practices while reflecting on, acknowledging, and embracing Indigenous ways of knowing/being with soil.

Chapter 2, "Soil Theories: Relational, Decolonial, Inhuman," is our attempt to set a program of research in social studies and cultural research on soils. In this chapter, we first address what we term the "un-theorization" of soil in the human and social sciences for most of the twentieth century. We propose that the invisibility of soil in contemporary social and political theory can be traced back to a range of sociohistorical separations that have transformed soil into a taken-for-granted, invisible infrastructure for modern cities, agriculture, and markets, as raw matter or a resource separate from society and emerging only as its residue—that which is left behind in post-apocalyptic narratives of the end of civilization as we know it. Then we delve into the shifting, heterogeneous, vertical layering of soil to explore instead how soil and society are assembled together; we thus suggest the generativity of "thinking with soil" for decentering social and political theory from the Anthropos, and for decolonizing narratives of conservation that we briefly touched on in this chapter, including an attentiveness to land, nature, and the geological, in order to develop better and more responsible attunements to socioecological entanglements in a time of ecological crisis. As we detail in Chapter 2, we propose four theoretical sensibilities through which to engage with soils and as a way of relating with the generative capacities of the more-than-human: assembling soils; the elemental ecologies of soil; inhumanness: earthly politics; and decolonizing soils. We take these sensibilities not as discrete conceptual containers but as a highly interconnected web of theoretical gestures and political moves that invoke multiple questions, practices, actions, and things.

In Chapter 3, "Mapping Soil, Losing Ground? Politics of Soil Mapping," Juliette Kon Kam King and Céline Granjou document the evolution of soil mapping since the 1960s at the French National Institute of Research on Agriculture (INRA). They account for the shift from soil surveying initiatives to the rise of soil digital mapping projects, including monitoring, modeling, and predicting soil quantitative properties, such as carbon content, at the global scale. The authors suggest that, as computer scientists reconceptualize soil as the underground part of the global environment monitored by earth system models and global change sciences, soil as a local and situated object of study and concern for pedologists tends to be lost from sight.

In Chapter 4, "Soils and Commodification," Salvatore Engel-Di Mauro and Levi Van Sant develop a critical approach to the economic valuation of soil in light of the Marxist theory of value. The authors recall that the economic value of natural entities does not, and cannot, rely on nature itself; instead, this value is always constructed or perceived by people through social relations of appropriation, expropriation, and domination. While soil is currently sold under a variety of guises—from land tenure to pot mixes—its appropriation and trade are in fact superimposed over and destructive of local socioecological interconnectedness and rural livelihoods. Thus, the notion that soil itself provides society with "ecosystem services" with an intrinsic economic value partakes in capitalist delusion.

In Chapter 5, "Knowing Earth, Knowing Soil: Epistemological Work and the Political Aesthetics of Regenerative Agriculture," Matthew Kearnes and Lauren Rickards work with the epistemological and aesthetic bricolage of regenerative agricultural practices designed to restore soil functionality and organic carbon content. Exploring the ways in which regenerative agriculture evokes a material form of biomimicry, what Kearnes and Rickards term an "assemblage of technoscientific, biochemical, and geo-aesthetic forces," they document the ways in which carbon-farming practices enroll both agrarian symbolism and calculative assessments in marking out a political terrain for visualizing alternative climatic futures. They close by calling for a recognition of the "hybrid epistemological work" necessary to craft a progressive land ethic in the context of climatic change.

In Chapter 6, "To Know, to Dwell, to Care: Towards an Actionable, Place-based Knowledge of Soils," Anna Krzywoszynska co-authors a contribution with a farmer, David Blacker, and a soil scientist, Steve Banwart. Bringing into dialogue David's practical, agronomic experiments in soil testing and observation with insights from critical zone sciences, the authors argue for a re-situating of human–soil relations as foundational to dwelling, that is to humans' knowledgeable action in places. The authors emphasize the need to break with the surface approach to soils, and to uncover their deep, dynamic, and interconnected natures through place-specific inquiries. Situating land users as participants in critical zone processes, the authors call for conceptual and practical tools which would "empower dwellers to become better dwellers" by bringing deep and dynamic soils into their practices of sensing and sense-making.

In Chapter 7, "Soiling Mars: 'To Boldly Grow Where No Plant Has Grown Before?,'" Filippo Bertoni presents an ongoing experiment conducted in a leading agricultural research center in the Netherlands aiming to develop future Martian agriculture through experimenting with earthworms. Bertoni unpacks the functionalist biogeochemical understandings of earth and Earth and the technoscientific efforts to "make a universal and unitary cosmos" at work in the experiment. He calls for developing alternative stories and analytics, and proposes a logic of *soiling* that would allow for situating soils, worms, and planets in specific histories and "destabilizing ongoing colonial and capitalist legacies of modern versions of the world."

In Chapter 8, "Geosocial Polar Futures and the Material Geopolitics of Frozen Soils," Juan Francisco Salazar and Klaus Dodds focus on a specific type of soil, the frozen soil of polar regions, and unpack the entangled socioecological histories of soil, ice, and people in the Arctic and Antarctica. While Arctic permafrost thaw is threatening local socioecologies, whose highest vulnerability to climate change is still denied by the US government, Antarctic soil attracts rising interest for biodiversity bioprospecting, including rare plants and bacteria adapted to the cold. Through focusing on the polar regions, Salazar and Dodds unpack the enrolment of soil in contrasting projects and expectations of socioenvironmental management, exploitation, and redemption in a time of ecological crisis.

In Chapter 9, "A Mend to the Metabolic Rift? The Promises (and Potential Pitfalls) of Biosolids Application on American Soils," Nicholas C. Kawa addresses current industrial initiatives of using sewage sludge to fertilize agricultural fields in the United

States. His contribution looks at both the hopes and critics surrounding the use of shit by the biosolids industry to grow crops, including fears related to toxic residues and contamination risks. He highlights the ambiguities of the industrial logics of upgrading waste, which seek to bridge the metabolic rift by developing a profitable trade.

In Chapter 10, "Reclaiming Freak Soils: From Conquering to Journeying with Urban Soils," Germain Meulemans tells the story of urban gardeners who have been growing soil and recreating a garden in a Paris wasteland through experimentation with compost materials and weeds. Through describing the everyday skills and efforts deployed by gardeners in order to manufacture soil and grow plants in this abandoned part of the capital city, Meulemans unsettles the connection of soil to place, and suggests the need to better acknowledge the value of mundane practices of soil reclaiming—far from the dominant and destructive industrial approaches to soil grabbing to provide for urban engineering needs.

In Chapter 11, "Soil Refusal: Thinking Earthly Matters as Radical Alterity," Manuel Tironi refers us to his decade-long work on soil–plant–human relations in Puchuncaví, a small rural area in central Chile. Tironi invites readers into the garden of Olivia, who establishes deep ethico-practical commitments with plants and soils in a context of chronic industrial violence, and in the way these human–soil–plant embroilments allow for a politics of intimate resistance. For Tironi, these are moments in which soils, in close proximity to plants, chemicals, and animals (human and otherwise), emerge as radical alterity—as a sovereign Other not fully amenable to relationality. Tironi calls this "soil refusal" to indicate situations of human–soil encounters in which the form and content of the encounter itself are alien to what "encounter" is supposed to be and do.

In Chapter 12, "Geophagiac: Art, Food, Dirt," Lindsay Kelley addresses art practices of eating soil or clay/dirt, called geophagy. To unsettle the clinical gaze that pathologizes geophagy, she recalls that clay and soil appear in a wide range of diets, from food supplements to diarrhea medicine and infants' tasting experiments. Kelley develops a critical stance to the racist colonial structures through which soil eating has been only seen in terms of a deviance to be found in underdeveloped, starving peoples and slaves of past centuries. Instead, she proposes a reading of geophagy "as socioculturally meaningful in multiple ways, with soil ingested as food, as miracle and medicine, and as protest," delving into three case studies: a land art exhibition, a collective religious ritual, and a historical mass slave protest.

This is a book to think and feel with all the human and nonhuman critters enveloped by and within soils. As Donna Haraway has eloquently put it:

> It matters what we use to think other matters with; it matters what stories we tell to tell other stories with; it matters what knots knot knots, what thoughts think thoughts, what descriptions describe descriptions, what ties tie ties. It matters what stories make worlds, what worlds make stories.
>
> Haraway 2016: 12

We invite readers to engage with these chapters as stories of soils so far. Stories of soils that make worlds, in this period of dithering, where sites of soily politics are more needed than ever. A return to dirt. A new terrestrial, grounded, geologic politics.

References

Ashley, G. M. (1998), "Where are We Headed? 'Soft' Rock Research into the New Millennium," *Geological Society of America Abstract Program*, 30 (7): A-148.

Bartkowski, B., B. Hansjürgens, S. Möckel, and S. Bartke (2018), "Institutional Economics of Agricultural Soil Ecosystem Services," *Sustainability*, 10 (7): 2447 [https://doi.org/10.3390/su10072447].

Blok, A. and C. B. Jensen (2019), "The Anthropocene Event in Social Theory: On Ways of Problematizing Nonhuman Materiality Differently," *The Sociological Review*, 67 (6): 1195–1211.

Bouma, J. (2014), "Soil Science Contributions Towards Sustainable Development Goals and Their Implementation: Linking Soil Functions with Ecosystem Services," *Journal of Plant Nutrition and Soil Science*, 177 (2): 111–20.

Bouma, J. (2015), "Reaching Out from the Soil-Box in Pursuit of Soil Security," *Soil Science and Plant Nutrition*, 61 (4): 556–65.

Brevik, E. C., A. Cerdà, J. Mataix-Solera, L. Pereg, J. N. Quinton, J. Six et al. (2015), "The Interdisciplinary Nature of *SOIL*," *SOIL*, 1: 117–29.

Cavicchioli, R., W. J. Ripple, K. N. Timmis, F. Azam, L. R. Bakken, M. Baylis et al. (2019), "Scientists' Warning to Humanity: Microorganisms and Climate Change," *Nature Reviews Microbiology*, 17: 569–86 [https://www.nature.com/articles/s41579-019-0222-5].

Crawford, J. (2012), "What If the World's Soil Runs Out?," *TIME*, December 14 [http://world.time.com/2012/12/14/what-if-the-worlds-soil-runs-out; accessed March 1, 2019].

Davies, J. (2017), "The Business Case for Soil," *Nature*, 543 (7645): 309–11.

Dibley, B. (2012), "'The Shape of Things to Come': Seven Theses on the Anthropocene and Attachment," *Australian Humanities Review*, 52: 139–53.

Dudal, R. (2005), "The Sixth Factor of Soil Formation," *Eurasian Soil Science C/C of Pochvovedenie*, 38: S60.

Eisenhauer, N., P. M. Antunes, A. E. Bennett, K. Birkhofer, A. Bissett, M. A. Bowker et al. (2017), "Priorities for Research in Soil Ecology," *Pedobiologia*, 63: 1–7.

Engel-Di Mauro, S. (2014), *Ecology, Soils, and the Left: An Ecosocial Approach*, New York: Palgrave Macmillan.

Engel-Di Mauro, S. (2020), "Learning Dialectics to Grow Better Soils Knowledge, not Bigger Crops: A Materialist Dialectics and Relationality for Soil Science," *Capitalism Nature Socialism*, 31 (1): 52–69.

Escobar, A. (2018), *Designs for the Pluriverse: Radical Interdependence, Autonomy, and the Making of Worlds*, Durham, NC: Duke University Press.

FAO (2015), *Status of the World's Soil Resources: Main Report*, Rome: Food and Agriculture Organization of the United Nations [http://www.fao.org/documents/card/en/c/c6814873-efc3-41db-b7d3-2081a10ede50/].

Granjou, C. and Phillips, C. (2018), "Living and Labouring Soils: Metagenomic Technologies and a New Agricultural Revolution?," *BioSocieties*, 13: 1–23.

Haraway, D. J. (2015), "Anthropocene, Capitalocene, Plantationocene, Chthulucene: Making Kin," *Environmental Humanities*, 6: 159–65.

Haraway, D. J. (2016), *Staying with the Trouble: Making Kin in the Chthulucene*, Durham, NC: Duke University Press.

Jasanoff, S. (2004), *States of Knowledge: The Co-production of Science and the Social Order*, Abingdon: Routledge.

Koch, A., A. McBratney, M. Adams, D. Field, R. Hill, J. Crawford et al. 2013. "Soil Security: Solving the Global Soil Crisis," *Global Policy*, 4 (4): 434–41.

Krzywoszynska, A. (2019), "Caring for Soil Life in the Anthropocene: The Role of Attentiveness in More-than-Human Ethics," *Transactions of the Institute of British Geographers*, 44 (4): 661–75.

Krzywoszynska, A. and G. Marchesi (2020), "Towards a Relational Materiality of Soils: Introduction to the Special Issue 'Conceiving Soils and Humans in the Anthropocene,'" *Environmental Humanities*.

Latour, B. (2018), *Down to Earth: Politics in the New Climatic Regime*, Cambridge: Polity Press.

Malm, A. (2018), *The Progress of This Storm: Nature and Society in a Warming World*, London: Verso.

Meulemans, G. (2020), "Urban Pedogeneses: The Making of City Soils from Hard Surfacing to the Urban Soil Sciences," *Environmental Humanities*.

Mol, A. (1999), "Ontological Politics: A Word and Some Questions," *The Sociological Review*, 47 (suppl. 1): 74–89.

Mol, A. (2002), *The Body Multiple: Ontologies in Medical Practice*, Durham, NC: Duke University Press.

Puig de la Bellacasa, M. (2014), "Encountering Bioinfrastructure: Ecological Struggles and the Sciences of Soil," *Social Epistemology*, 28 (1): 26–40.

Puig de la Bellacasa, M. (2015), "Making Time for Soil: Technoscientific Futurity and the Pace of Care," *Social Studies of Science*, 45 (5): 691–716.

Puig de la Bellacasa, M. (2017), "When the Word for World is Soil: Transforming Human-Soil Communities," *Book of Abstracts and Conference Program*, Knowledge/Culture/Ecologies (KCE) International Conference, November 15–18, 2017, Santiago de Chile.

Robinson, K. S. (2012), *2312*, New York: Orbit Books.

Shiva, V. (2009), *Soil, Not Oil: Climate Change, Peak Oil and Food Insecurity*, London: Zed Books.

Steffen, W., W. Broadgate, L. Deutsch, O. Gaffney and C. Ludwig (2015), "The Trajectory of the Anthropocene: The Great Acceleration," *The Anthropocene Review*, 2 (1): 81–98.

Stengers, I. (2005), "The Cosmopolitical Proposal," in B. Latour and P. Weibel (eds.), *Making Things Public: Atmospheres of Democracy*, 994–1003, Cambridge, MA: MIT Press.

Stengers, I. (2017), "Autonomy and the Intrusion of Gaia," *South Atlantic Quarterly*, 116 (2): 381–400.

Timmis, T., R. Cavicchioli, J. L. Garcia, B. Nogales, M. Chavarría, L. Stein et al. (2019), "The Urgent Need for Microbiology Literacy in Society," *Environmental Microbiology*, 21 (5): 1513–28.

2

Soil Theories: Relational, Decolonial, Inhuman

Manuel Tironi, Matthew Kearnes, Anna Krzywoszynska,
Céline Granjou, and Juan Francisco Salazar

Introduction

In the southern suburbs of Sydney, Australia, the rather curiously named garden supplier Soil 'n Stuff sells soil, gravel, and building supplies to gardeners, landscape designers, and builders. Soil arrives here, and is sold again, in neatly stacked and brightly colored plastic wrapping. Each package of soil is categorized for both its content—cow, chicken, and sheep manure and mushroom compost—and its function in an array of suburban gardening projects: vegetable propagation, annuals, lawn maintenance. For the more ambitious, at the back of the compound, larger quantities of soil, destined for industrial-scale uses, are organized in dark heaps, alongside various gradients of gravel, sand, and other landscaping supplies.

This scene will of course be familiar to those for whom soil is considered a commodity, divorced from its multiple and overlapping histories and from the vital forces that produced it and categorized for its productive qualities within prescribed limits. At the same time, Soil 'n Stuff raises a number of interesting questions, some ontological, some political: What is soil, and how is it different from other earthly materials—sand, gravel, manure, compost? What is soil's relationship with land and place? Is soil purely "natural" or are soils also brought into existence by sociocultural arrangements? Or, inversely, does soil have an independent existence, in and of itself, irrespective of the work of "stuff"? It is increasingly clear that soils, like "nature" in general, are never simply "out there," outside the social. But if this is the case, one question that remains is how to make sense of the resistance of soils to social determination. Soils seemingly maintain the curious ambivalence of the "'n stuff" moniker, manifest in their opacity and indifference to human fate, their recalcitrance as geochemical things and processes, and their potential to blur our most basic categories and dichotomies, such as the biotic and abiotic, the organic and the mineral, the bio- and the geo-, living and non-living "things."

Soil 'n Stuff is also the picture of abundance. The soils here are packaged in ways that distance them from the ongoing processes of soil loss, degradation, and overuse, and the intensive agricultural and industrial processes that underpin the exploitation of soils. The abundance of soils in this most prosaic and suburban context points to—

Figure 2.1 Soil n' Stuff. Local business in Sydney, Australia. Image by Matthew Kearnes.

Figure 2.2 Soil n' Stuff. Local business in Sydney, Australia. Image by Matthew Kearnes.

and yet also obscures—wider questions of how to address soil degradation and conserve soil. Soil care and conservation challenges the categories of nature conservation and activism. Soil is commonly presented as invisible, hidden under our feet, and lacking a recognizable "face." Compared with iconic animal species, such as the panda or polar bear (Yusoff 2010), soil is not easily accommodated within the representational and aesthetic registers that have constituted the eco-political narratives of endangered species conservation, and indeed of the possibility of grieving their loss (Yusoff 2012; Head 2016). As a result, soils challenge environmental ethics to cultivate new forms of attentiveness (Krzywoszynska 2019a) and an appreciation of soils' integrity as an assemblage of both process and form (O'Brien 2020)—even if these come in the shape of friction and resistance (Tironi 2019).

As a picture of sanitary cleanliness, Soil 'n Stuff also poses questions of the (potential) toxicity of soil. And if soils are messy, ungovernable, and even toxic, do they render something valuable for how politics is *defined* in the so-called Anthropocene? Perhaps soils preempt a form of politics in which object and subject do not exist in ontologically separate domains, or a way of being human that, like Indigenous peoples whose politics have always been soily, is not dependent on a strict separation between matter and thought, body and soul, humus and human (Boff 2008; Haraway 2016). Thinking with Soil 'n Stuff—and indeed with the "'n stuff" of soil—it is clear that an adequately soily social theory cannot simply reflect soils in the abstract, whilst conversely insisting that the mattering of soil is inseparable from social theory.

Diverse theoretical impulses and different conversations within the social sciences and the humanities have rendered visible different questions about soil's relationship to social life. Without trying to draw a linear history, in this chapter we propose a program for mapping out the theorization(s) of soil. We first address the un-theorization of soil—by which we mean the conspicuous non-theorization of soil—in the human and social sciences for most of the twentieth century. We propose that the invisibility of soil in contemporary social and political theory can be traced back to a range of sociohistorical separations that have transformed soil into a taken-for-granted, invisible infrastructure for modern cities, agriculture, and markets, as raw matter or a resource separate from society and emerging only as its residue—that which is left behind in post-apocalyptic narratives of the end of civilization as we know it.

We then explore the ways in which contemporary social theories have engaged with soils as both a process and a physicality to think about the human–nature nexus: theories that dwell in the shifting, heterogeneous, vertical layering of soil to explore how soil and society are assembled together—even if as divergence. We suggest that these contemporary developments are characterized by two conceptual gestures. On the one hand, they locate soils as *generated* by multifarious practices, apparatuses, and modes of attention. On the other, they take soils as *generating* publics, politics, and relations. The socialization of soils, and the soiling of the social. Taken together, these theories mobilize the generativity of "thinking with soil" for decentering social and political theory from the Anthropos, and for decolonizing narratives of conservation and attentiveness to land, nature, and the geological to develop better and more responsible attunements to socioecological entanglements in a time of ecological crisis.

Soil Separations, and the Un-theorization of Soil

Given the breadth of social-scientific analyses of contemporary environmental politics, it is striking that soil remains relatively untheorized in contemporary socio-spatial thinking. Nigel Clark suggests that "for complex historical and political reasons ... the social sciences have an inheritance of disinterest in the geologic" (2013: 2829).[1] The same might be said for soil. In Western accounts, the biblical image of God fashioning the first man from clay echoes with common understandings of soil as raw matter that is teleologically shaped and given form and meaning by people and societies—the blank page on which civilization writes its history.[2] Soil is that Nature which comes before Culture, the dark and shapeless matter offering its blank substrate to humans for their endeavors of cultivation and creation. Soil thus appears as both the seminal material—the humus—from which we humans are made and on which we live, and the final state of matter to which we return after death. Soil is that which is left over, and left after. It provides "the basic kinaesthetic experience of having our feet planted on the earth" (Clark 2011: 6) for the time of our existence.

While soil is regarded as both primary and primordial, the direct material and embodied experience of soil, dirt and mud, is commonly cast as polluting. For example, as Ogborn's (1998) history of modernist urban planning, street design, and the construction of pavements in London suggests, having feet "planted on the earth" has become an increasingly rare experience in many world cities. Indeed, modern cities function to insulate urban dwellers from an embodied and kinesthetic experience of soil, mud, and dirt. Building on Ogborn's analysis, Ingold captures the ways in which the sensual and embodied experience of soil is increasingly obscured in highly urbanized landscapes:

> No longer did [the pedestrian] have to pick [their] way, with care and dexterity, along pot-marked, cobbled or rutted thoroughfares, littered with the accumulated filth and excrement of the countless households and trades whose businesses lay along them. Dirt is the stuff of tactile (and of course, olfactory) sensation. It could trip you up, or soil your boots.
>
> 2004: 326

Indeed, this relegation of soils to the background has been central to the rise of the modern city in which separation from and the invisibility of the soil is the norm rather than the exception, and in which a responsibility for "dealing with" soils becomes attached to specific groups of experts (Meulemans 2020b). As Meulemans argues, the modernist drive to "separat[e] soil from sky [and] obtain a dry, smooth, non-slippery surface that affords easy walking and driving" is maintained "by an army of street sweepers, who, every day, actualise the 'metabolic rift' that leads us to look at urban ways as transport surfaces rather than as soils" (2017: 67).

Soil as Residue

The separation between soil and the lived experience of social life has social and ontological consequences. Indeed, one correlation of this separation, what we might think of as a relative "un-theorization" of soil, is the naturalization of a form of soil determinism which conceptualizes soil health as *essential* to human life, agricultural productivity rates, and adaptation to environmental change, whilst at the same time *essentializes* soil as outside the ambit of sociality. In this frame, soil is rendered simultaneously as an essence and as a residue, as an element that comes before and is left after the processes of exploitation.

In one of the few recent works that seek to combine critical theory with a materially sensitive account of soil and the specificities of soil science, Salvatore Engel-Di Mauro argues that when it is defined as dirt "soil becomes . . . a disruptor of hygienic norms— precisely when it is detached from itself" (2014: 2). Echoing Mary Douglas's (1966) well-known characterization of dirt as "matter out of place," Engel-Di Mauro's argument is that when soil is defined as a residue, as the "left behind" and the "under our feet," it is actively excluded from accounts of sociality, thus leading to the long-standing absence of soil from most social and political accounts.

The depiction of depleted soil as the ultimate residue of civilization, that which remains after the end of civilization as we know it, also vividly emerges from images depicting soil loss and erosion. Here, depictions of soil loss draw on a repertoire of images of the US Dust Bowl of the 1930s. Pictures of denuded agricultural landscapes and shattered communities circulated widely and became aesthetic proxy for contemporary tropes of ecological concern (Worster [1979] 2004; Bailey 2016). Soil is depicted as a figure of loss, where all that is left behind is dirt, dust, and the remnants of former farming settlements. So, images of dirt and dust constitute a post-apocalyptic trope in contemporary science fiction. For example, *The Maze Runner*—based on the young-adult novel series by James Dashner—depicts a group of young heroes as they leave their leafy and grassy labyrinth only to find that the real world has turned into a vast desert wasteland after a series of huge, unstoppable blasts of dust that have terminated any former, livable "geosocial" formation (Clark and Yusoff 2017). However, as Holleman suggests, while the iconic images of the Dust Bowl "are poignant and important reminders of the class dynamics and ecological rapaciousness of the ruling 'capitalist ethos' . . . they do not capture the broader context of the rapid expansion of colonialism and imperialism from which the international problem of soil erosion emerged" (2017: 237). In this sense, the figuring of soil as an homogeneous civilizational residue functions to obscure the specific and situated processes that condition the exploitation of soil.

Soil, Land, and Governance

The essentializing logic that has underpinned much thinking on soil has an extensive heritage in the histories of Western social and political thought, particularly in reference to the idealized relation between land and its people in the building of nation-states. Soil is commonly linked to blood, conceived of as the essence of sociohistorical identity, and presented in elemental terms as central to kinship and the construction of natural and political unity. In his recent genealogy of the birth of territory as a concept in Western legal, religious, and political thinking, Stuart Elden records that "in the myths from autochthony . . . the people are directly linked to the soil of which they are born"

(2013: 51). Perhaps the most extreme version of this determinist logic is found in the fascist projects of the mid-twentieth century. It is perhaps telling that the most systematic soil theory—that of Schmitt's ([1950] 2006) *Nomos of the Earth*—was wrapped up in the projection of a fascist spatiality. Schmitt opens this work with the striking claim that the "earth became known as the mother of law" and that "soil that is cleared and worked by human hands manifests firm lines, whereby definite divisions become apparent. Through the demarcation of fields, pastures, and forests, these lines are engraved and embedded. Through crop rotation and fallowing, they are even planted and nurtured. In these lines, the standards and rules of human cultivation of the earth become discernible" ([1950] 2006): 42). In Schmitt's account, we see what is perhaps the clearest articulation of the proposition that soil cultivation is entangled with the eugenic projects of shaping, and purifying, a national body. In his more popular writing, Schmitt outlined the political intent of this definition of soil, earth, and blood. For example, in a 1939 lecture, celebrating Hitler's assumption of power, Schmitt commented that the German *volk* are "an empirical reality determined by species and origin, blood and soil" (quoted in Hell 2009: 294).[3]

Compared with the explicitly racist and fascist ideologies of blood and soil, where soil represents a primordial grounding for a nationalist body politic, we are of course mindful of the ways in which the notion of making soils—and indeed the cultivation and improvement of soils—is also encoded by the logics of contemporary statecraft (Engel-Di Mauro 2002; Van Sant 2018), agrarian sensibilities (Hodge 2007; Guthman 2014; Lowe 2015), and implicit heteronormative discourses (Engel-Di Mauro 2006; Rickards 2006; Jacobs 2010; Bryant and Garnham 2015), and is underpinned by histories of colonial appropriation (Munro 2020). The selective recognition of some forms of cultivation practices and not others—for example, Indigenous land-management practices (Gammage 2011; Neale et al. 2019a)—has been, and continues to be, a central element of colonial projection.

This heritage is evident in the etymology of the term cultivation, which considers land improvement and agriculture as breaking with the state of nature and establishing the possibility of culture. Cultivation, from the Late Latin *cultivus* ("tilled"), is associated both with labor and with the notion of moral improvement. Indeed, Western liberalism defined soil cultivation as central to a definition of property, and thereby to the establishment of notions of political jurisdiction and the extension of these models of territorial dominance through colonialism (Arneil 1996). Here we see the links between the concepts of soil, land, and culture, where the notion of cultivation signals something of the labor of bringing the natural within the realm of the cultural and its association with concepts of religious practice and worship (cult) and geopolitical machination (colony, settlement, recognizable cultivation, *terra nullius*). In this context, it is notable that progressive projects that aim to mix "culture" with "nature" through agri-cultural improvement of soils have formed the basis of land claims and the resulting expropriation of land from "undesirable" communities, such as black farmers in the United States (Van Sant 2018). The French notion of terroir, which has become associated with fashionable gastronomic pleasures and wine degustation, also reproduces a kind of essentialization of the link between soil and the people who inhabit and cultivate it, through projections of the influence of the situated, historical savoir-faire of cultivating and manufacturing food combined with place-specific, belowground microbiota. Like with the entrenching of nationalist projects, terroir too implicates complex systems of land governance and regulation in which appropriate forms of cultivation and land rights reinforce one another (Demossier 2011).

Soil, Agriculture, and Capital

Perhaps the most significant influence on contemporary un-theorizations of soil is Marx's brief references to soil degradation in his work on social metabolism. In a memorable passage from the first volume of *Capital*, Marx argues for a structural link between soil degradation, modes of production, and the process of economic abstraction and alienation. Introducing the notion of "metabolic rift," he indicates the intimate interconnections between the "vitality of soil" and a "social metabolism" that is "prescribed by the natural laws of life." It is in these passages that Marx famously develops his analysis of the structural linkages between soil depletion and political exploitation, arguing that "capitalist production ... only develops the techniques and the degree of combination of the social process of production by simultaneously undermining the original sources of all wealth—the soil and the worker" ([1887] 1976: 638).

Marx's accounts of soils degradation have been exceptionally influential in the field of political ecology and in critical analyses of the destructive exploitation of soils, identified in a range of recent accounts as characteristic of a "productionist drive" toward intensive cultivation and artificially enhanced nutrient yield (Blaikie 1985; Peet and Watts 1996). At the same time, the historical specificity of Marx's thought on this topic is only now starting to be explored. For example, Marxian notions of a metabolic rift essentialized both humans and soils, failing to appreciate the interrelatedness of land use and soil fertility and the centrality of labor as an actual (not abstract) process for the shape of human–soil relations and their sustainability (Schneider and McMichael 2010).

What is striking is the degree to which this metabolic theory of soil degradation—which ties soil to structures of social and economic exploitation, expropriation, and urbanization—does not significantly depart from the depiction of soil as a residue (Engel-Di Mauro 2014), figuring soil as that which is left behind *after* processes of weathering and agricultural depletion. For example, the commodification of soils, as embodied by the commercialization and abstraction of soil, is a core element of the broader project of turning soils and lands into economic resources—"bits" of nature separated from, and exploitable for, capital accumulation. While soil commodities are bought and sold, the principal way for soils to participate in capital markets has been as an agricultural resource: something which participates in the creation of commodities (crops and animal bodies) but is not in itself normally commodified. This capacity of soils to participate in commodity creation has led to a focus on soil fertility as the principal mode of engaging with soils. Soil fertility as the only thing that "counts" about soils in turn forms a key element of what the environmental ethicist Paul Thompson (2005) characterizes as the "paradigm of productionism." Basing his account on an evolutionary history of human settlement and civilization—one that locates the development of permanent human settlements and social structures with the "social evolution of human activities" from hunting and foraging to agriculture, domestication, and cultivation—Thompson characterizes productionism as "the philosophy that emerges when production is taken to be the sole norm for ethically evaluating agriculture" (2005: 47)—and, we could add, for engaging with soil materialities.

The importance of markets to valuing and engaging with soils is seen in a similar way in the recent efforts of soil mapping, which have been focusing on what soils contain and do rather than what soils are: if they are worthy of mapping and modeling (and prospecting, enhancing, or conserving), relying on ever more sophisticated techniques of satellite imagery, this is because soils host a variety of mineral and organic substances such as carbon, manganese, and nickel—not because they are unique bodies or "types" resulting from specific, long-term pedogenesis mechanisms that tend to be of interest only to pedologists (see Kon Kam King and Granjou, this volume). In the proliferation of carbon markets, the value of soil is defined by the degree to which it can be operationalized as a more or less stable sink through which carbon can be cycled (Kearnes and Rickards 2017). Similarly, research into soil microbiomes and the hopes invested in their potential to reconfigure agricultures and ecologies is leading to new conceptualizations of soils as biocapital and opening up the world's soils to new forms of bioprospecting (Granjou and Phillips 2018). It is important to note that soils' capacities to participate in productionism and in capital accumulation are not inherent but rather develop through forms of human and nonhuman labor which reconfigure both soils and their "users" (Krzywoszynska 2020). As new soil resource frontiers are "opened up," it is worth paying attention to the changing shape of the assemblages of humans and nonhumans which make the existence of these frontiers possible.

This resource-ing of soils, in which soils' capacities are valued and evaluated in relation to capital markets, can be contrasted with emergent socioecological approaches to soil relations. Puig de la Bellacasa contrasts agriculture's productionist drive with what she terms the alter-ontologies of diverse agricultural systems—the "foodweb" concept of soil life and permaculture, for example, which functions to "'slo[w] down'. . . the pace of productivist appropriation of soil life as a resource" (2005: 709), or the careful work of alternative soil cultivation techniques (e.g., organic farming, permaculture, "foodweb" philosophies of soil structure)—while in practice this opposition has rarely been a clean-cut one. The promotion of organic and low-tillage farming techniques— and indeed a range of soil improvement strategies by large agribusiness, for example—is indicative of the relatively fluid traffic between alternative soil management strategies and mainstream agricultural practice (Krzywoszynska 2019b).

Down to Dirt: Thinking-with Soils

Despite the notable absence from contemporary social theory that we note above, soils has begun to make important inroads in recent years and across many disciplines. Perhaps one of the most salient gestures of contemporary theorizations on soil is precisely the activation of soils as generative matter that cannot be dissociated from the configuration of the social. From being a residue that appears once the social has happened, or figured as a raw material external to the social, soil has become a constitutive power that is inseparable from the social itself. By virtue of its sociotechnical configuration and its world-making affordances, soil is conceptualized as both the result of social relations and the producer of them. Taken together, these moves unsettle the idea of soils as simply an elemental substance that exists laterally, before sociocultural formations, and destabilizes the notion that the latter are independent from the vicissitudes and proclivities of the former. Work in human geography (Engel-Di Mauro 2014; Kearnes and Rickards 2015, 2017; Krzywoszynska 2019a; Krzywoszynska and Marchesi 2020), science and technology studies (Granjou and Phillips 2018; Kon Kam King et al. 2018), environmental sociology (Granjou and Salazar 2019), Indigenous climate change studies (Whyte 2017), and history (McNeill 2001; Bashford 2014; Marchesi 2020) has variously engaged with novel approaches to soil and perspectives from the environmental sciences, to highlight the transformative potential of different characteristics and affordances of soils on the way societies assemble. These new approaches to the study of soils go beyond the classic explorations of human–soil relations in political ecology (Blaikie 1985) and attend more carefully, more creatively, and more critically to the ways in which we think- and act-with soil, both materially and theoretically.

In what follows we account for four theoretical sensibilities that have engaged with soils as a way of relating with the generative capacities of the more-than-human. We take these sensibilities not as discrete conceptual containers but as a highly interconnected web of theoretical gestures and political moves that invoke multiple questions, practices, and objects.

Assembling Soils

Soils are assembled through a diverse array of human and nonhuman forces. This is, bluntly, a key conceptual and analytical agenda energizing contemporary soil theories. The inauguration of this thread can be traced to the work of Bruno Latour. In following a team of pedologists on a sampling trip to the Amazon in the late 1990s, he ethnographically explored the way that "soils" are produced through a complex set of cultural practices engaged in by real people, rather than simply being a bundle of natural determinations waiting for the expert's successful unveiling (Latour 1999; Lyons 2014). Latour documents the "small anthropological mysteries" (1999: 47) through which "the earth becomes a sign, takes on a geometrical form, becomes the carrier of a numbered code, and will soon be defined by a color" (1999: 49).

Against the purification of soil as a residue existing either before or after social life, Latour indicated a research program into the entanglement between soils and politics, between science and culture. Following this trail, for Elden (2013) soil is made to work cartographically, legally, and politically in the ways it is translated into concepts of land and territory. Similarly, in her discussion of the concept of land in geopolitical thought, Tania Murray Li argues that "the axe, the spade, the plough, the title deed, the tax register, maps, graphs, satellite images, ancestral graves, mango trees—do more than simply record the presence of land as a resource: they are integral to assembling it as a resource for different actors" (2014: 589). For Li, soil is worked *into* land, and its form retains traces of its material and discursive assemblage.

Importantly, the assembling of soils does not indicate a return to social constructionism. Soil does not become a purely semiotic sign for phenomenological interpretation and articulation. Rather, soil emerges as an entity with which the social *becomes-with*. The work of Donna Haraway has been crucial in the instantiation of this sensibility. For Haraway, soil, compost, and composting are crucial elements for the sustenance of life, but also a reminder that "critters—human and not—become-with each other, compose and decompose each other" (Haraway 2016: 97). We will return to Haraway's composting later. For now, it suffices to say that here Haraway thinking-with compost gestures toward the formulation, even if speculatively, of a political program: an ethical and practical guide for activism and intervention, for defining where the problem resides, what the commons means, and which collaborations are needed—in brief, what politics is about.

Along these lines, Kristina Lyons, for example, describes a range of experimental practices conducted by Colombian farmers that emerge *along with* the forest, *la selva*, in a process in which farmers "learn to *see with la selva*" and engage in practices of "becoming the *selva's* apprentice" (2014: 223). In a similar vein, Angela Lederach has examined how practices of territorial peacebuilding, also in Colombia, "emerge from within a relational framework" in which "the interconnected lives of campesinos, avocado forests, traditional crops, mountain landscapes, and monkeys that form a distinctive niche in the Alta Montaña to uncover a particular ecological imagination that infuses grassroots peacebuilding" (2017: 592). Relatedly, in his wonderful book *Amazonia in the Anthropocene: People, Soils, Plants, Forests*, Nicholas Kawa (2016) documents the phenomenon of *terra preta* (black soils) in Brazilian Amazonia. Engaging with contemporary farmers, he described long-term evidence of human alteration of soils, allowing for a problematizing of technoscientific models of controlled sustainable agriculture and opening up a reflection on the social lives of soils and plants as actants with agency to heal.

Seen in this light, the notion of soil *cultivation* might be repurposed in ways that retain something of the notion of earthly inscription—which have been central to its broader political and legal resonance—whilst also insisting on the practical and material labor entailed in cultivating soils. What we have in mind here is something similar to Thompson's (2013) notion of choreography in her ethnographic study of stem cell science. In this work, she demonstrates the ways in which diverse research resources, devices, and materials are not simply *assembled* but are actively configured to produce standardized research objects. For Thompson—and for the notion of cultivation we advance here—this active configuration also entails the enactment of both markets and notions of virtue in the definitional work involved in demarcating "good" science. Attending to the cultivation of soils reveals that questions of what constitutes "good soil"—soils that are innately "good," but also "good for" the Earth and the climate—are rarely far from the surface.

The Elemental Ecologies of Soil

Depicting soils as complex articulations brought into being by a myriad of interventions, solidarities, and apparatuses provides a vantage point for the recognition of soils as ecological beings in a permanent state of chemical and physical mutation and expansion. In other words, soil has become a rich milieu for rendering visible the logics of entanglement and co-dependence. This points to the possibility of broadening conceptions of, and relationship to, soil. By more fully considering the microscopic beings—bacteria, fungi, and earthworms—that reside in, eat, digest, make, and transform it, soil appears altogether more active and characterized by diverse capacities (Granjou and Salazar 2019). This centrality of soil biota is a source of both hope and hype within the scientific community, that increasingly invests in soil biota research in pursuit of more profitable and more ecologically sensitive agricultural practices (Granjou and Phillips 2018). These new material practices and discursive framings of soil biota as labor are supporting and intensifying a preexisting direction of improvement of soils, understood as their more successful enrolment in processes of capital (Krzywoszynska 2020).

As a heterogeneous mix of living, decaying, dying, and dead things stitched together to form what soil scientists term "soil aggregates" as the basic unit of soil ontologies, soil contradicts any quest for purity, understood as the "attempt to delineate and delimit the world into something separable, disentangled, and homogenous" (Shotwell 2016: 15): it is indeed soil's impurity and propensity to decomposing and rotting that are generative of unique possibilities for recomposition and rebirth (Lorimer 2016). These stories capture something of Haraway's compost-ist ethic and reflections on compost and composting. While compost is the result of various beings—vermin, fungi, bacteria, oxygen, plants, and humans—collaborating in ecological embroilments, this process resists any teleological framing, and is continually overflowing and expanding with and towards new relations and matters. Haraway claims that "I am a compost-ist, not a posthuman-ist: we are all compost, not posthuman" (2015: 161). A notion of the (de) composition of soil—meaning that all soil is *made, composed, and assembled; indeed composted*—provides a vantage point for exploring the idiosyncratic effects of the ways in which soil and land—in addition to grass, cows, and people—are being enlisted in the specifically technocratic and promissory logics of environmental control and climate capitalism (Kearnes and Rickards 2017; Kon Kam King et al. 2018; Granjou and Salazar 2019; Krzywoszynska 2019a).

Here, soil raises particular issues regarding its unique opacity and resistance to our capacities of perception. It is not possible to consider soil as one does when looking into air or water. The first microscopes developed by Hooker in the late seventeenth century allowed Van Leeuwenhoek to offer the first descriptions of bacteria and protozoa in 1673. Since then, environmental microbiologists have relentlessly endeavored to develop instruments and methods to gain a clearer picture of the properties and activities of soil samples. However, soil is rarely transparent in this manner. Yet, as underlined by Clark and Hird, there is very little recognition of soil as a living environment because its living being resists the technologies of presence-making that underpin the environmentalist focus on biodiversity loss on the Earth's surface: "a great many of the living lineages that are now likely to be 'disappearing' have never appeared to us in the first place ... Too small, too obscure, too reticent to have graced our archives, these beings blink out of existence without even making their presence felt" (2014: 45).

Here we want to insist that, rather than simply being made and actively cultivated (by humans), soils are entangled with larger, and smaller, physical-chemical ecologies that expand—and defy—our "natural" imaginaries. Soils are inseparable, for example, from the active processes of weathering, erosion, and decomposition, aided and abetted by all manner of fungal and microbial life (Hird 2009). In her recent work on what she terms "the possibility of life in capitalist ruins," Anna Tsing insists that "making worlds is not limited to humans .... Bacteria made our oxygen atmosphere, and plants help maintain it. Plants live on land because fungi made soil by digesting rocks" (2015: 22). The crucial agencies of living beings—from bacteria to fungi—were already signaled in the early nineteenth century by Darwin's observations about the role of earthworms in soil formation and social existence.

The fact that soil's internal dynamics and mutations are not easily visible and perceptible becomes an onto-political issue in itself, rather than being an obstacle for the politicization of soils. Kathryn Yusoff (2012) has emphasized how conservation biology practices hang on visibility-making technologies and representational politics: making living beings visible is foundational to the subject-making process that is fundamental to the will to conserve and care for them. However, this is especially problematic for soil's living beings: not only does their small size often make them invisible to the naked eye, the soil in which they live is not open and transparent but rather closed and opaque to our view. At the same time, Krzywoszynska cautions against a simple equating of visibility and sense-ability with care, especially in relation to soils. As she argues, in conditions of conflicting land-use objectives, "while attentiveness in relations of care does have a potential to generate an expansive and transformative ethic, this can be limited by the necessity of achieving care for specific things" (2019a: 5). She thus calls for care practices to be rooted in a speculative, probing attentiveness which pushes beyond what can be directly experienced by individual bodies, and which continually reveals the interconnectedness of different care practices and their subjects. This probing attentiveness is what will make possible a continual and conflictual reconfiguring of human–soil relations as different communities discover and reconfigure their earthly attachments.

Inhumanness: Earthly Politics

By emphasizing how soils are assembled through multiple practices and entanglements, social theory has also made visible the capacity of soil and soil ecologies to contest dominant technoscientific discourses on human–nature relations. Importantly, feminist approaches to social studies of science, led by the pioneering work of Maria Puig de la Bellacasa, have opened up the potential of soils to resist entrenched Western onto-epistemics. Puig de la Bellacasa's work has explored the manifold manifestations of transforming human–soil communities that reverse the simplified sense of human–environment relations bound to destruction and extinction. Following the turn to soil ecology within soil sciences, Puig de la Bellacasa has focused on soil temporalities as challenging the dominant narratives of future-oriented and technoscience-driven human–soil relations. The tension between the long-time spans needed for soil transformation and regeneration and the "relentless futurity" of agricultural productivism lays bare the disjuncture between societal and soil temporalities which will have to be redressed. Her exploration of the soil foodweb as the basis for a different material and temporal way of organizing human–soil relationalities has been highly influential (Puig de la Bellacasa 2014).

We want to propose that the problematization of conventional categories for thinking "about" soils resonates with the attempt to push politics away from "the human" as the pivotal reference of knowledge and action. In the context of the call for an "earthly politics" (Lorimer 2007; Whatmore 2013a; Tironi 2019)—a politics that, in the words of Sarah Whatmore, takes "stuff of all sorts as *forceful* and [...] experiment[s] with what it means to incorporate this forcefulness into ethico-political conduct" (2013a: 38)—soil, as matter or as a symbol or process, has been invoked for the cultivation of a particular genre of ecological politics. Put differently, soil becomes a potentiated matter that is not just a domain of politics but also a reference for what earthly politics is and means when the "human" is no longer the point of reference or the epistemic medium through which the world is conceptualized.

The elementality of soil—and accounting for soil's irreducible and even recalcitrant existence—seems crucial here. This extends to a recognition of the multiple ways in which soil is enrolled in and essential to the "creative energies of the earth itself" (Whatmore 2013b). Forty-five percent mineral, 5% organic matter, between 20 and 30% water, with air making up the rest. Clay, sand, and silt; humus, earthworms, and insect corpses; hydrogen and oxygen; nitrogen and phosphorous. This is soil, as social scientists have come to realize. A geochemical accomplishment, an entanglement of interactive, irritable, and irritating things which forms the basis of "life" but which, we seem to forget, is not always available for *relation*—at least as defined when the "human" is foregrounded.

Soils retain a creative, irreducible power that forces things, affect, and relations into being. Indeed, soils *are* a force of their own. The call made by these social theorists, and which we second, is to take soil as the "material background of our habits and habitat ... the conditions of possibility of being and matter" (Neale et al. 2019b). Developing processual and object-oriented philosophies, these elemental approaches point to the possibility of thinking human–nature relations outside anthropocentric ontologies. From this vantage point, the political and conceptual challenge is not simply that of understanding the processes and effects of socializing soils, but also, paraphrasing Clark and Gunaratnam (2017), in the possibility of soiling the social.

Here, we suggest, social theory has taken two different yet complementary roads. In a first strand, which draws inspiration from work in new materialism (Pilgrim 2013; Granjou and Salazar 2019) and particularly that of Jane Bennett (2010), social theorists have rendered visible the active and vibrant life of non-living soil components. For example, in Meulemans's (2020a) account of the making of "living soils," the relationality of soils is inseparable from their capacity to animate otherwise inert minerals, and thus force new practices of care and co-laboring. Similarly, Ureta (2016) indicates that toxic soils subjected to sustained chemical violence "are characterized by an exuberant vitality, [as] their multiple components are continually mutating, forging new bonds." In this view, soiling the social implies accounting for non-living socialities (in the Tardean sense) in which mineralogical and inorganic elements generate relations and processes that have an impact on the social but that are indifferent to its logics.

A second strand of work articulates what soiling the social means ontologically and politically by drawing on work in speculative realism (Clark 2011) and feminist and anti-colonial geophilosophies (Povinelli 2016; Yusoff 2019) and insisting on the radical alterity of soils. This call, with which this book is aligned, entails, first and foremost, accounting for the *inhumanness* of soils. The invocation of the inhuman condition of soils has no simple normative claim: we are not trying to draw an agonistic spectacle in which soils act *against* the human. Rather, the inhumanness of soils indicates a complex twofold tension inherent to soil existence: while it is an element intimately necessary for human earthly existence, it is also radically and even violently other to humanness (Cohen 2015). Identifying similarly profound challenges to dominant human–soil ontologies, Nigel Clark (2017) —in his work on the politics of strata (see also Salazar and Dodds, this volume)—highlights how our classical view of the ground as a stable and eternal foundation has been deeply unsettled by the development of geosciences since the 1980s. Its focus on tectonic shifts illustrates how movement, change, and even brutal upheavals are part of the normal and usual bearing of the Earth's surface. Drawing insights from the deepness of the soil and the (inter) dependencies of the life buried in and growing from it, he proposes, provide a way of extending social theoretical reflection into "in-human" regions devoid of any trace of human presence and activity, as well as into the margins and trading zones between non-living matter and the living.

The turn to the inhumanness of soils is, then, closely related to the recognition of soils not simply as actors in the abundance of the *bios* but also as elements of the *geos*— the non-life existence of the geological (see Tironi, this volume). This geological turn is not meant to fall back into the figure of soil as an inert, stable, taken-for-granted component of anterior (and buried) life. Rather, the attempt is to unsettle entrenched ontologies in which (soil) existence is measured solely according to the categories and in the realms of "life" (Povinelli 2016).

Writing with Kathryn Yusoff, Clark (2017) expands on the exuberance and dynamism of the Earth, emphasizing how its rhythmical upheavals and obdurate mutations (including earthquakes and tectonic plate deformation) have been putting societies and their achievements in a state of intolerable vulnerability—which Enlightenment philosophers did their best to forget while elaborating on the autonomy of human reason and freedom. More recently, the geological realm also proved rather resistant to academic attempts to rethink social existence in terms of relational, co-productionist, and network-related collective performance: "While the fleshy exuberance of biological life and the 'spooky' indeterminacy of sub-atomic particles were roundly enrolled in efforts to reimagine collective life, the basal depths and *lumpen* masses of the inorganic, the mineral, the geologic have proved rather more recalcitrant" (Clark and Yusoff 2017: 13). The challenge of what Clark (2017: 18) terms "trying to think the social and the political *stratigraphically*," is in part related to the difficulty of unsettling considerations of the geological as the realm of the unchanging, the stable and inert backdrop for the deployment of human technological mastery (Kearnes and Rickards 2017).

Decolonizing Soils

The decentering of the human is also present in the contestation of the "we" (de la Cadena 2020) often invoked in social theories on soil and soil ecologies. It is important, we argue throughout this book, to account for how decolonial theory and praxis, and Indigenous scholarship from diverse geographies, have challenged the way Western politics—and Western politics of nature—have thought soils and soil practices. Put differently, questions of belonging to soil, being part of and attuned to soils and the radical autonomy of soils as irreducible beings, in addition to broader questions of reciprocal relationships and associated responsibilities between soil and social worlds, have provided the very foundation for the resurgence of Indigenous worlds across the world. In this specific regard, the question of a lack of engagement with "matters of soil" in social theory cannot be separated from ongoing questions of colonialism, and what Aníbal Quijano (2000) has termed the "coloniality of power" and the geopolitics of knowledge production between academic and other epistemologies, and between the Global South and the Global North. Hence, at the outset it must be said that we consider that Indigenous epistemologies and ontologies have a vital contribution to sustainable conservation practices, certainly not as a panacea for the planet's tribulations, but above all in leading a rethinking of human–soil relations at this critical juncture and as a path toward learning the urgent "arts of living" on a damaged planet (Tsing et al. 2017).

A critical framework offered by Indigenous theories and practices is to think soils as always emplaced (Escobar 2008) or in-*ayllú* (de la Cadena 2015): a relational force whose existence is always in, with, and for the land. In their recent work with Bawaka Country and Bawaka people in northeast Arnhem Land, Australia, Sarah Wright, Sandie Suchet-Pearson, Kate Lloyd, and Jill Sweeney (Bawaka Country et al. 2016) depict Country not simply as background but rather as storied, as making demands on us, calling us into relations. They suggest that in the context of Bawaka Yolŋu ontology, "knowing and valuing place/space comes from living within it, learning (hearing, feeling) the language of its soils and winds and birds, and in becoming together" (2016: 10). This moral, spiritual and ecological intimacy also emerges in Mapuche philosophy, in which *Mapu* (territory, land, soil) is indivisible from *Che* (person): *Che* must be understood as a process of becoming a being and a person, a situated process impossible to understand outside the *Mapu* (Melín et al. 2019). Similarly, in the North American context Vanessa Watts (2013: 27, cited in Davis and Todd 2017: 769) points out that "Our truth, not only Anishnaabe and Haudenosaunee people but in a majority of Indigenous societies, conceives that we (humans) are made from the land; our flesh is literally an extension of soil." For the "immense minorities" of the world that do not separate society from nature (Danowski and Viveiros de Castro 2017), soil and human, *humus* (Boff 2008; Haraway 2016), have always been entangled.

At the center of Indigenous theories on soils-in-place lies, we suggest, a powerful critique of Western politics of knowledge production. And this is as much a critique of modern science as it is a call for respecting other wisdoms and forms of knowledge creation, perhaps parallel to what Silvia Rivera Cusicanqui (2006) calls "oral history," or oral construction of knowledge as a counter methodology to Western/modern ways of doing (natural and social) science. The call, which we attend to throughout this book, is to be careful with the concepts with which we conceptualize concepts, to borrow from Strathern (1992). This is what prominent shaman Davi Kopenawa Yanomami pointed out to Bruce Albert in their candid ethno-political manifesto *The Falling Sky*: "When they think their land is getting spoiled, the white people speak of 'pollution.' In our language, when sickness spreads relentlessly through the forest, we say that *xawara* [epidemic fumes] have seized it and that it becomes ghost" (Kopenawa and Albert 2013: 391). As Cesarino (2014) observes, Kopenawa's shamanic speculations point to the weakness of "paper skin" and its drawings, responsible for producing an atrophy of memory and for the replication of "smoky and obscure words" (Kopenawa and Albert 2013: 23, in Cesarino 2014: 289). It is as if through Indigenous intimations with soil we—in the West—have come to recognize our "sanctioned epistemic ignorance," as labelled by Kuokkanen (2007).

The recognition of Indigenous conceptualizations of soil opens not only new avenues for epistemological diversity but also new terrains for political action, particularly in the face of climate change. Kyle Whyte writes about how Indigenous studies "arise from memories, knowledges, histories, and experiences of oppression that differ from many of the nonindigenous scientists, environmentalists, and politicians who are prominent in the framing of the issue of climate change today" (2017: 153). Indigenous societies with deep collective histories of having to be well organized to adapt to environmental change and that must constantly reckon "with the disruptions of historic and ongoing practices of colonialism, capitalism, and industrialization" (2017: 154) are not alone, as a range of rural movements attest. For instance, the transnational rural social movement La Vía Campesina, as Martínez-Torres and Rosset vividly illustrate,

> has been critically sustained and shaped by the encounter and *diálogo de saberes* (dialog among different knowledges and ways of knowing) between different rural cultures (East, West, North and South; peasant, indigenous, farmer, pastoralist and rural proletarian, etc.) that takes place within it, in the context of the increasingly politicized confrontation with neoliberal reality and agribusiness in the most recent phase of capital expansion. This dialog among the "absences" left out by the dominant monoculture of ideas has produced important "emergences" that range from mobilizing frames for collective action—like the *food sovereignty* framework—to social methodologies for the spread of *agroecology* among peasant families.
>
>   2014: 979

Crucial here is the possibility opened up by Indigenous theories of, and practices with, soils to redraw the parameters of politics. For example, Tironi (2018) suggests that the practices of care rehearsed by peasants to heal their plants and soils harmed by chemical pollution render possible a form of "hypo-politics"—or interventions attuned in the register of affection and conducted in the space of intimacy—that defy the conventional repertoire of activism. Similarly, and inheriting from ancestral engagements with soils, Maria Mies and Vandana Shiva claim that in so far as soil "is the womb not only for the reproduction of biological life but also of cultural and spiritual life" (2014: 343), soil demands a form of politics that defies conventional definitions of conservation but also of "politics" as a specific domain of the public sphere. Shiva calls not just for the politicization of soils but also for the invention *with* soils of new modes of intervention that rejoin the affective and the scientific, the sacred and the technical, and that weave together a form of resistance that does not disentangle the conjoined violence of industrialism, positivism, patriarchy, colonialism, and capitalism.

In brief, this book suggests that the political provocation of soil is, in many ways, the proposition of a decolonial gesture. If soils help in "taking the interdependence of human and non-human lives seriously," as indicated by Anna Krzywoszynska (2019a), they also help in revealing that the ontological split between humans and nonhumans is anything but universal—and that Indigenous epistemes take interdependence very seriously, to borrow from Sundberg (2014: 37).

Conclusion

How may we take the lessons of the soil seriously, and how may we take them further in the multi-scalar politics of regeneration and renewal of human–soil worlds? As Krzywoszynska et al. show (this volume), the first step is overcoming the epistemic hurdle of developing new modes of attending to soils as more than surfaces upon which humans live and act; engaging with soils as volumes and relational processes in the making of which humans are implicated and whose making also implicates humans. Changing soil epistemes by making available practical engagements with soil powers in turn brings about new soil ontologies in which separations between soils and (their) humans become blurred, and moreover, in which soil is not predicated on any type of relation beyond its own internal, inorganic becoming. As the dependencies and relations become not only known but also felt, they become available to be responded to, changing human practices and indeed the humans in question. In this regard, the decolonization of both soil itself and social theoretical soil narratives is critical for the radical interruption of the "human" front-staging the ecological dramaturgy of the Anthropocene: soil is not only more-than-human and even inhuman, it is also in relation to the human-in-divergence, or to different forms of being human—and of being soil. Engaging with imaginaries of lively and interconnected yet divergent and excessive soils in the arts and in the sciences further troubles ingrained assumptions about soils' residual and essentialized nature, shifting perceptions of who is being animated by whom in eco-social relations between humans and soils (Puig de la Bellacasa 2019). Thinking with soils thus leads to acting with soils, as "the political decisions about land use are inseparable from strategies for socio-ecological survival" (Krzywoszynska and Marchesi 2020).

As we show in this volume, the ways in which soil conservation, improvement, and technoscientific development practices are being marshaled in response to interlocking concerns regarding climate change, food security, and rural livelihoods is indicative of the deep connections between soils and social processes. As soil improvement and management are increasingly being incorporated into a range of social and political projects in response to environmental and humanitarian concerns, soil appears today as both a figure of concern—through images of soil degradation and desertification—and a figure of hope, through rising expectations of "good land management" and "healthy soils," underpinned by practices and innovation pathways that would contribute to addressing challenges of food security, sustainable development, poverty, and climate change.

While this book takes seriously soils as critical zones for intervention and reparation in the Anthropocene, we also want to be careful with contemporary calls to action. The contributions in this book force us to recognize the problematic connections between soil and capitalist logics of accumulation and reification. At the same time, the contributors do not take for granted how knowledge about soils is produced, and which are the best alliances for soil remediation and care. Soil itself appears, throughout the book, as an eerie entity that takes different forms and that demands different questions and practices. For example, we see the entanglements between the surface and the subsurface increasingly constituted as a key horizon in contemporary ecological politics. In the project of thinking-with soils, we have in mind the possibilities for exploring the emergent horizons arising from engagements with the belowground, as well as their coming into being.

Indeed, our thinking-with soils is also animated by an enchantment and fascination with the affordances of the belowground, where life abounds and yet is often neglected, and where unseen communities drive numerous ecological processes—energy flow, nutrient cycling, waste removal—essential for growing our food and sustaining the ecosystems we share. This volume is fueled by what William Connolly has evocatively termed a "sensitivity to nonhuman processes—such as to the seasons, or to changes in a climate pattern, or to the musical capacities of whales, or to bird–human disease crossings, or to delicate soil processes of self-renewal"—which often goes together with "a desire to slow down human processes so as to commune with a holistic nature that moves slowly" (2013: 10). Thinking-with soils is thus also an attempt to resonate with soils, not only recognizing their agential power over us but also opening up to the ways in which soils may reconfigure the meaning of "us" through new patterns of thought, practice, affect, and attachment.

Notes

1   There are, however, significant exceptions to Clark's characterization. These include work in the philosophy of geology (Frodeman 1995, 2003), archaeology (Boivin and Owoc 2004), and literary and cultural studies (Williams 2008), and burgeoning interest in subterranean spatialities (Pérez 2013, 2019; Kinchy et al. 2018; Melo Zurita et al. 2018; Ballestero 2019; Melo Zurita 2019; Melo Zurita and Munro 2019), geological modes of knowing (Tironi 2019), and political geologies (Bobbette and Donovan 2019).

2   It is important to note that religion and theology's abstraction from soil is a relatively recent and partial phenomenon, and as Kelley (this volume) demonstrates, the devotional interaction with and use of soil, dirt, and mud remains widespread in a range of pilgrimage, ceremonial, and ritualistic practices (Shiva 2017). At the same

time, figures of earth "groaning" and the spiritual sickness of soil remain a consistent theme of contemporary eco-theological concern (Pope Francis 2015; Grenfell-Lee 2017).

3   While this connection between soil and blood, and the attempt to ground kinship in earth, is deeply intertwined with the eugenic politics of twentieth-century fascism, soil also figures in more mundane ways in the construction of notions of territorial sovereignty. In Locke we see how the cultivation of soil is central to a definition of property, to the establishment of notions of political jurisdiction, and to the extension of these models of territorial dominance through colonialism and imperial projection (Arneil 1996).

References

Arneil, B. (1996), *John Locke and America: The Defence of English Colonialism*, Oxford: Oxford University Press.

Bailey, J.-S. (2016), *Dust Bowl: Depression America to World War Two Australia*, New York: Palgrave Macmillan.

Ballestero, A. (2019), "Touching with Light, or, How Texture Recasts the Sensing of Underground Water," *Science, Technology, & Human Values*, 44 (5): 762–85.

Bashford, Alison (2014), *Global Population: History, Geopolitics, and Life on Earth*, New York: Columbia University Press.

Bawaka Country, S. Wright, S. Suchet-Pearson, K. Lloyd, L. Burarrwanga, R. Ganambarr et al. (2016), "Co-becoming Bawaka: Towards a Relational Understanding of Place/ Space," *Progress in Human Geography*, 40 (4): 455–75.

Bennett, J. (2010), *Vibrant Matter: A Political Ecology of Things*, Durham, NC: Duke University Press.

Blaikie, P. (1985), *The Political Economy of Soil Erosion in Developing Countries*, London: Longman.

Bobbette, A. and A. Donovan (2019), *Political Geology: Active Stratigraphies and the Making of Life*, Cham, Switzerland: Palgrave Macmillan.

Boff, L. (2008), *Essential Care: An Ethics of Human Nature*, Waco, TX: Baylor University Press.

Boivin, N. and M. A. Owoc, eds. (2004), *Soils, Stones and Symbols: Cultural Perceptions of the Mineral World*, Abingdon: Routledge.

Bryant, L. and B. Garnham (2015), "The Fallen Hero: Masculinity, Shame and Farmer Suicide in Australia," *Gender, Place & Culture*, 22 (1): 67–82.

Cesarino, P. de N. (2014), "Ontological Conflicts and Shamanistic Speculations in Davi Kopenawa's *The Falling Sky*," *HAU: Journal of Ethnographic Theory*, 4 (2): 289–95.

Clark, N. (2011), *Inhuman Nature: Sociable Life on a Dynamic Planet*, London: Sage.

Clark, N. (2013), "Geoengineering and Geologic Politics," *Environment and Planning A*, 45 (12): 2825–32.

Clark, N. (2017), "Politics of Strata," *Theory, Culture & Society*, 34 (2/3): 211–31.

Clark, N. and Y. Gunaratnam (2017), "Earthing the *Anthropos*? From 'Socializing the Anthropocene' to Geologizing the Social," *European Journal of Social Theory*, 20 (1): 146–63.

Clark, N. and M. J. Hird (2014), "Deep Shit," *O-Zone: A Journal of Object-Oriented Studies*, 1: 44–52.

Clark, N. and K. Yusoff (2017), "Geosocial Formations and the Anthropocene," *Theory, Culture & Society*, 34 (2/3): 3–23.

Cohen, J. J. (2015), *Stone: An Ecology of the Inhuman*, Minneapolis, MN: University of Minnesota Press.

Connolly, W. E. (2013), *The Fragility of Things: Self-Organizing Processes, Neoliberal Fantasies, and Democratic Activism*, Durham, NC: Duke University Press.

Cusicanqui, S. R. (2006), "El potencial epistemológico y teórico de la historia oral: De la lógica instrumental a la descolonización de la historia," *Voces Recobradas, Revista de Historia Oral*, 8 (21): 12–22.

Danowski, D. and E. Viveiros de Castro (2017), *The Ends of the World*, Cambridge: Polity Press.

Davis, H. and Z. Todd (2017), "On the Importance of a Date, Or, Decolonizing the Anthropocene," *ACME: An International Journal for Critical Geographies*, 16 (4): 761–80.

de la Cadena, M. (2015), *Earth Beings: Ecologies of Practices Across Andean Worlds*, Durham, NC: Duke University Press.

de la Cadena, M. (2020), "An Invitation to Live Together: Making the 'Complex We,'" *Environmental Humanities*.

Demossier, Marion (2011), "Beyond *Terroir*: Territorial Construction, Hegemonic Discourses, and French Wine Culture," *Journal of the Royal Anthropological Institute*, 17 (4): 685–705.

Douglas, M. (1966), *Purity and Danger: An Analysis of Concepts of Pollution and Taboo*, London: Routledge.

Elden, S. (2013), *The Birth of Territory*, Chicago, IL: University of Chicago Press.

Engel-Di Mauro, S. (2002), "Gender Relations, Political Economy, and the Ecological Consequences of State-Socialist Soil Science," *Capitalism Nature Socialism*, 13 (3): 92–117.

Engel-Di Mauro, S. (2006), "From Organism to Commodity: Gender, Class, and the Development of Soil Science in Hungary 1900–89," *Environment and Planning D: Society and Space*, 24 (2): 215–29.

Engel-Di Mauro, S. (2014), *Ecology, Soils, and the Left: An Ecosocial Approach*, New York: Palgrave Macmillan.

Escobar, A. (2008), *Territories of Difference: Place, Movements, Life, Redes*, Durham, NC: Duke University Press.

Frodeman, R. (1995), "Geological Reasoning: Geology as an Interpretive and Historical Science," *Geological Society of America Bulletin*, 107 (8): 960–68.

Frodeman, R. (2003), *Geo-Logic: Breaking Ground between Philosophy and the Earth Sciences*, Albany, NY: State University of New York.

Gammage, B. (2011), *The Biggest Estate on Earth: How Aborigines Made Australia*, Sydney: Allen & Unwin.

Granjou, C. and C. Phillips (2018), "Living and Labouring Soils: Metagenomic Ecology and a New Agricultural Revolution?," *BioSocieties*, 14 (3): 393–415.

Granjou, C. and J. F. Salazar (2019), "The Stuff of Soil: Belowground Agency in the Making of Future Climates," *Nature and Culture*, 14 (1): 39–60.

Grenfell-Lee, T. Z. (2017), "Earth as Community Garden: The Bounty, Healing, and Justice of Holy Permaculture," in D. M. Hart (ed.), *The Wiley Blackwell Companion to Religion and Ecology*, 410–26, Oxford: Wiley.

Guthman, J. (2014), *Agrarian Dreams: The Paradox of Organic Farming in California*, Oakland, CA: University of California Press.

Haraway, D. (2015), "Anthropocene, Capitalocene, Plantationocene, Chthulucene: Making Kin," *Environmental Humanities*, 6: 159–65.

Haraway, D. (2016), *Staying with the Trouble: Making Kin in the Chthulucene*, Durham, NC: Duke University Press.

Head, L. (2016), *Hope and Grief in the Anthropocene: Re-conceptualising Human–Nature Relations*, Abingdon: Routledge.

Hell, J. (2009), "*Katechon*: Carl Schmitt's Imperial Theology and the Ruins of the Future," *The Germanic Review: Literature, Culture, Theory*, 84 (4): 283–326.

Hird, M. J. (2009), *The Origins of Sociable Life: Evolution After Science Studies*, New York: Palgrave Macmillan.

Hodge, J. M. (2007), *Triumph of the Expert: Agrarian Doctrines of Development and the Legacies of British Colonialism*, Athens, OH: Ohio University Press.

Holleman, H. (2017), "De-naturalizing Ecological Disaster: Colonialism, Racism and the Global Dust Bowl of the 1930s," *Journal of Peasant Studies*, 44 (1): 234–60.

Ingold, T. (2004), "Culture on the Ground: The World Perceived Through the Feet," *Journal of Material Culture*, 9 (3): 315–40.

Jacobs, S. (2010), *Gender and Agrarian Reforms*, Abingdon: Routledge.

Kawa, N. C. (2016), *Amazonia in the Anthropocene: People, Soils, Plants, Forests*, Austin, TX: University of Texas Press.

Kearnes, M. and L. Rickards (2015), "Growing the Social Life of Soil," *Australian Policy Online* [http://doi.org/10.4225/50/5668B815A9E22].

Kearnes, M. and L. Rickards (2017), "Earthly Graves for Environmental Futures: Techno-burial Practices," *Futures*, 92 (suppl. C): 48–58.

Kinchy, A. J., R. Phadke, and J. M. Smith (2018), "Engaging the Underground: An STS Field in Formation," *Engaging Science, Technology, and Society*, 4: 22–42.

Kon Kam King, J., C. Granjou, J. Fournil, and L. Cecillon (2018), "Soil Sciences and the French 4 per 1000 Initiative—The Promises of Underground Carbon," *Energy Research & Social Science*, 45: 144–52.

Kopenawa, D. and B. Albert (2013), *The Falling Sky*, Cambridge, MA: Harvard University Press.

Krzywoszynska, A. (2019a), "Caring for Soil Life in the Anthropocene: The Role of Attentiveness in More-than-Human Ethics," *Transactions of the Institute of British Geographers*, 44 (4): 661–75.

Krzywoszynska, A. (2019b), "Making Knowledge and Meaning in Communities of Practice: What Role May Science Play? The Case of Sustainable Soil Management in England," *Soil Use and Management*, 35 (1): 160–68.

Krzywoszynska, A. (2020), "Nonhuman Labor and the Making of Resources: Making Soils a Resource through Microbial Labor," *Environmental Humanities*.

Krzywoszynska, A. and G. Marchesi (2020), "Towards a Relational Materiality of Soils: Introduction to the Special Issue 'Conceiving Soils and Humans in the Anthropocene,'" *Environmental Humanities*.

Kuokkanen, R. (2007), *Reshaping the University: Responsibility, Indigenous Epistemes, and the Logic of the Gift*, Vancouver: University of British Columbia Press.

Latour, B. (1999), *Pandora's Hope: Essays on the Reality of Science Studies*, Cambridge, MA: Harvard University Press.

Lederach, A. J. (2017), "'The *Campesino* was Born for the *Campo*': A Multispecies Approach to Territorial Peace in Colombia," *American Anthropologist*, 119 (4): 589–602.

Li, T. M. (2014), "What Is Land? Assembling a Resource for Global Investment," *Transactions of the Institute of British Geographers*, 39 (4): 589–602.

Lorimer, H. (2007), "Cultural Geography: Worldly Shapes, Differently Arranged," *Progress in Human Geography*, 31 (1): 89–100.

Lorimer, J. (2016), "Rot," *Environmental Humanities*, 8 (2): 235–39.

Lowe, K. M. (2015), *Baptized with the Soil: Christian Agrarians and the Crusade for Rural America*, Oxford: Oxford University Press.

Lyons, K. M. (2014), "Soil Science, Development, and the 'Elusive Nature' of Colombia's Amazonian Plains," *Journal of Latin American and Caribbean Anthropology*, 19 (2): 212–36.

Marchesi, G. (2020), "Justus von Liebig Makes the World: Soil Properties and Social Change in the 19th Century," *Environmental Humanitites*.

Martínez-Torres, M. E. and P. M. Rosset (2014), "*Diálogo de Saberes* in La Vía Campesina: Food Sovereignty and Agroecology," *Journal of Peasant Studies*, 41 (6): 979–97.

Marx, K. ([1887] 1976), *Capital: A Critique of Political Economy*, Vol. 1, Harmondsworth: Penguin Books.

McNeill, J. R. (2001), *Something New Under the Sun: An Environmental History of the Twentieth-Century World*, New York: W. W. Norton.

Melín, M., P. Mansilla and M. Royo (2019), *Cartografía Cultural del Wallmapu*, Santiago: LOM Ediciones.

Melo Zurita, M. de L. (2019), "Holes, Subterranean Exploration and Affect in the Yucatan Peninsula," *Emotion, Space and Society*, 32: 100584 [https://doi.org/10.1016/j.emospa.2019.100584].

Melo Zurita, M. de L. and P. G. Munro (2019), "Voluminous Territorialisation: Historical Contestations over the Yucatan Peninsula's Subterranean Waterscape," *Geoforum*, 102: 38–47.

Melo Zurita, M. de L., P. G. Munro and D. Houston (2018), "Un-earthing the Subterranean Anthropocene," *Area*, 50 (3): 298–305.

Meulemans, G. (2017), "The Lure of Pedogenesis: An Anthropological Foray into Making Urban Soils in Contemporary France," PhD thesis, University of Aberdeen and University of Liège.

Meulemans, G. (2020a), "Wormy Collaborations in Practices of Soil Construction," *Theory, Culture & Society*, 37 (1): 93–112.

Meulemans, G. (2020b), "Urban Pedogeneses: The Making of City Soils from Hard Surfacing to the Urban Soil Sciences," *Environmental Humanities*.

Mies, M. and V. Shiva (2014), *Ecofeminism*, London: Zed Books.

Munro, P. (2020), *Colonial Seeds in African Soil: A Critical History of Forest Conservation in Sierra Leone*, New York: Berghahn Books.

Neale, T., R. Carter, T. Nelson, and M. Bourke (2019), "Walking Together: A Decolonising Experiment in Bushfire Management on Dja Dja Wurrung Country," *Cultural Geographies*, 26 (3): 341–59.

Neale, T., T. Phan, and C. Addison (2019), "An Anthropogenic Table of Elements: An Introduction," *Cultural Anthropology* [https://culanth.org/fieldsights/an-anthropogenic-table-of-elements-an-introduction].

O'Brien, A. (2020), "Ethical Acknowledgement of Soil Ecosystem Integrity Amid Agricultural Production in Australia," *Environmental Humanities*.

Ogborn, M. (1998), *Spaces of Modernity: London's Geographies 1680–1780*, New York: Guilford Press.

Peet, R. and M. Watts (1996), *Liberation Ecologies: Environment, Development, Social Movements*, London: Routledge.

Pérez, M. A. (2013), "Lines Underground: Exploring and Mapping Venezuela's Cave Environment," *Cartographica: The International Journal for Geographic Information and Geovisualization*, 48 (4): 293–308.

Pérez, M. A. (2019), "Forging a Regional Speleology: Publications, Friendship, and Identity in Cuban and Venezuelan Cave Science and Exploration," *Journal of Latin American Geography*, 18 (2): 60–87.

Pilgrim, K. (2013), "'Happy Cows,' 'Happy Beef': A Critique of the Rationales for Ethical Meat," *Environmental Humanities*, 3 (1): 111–27.

Pope Francis (2015), "Encyclical Letter Laudato Si' of the Holy Father Francis on Care for our Common Home" [http://w2.vatican.va/content/francesco/en/encyclicals/documents/papa-francesco_20150524_enciclica-laudato-si.html].

Povinelli, E. A. (2016), *Geontologies: A Requiem to Late Liberalism*, Durham, NC: Duke University Press.

Puig de la Bellacasa, M. (2014), "Encountering Bioinfrastructure: Ecological Struggles and the Sciences of Soil," *Social Epistemology*, 28 (1): 26–40.

Puig de la Bellacasa, M. (2015), "Making Time for Soil: Technoscientific Futurity and the Pace of Care," *Social Studies of Science*, 45 (5): 691–716.

Puig de la Bellacasa, M. (2019), "Re-animating Soils: Transforming Human–Soil Affections through Science, Culture and Community," *Sociological Review*, 67 (2): 391–407.

Quijano, A. (2000), "Coloniality of Power and Eurocentrism in Latin America," *International Sociology*, 15 (2): 215–32.

Rickards, L. (2006), "Capable, Enlightened and Masculine: Constructing English Agriculturalist Ideals in Formal Agricultural Education, 1845–2003," PhD thesis, University of Oxford.

Schmitt, C. ([1950] 2006), *The Nomos of the Earth in the International Law of the* Jus Publicum Europaeum, trans. and annot. G. L. Ulmen, New York: Telos.

Schneider, M. and P. McMichael (2010), "Deepening, and Repairing, the Metabolic Rift," *Journal of Peasant Studies*, 37 (3): 461–84.

Shiva, V. (2017), "*Swaraj*: From *Chipko* to *Navdanya*," in J. Hart (ed.), *The Wiley Blackwell Companion to Religion and Ecology*, 12–19, Oxford: Wiley.

Shotwell, A. (2016), *Against Purity: Living Ethically in Compromised Times*, Minneapolis, MN: University of Minnesota Press.

Strathern, M. (1992), *After Nature: English Kinship in the Late Twentieth Century*, Cambridge: Cambridge University Press.

Sundberg, J. (2014), "Decolonizing Posthumanist Geographies," *Cultural Geographies*, 21 (1): 33–47.

Thompson, C. (2013), *Good Science: The Ethical Choreography of Stem Cell Research*, Cambridge, MA: MIT Press.

Thompson, P. B. (2005), *The Spirit of the Soil: Agriculture and Environmental Ethics*, London: Routledge.

Tironi, M. (2018), "Hypo-interventions: Intimate Activism in Toxic Environments," *Social Studies of Science*, 48 (3): 438–55.

Tironi, M. (2019), "Lithic Abstractions: Geophysical Operations against the Anthropocene," *Distinktion: Journal of Social Theory*, 20 (3): 284–300.

Tsing, A. (2015), *The Mushroom at the End of the World: On the Possibility of Life in Capitaist Ruins*, Princeton, NJ: Princeton University Press.

Tsing, A., H. Swanson, E. Gan, and N. Bubandt (2017), *Arts of Living on a Damaged Planet: Ghosts and Monsters of the Anthropocene*, Minneapolis, MN: University of Minnesota Press.

Ureta, S. (2016), "Chemical Rubble: Historicizing Toxic Waste in a Former Mining Town in Northern Chile," *Arcadia*, 20 [https://doi.org/10.5282/rcc/7704].

Van Sant, L. (2018), "'The Long-Time Requirements of the Nation': The US Cooperative Soil Survey and the Political Ecologies of Improvement," *Antipode* [https://doi.org/10.1111/anti.12460].

Watts, V. (2013), "Indigenous Place-thought & Agency amongst Humans and Non-humans," *Decolonization: Indigeneity, Education & Society*, 2 (1): 20–34.

Whatmore, S. (2013a), "Earthly Powers and Affective Environments: An Ontological Politics of Flood Risk," *Theory, Culture & Society*, 30 (7/8): 33–50.

Whatmore, S. (2013b), "Nature and Human Geography," in P. Cloke, P. Crang, and M. Goodwin (eds.), *Introducing Human Geographies*, 3rd edition, 152–62, Abingdon: Routledge.

Whyte, K. (2017), "Indigenous Climate Change Studies: Indigenizing Futures, Decolonizing the Anthropocene," *English Language Notes*, 55 (1/2): 153–62.

Williams, R. (2008), *Notes on the Underground: An Essay on Technology, Society, and the Imagination*, 2nd edition, Cambridge, MA: MIT Press.

Worster, D. ([1979] 2004), *Dust Bowl: The Southern Plains in the 1930s*, Oxford: Oxford University Press.

Yusoff, K. (2010), "Biopolitical Economies and the Political Aesthetics of Climate Change," *Theory, Culture & Society*, 27 (2/3): 73–99.

Yusoff, K. (2012), "Aesthetics of Loss: Biodiversity, Banal Violence and Biotic Subjects," *Transactions of the Institute of British Geographers*, 37 (4): 578–92.

Yusoff, K. (2019), *A Billion Black Anthropocenes or None*, Minneapolis, MN: University of Minnesota Press.

3

Mapping Soil, Losing Ground? Politics of Soil Mapping

Juliette Kon Kam King and Céline Granjou

Cartography and mapping have never been neutral instruments of description and knowledge of space: they promote certain conceptions of what mapping means, and what territories are—making them amenable to certain projects of government (Turnbull 1989; Jacob 1992; Cosgrove 1999). Soil mapping aims to account for the diversity of vertical layering and horizontal distribution of soil. As with any kind of cartographic enterprise, soil maps are far from being mere tools or resources for representing an outside world that is already "out there," waiting to be measured and mapped; instead, soil maps materialize struggles for the imposition of value-laden views of what soils are, who soil experts are, and what knowing and governing soils means. In this chapter, we propose to reflect on the constitutive powers of soil maps, i.e., the notion that they do not merely hold instrumental value as transparent tools of representation and knowledge but also have the capacity to constitute soil issues and soil ontologies. As part of this book's broader attempt to articulate a material politics of soil, our reflection on soil maps draws inspiration from Bruce Braun and Sarah Whatmore's program to rethink the "constitutive nature of material processes and entities in social and political life" and to understand "the way that things ... help constitute the common worlds that we share" (2010: ix). As with any kind of knowledge enterprise, soil mapping relies on a range of material and social "inscriptions" (Latour 1999) and "infrastructures" (Star 1999), including soil maps and nomenclatures, soil samplings, measurement and analysis guidelines and tools, soil data and databases, and research institutions and organizations funding and fostering soil mapping. In this chapter, we are interested in the material politics of soil mapping, how soil maps and soil mapping infrastructures contribute to making soil thinkable and governable in some ways rather than others. As Turnbull put it, "we should perhaps recognize that all maps ... can be related to experience and that instead of rating them in terms of accuracy or scientificity we should consider only their 'workability'—how successful are they in achieving the aims for which they were drawn" (1989: 42). By retracing the history of soil mapping in France from the 1960s to the present, we show how shifting material infrastructures of soil mapping have been making soil amenable to various forms of management and governance—thus accounting for "the relationship between scientific and political practices and orderings" (Braun and Whatmore 2010: x).

In France, national soil mapping efforts developed as part of the broader national endeavor to "enhance" and exploit the newly colonized territories overseas and, in particular, to subject colonized soils to agricultural exploitation in the nineteenth and first half of the twentieth century—confirming classical insights into cartography as the quintessential imperial science, as it accounts for the land resources available for imperial expansion, occupation, and use (Edney 1997).[1] As numerous French soil scientists returned to the mainland in the wake of French former colonial territories' independence processes, soil cartography began to develop in relation to the rise of land-use planning needs and strategies in continental France: soil maps provided the French state with knowledge of the spatial distribution of soils as national resources amenable to political projects of land-use planning and agricultural development. The French Interministerial Delegation of Land Planning and Regional Attractiveness (DATAR) was, for instance, implemented in 1963 together with the first French Office of Soil Study and Soil Mapping (SESCPF) in 1968.

In this chapter, heeding Turnbull's (1989) provocative call to consider maps themselves as territories, we scrutinize which visions of soil and which types of soil governance soil maps contribute to asserting and imposing; we also ask how soil maps help certain groups and profiles of cartographers gain legitimacy and recognition over other, concurrent, groups. We scrutinize the shift from SESCPF's national, field-based soil surveying initiatives toward the current rise of digital techniques and approaches to soil mapping, which aim to monitor and predict soil properties and their changes over time at both the national and planetary levels. We suggest that this corresponds to a shift in academic and professional hierarchies within soil science, with statistical, computer-modeling, and big-data skills and disciplines gaining the upper hand over field-based soil expertise dedicated to characterizing and classifying local soils according to place-based formation mechanisms. In addition, as new digital soil maps tend to represent soil as a global, continuous cover, with varying properties and providing a range of "services" at the planetary scale, they also convey new understandings of what soils are, and how they should be governed. Digital soil maps suggest that soil itself is increasingly monitored, studied, and managed as the belowground part of the global environment, detached from pedologists' place-based experiences and research, and subjected instead to Earth system modeling and scientific global change monitoring.

Our findings draw on data collected during a sociological investigation into InfoSols, the research and development unit in charge of managing soil surveying and monitoring in France, which replaced SESCPF in 2000. InfoSol is part of the French National Institute of Research on Agriculture (INRA) and has had an important role in the development of digital soil mapping at the international level (in particular through the role played by its founder and former head, Dominique Arrouays). Throughout our investigation, we examined InfoSol archives (i.e., strategic and reporting literature), conducted ten interviews with InfoSol and SESCPF pedologists, researchers, and technicians, and attended InfoSol meetings as observers. This material is supported by a range of interviews conducted in 2017 with French soil scientists at INRA, as part of a broader research project addressing the development of French soil sciences and policies. To trace this history of soil mapping development, we rely on a range of articles written by soil scientists, including former heads of SESCPF (Marcel

Jamagne and Jean Boulaine) and InfoSol (Dominique Arrouays). We use these articles as both a source of historical information and an indication of the level of contestation surrounding the status and utility of soil maps, in a context where soil mapping has often been considered a low-status activity accessory to "true" research by other scientists and decision-makers (Hartemink and McBratney 2008). In this chapter, we distinguish between pedologists, i.e., researchers and technicians who have training in field soil science, and other researchers and technicians trained in statistics or computer modeling.

We first account for the shift in how soil has been represented and investigated, from SESCPF soil surveying programs in the 1970s to the rise of new soil mapping infrastructures in the 1990s, suggesting how these new infrastructures (including the types of maps but also soil science skills, tools, databases, and research organizations) fostered the reconceptualization of soil as a range of belowground quantitative properties associated with the provision of various functions and "services" to be monitored and managed—also offering new tools for soil policy. Then we account for the more recent rise of digital soil mapping technologies and unpack the tensions and criticisms within the soil science community regarding the way in which digital mapping technologies are challenging field-based expertise and understandings of local soils. As soil tends to be reconfigured from an object of study and concern for field experts into the belowground part of the "global environment" subjected to Earth system sciences modeling and global-change monitoring efforts, digital soil mapping projects may be at risk of "losing ground", i.e., losing soils themselves as situated and coherent objects of study and concern.

The Rise and Transformation of French Soil Mapping: 1970s–1990s

SESCPF was created in 1968 as part of INRA to provide agricultural managers and land-use planners with national soil inventories and maps. SESCPF's establishment in the 1960s resonated with "the period's renewed emphasis on planning" and the associated "promise of a global inventory of the world's soil resources" that were also at stake in the enterprise of making a global soil map of the world launched by the Food and Agriculture Organization (FAO) and the United Nations Educational, Scientific and Cultural Organization (UNESCO) in the 1960s and 1970s (Selcer 2015: 180). SESCPF maps aimed to make national soils amenable to political projects of planning and exploiting the national territory as a whole. In particular, they aimed to identify "zones to be kept for intensive agriculture and for forestry production, and those that can be assigned to other uses," as explained by former SESCPF members (SESCPF archives).

SESCPF soil maps drew on a classification created in 1956 by Georges Aubert, a French soil scientist working at the national research office dedicated to French former colonies (ORSTOM), and his colleague Philippe Duchaufour, an influential soil scientist who trained a number of French soil researchers. Their classification ordered soils in series, types, subtypes, and varieties, very much in the same way that natural history classified living beings in kingdoms, genres, and species. Soil types were primarily defined in accordance with what soil scientists call *pedogenesis*, meaning the dynamic processes of soil formation and weathering associated with different geological factors and, secondarily, with climate-related mechanisms. The description of soil pedogenesis mechanisms was grounded in painstaking fieldwork, including digging soil pits several meters deep, extracting soil samples with soil drills, and carrying them back to the lab for further analysis—in sometimes very poorly accessible sites, such as forests and mountains—as explained by Claude, a pedologist who worked at SESCPF:

> Soil scientists study something that they do not see ... ornithologists see birds— they even hear them. As for me, I have to dig .... Digging pits is very constraining: either it is done by hand and takes four hours, or we bring an excavator, which needs to gain access to the field site and many other things.

Most soil identification was indeed carried out directly in soil pits, relying on pedologists' experience and senses, i.e., sight, smell, and touch, as Isabelle, a pedologist at InfoSol, told us (see also Meulemans 2018):

> When a pedologist digs a hole and looks at the soil, she[2] will describe it, saying: "It has this color, I can see this layer, I see different colors, structures ... those aggregates are somewhat different here, here we have stones, here there isn't any stone ..." and all this information allows her to determine grossly ... whether that soil has developed following this or that soil formation mechanism.

Soil identification was mostly based on physicochemical parameters, without taking into account biology: the presence of microscopic life played no role in determining soil types. SESCPF soil maps' focus on physicochemical weathering helped to convey the notion that soil could only change over the very long term, as a very slow process in which humans played no part. The very fact that maps in the 1960s and 1970s were painstakingly drawn and expensively printed on paper further contributed to SESCPF pedologists favoring stable criteria for describing soils, and leaving aside human activities as subject to too many variations. Marcel Jamagne, pedologist and head of SESCPF, wrote: "We took into account only permanent characteristics in order for the map that was developed to be of long-term value" (1977: 24).

SESCPF aimed at mapping French soils at a scale of 1:100,000. On SESCPF maps, soils were represented as bounded polygonal areas, i.e., separate "soil individuals" (following an expression used by soil scientists) also called "pedons." To social thinker Salvatore Engel-Di Mauro, the pedon concept is "one of the contrivances" through which "soils' seamlessness" has been addressed by soil scientists (2020: 57–58). Underlying a "tendency to decontextualise and atomise soils to pedons" (2020: 60), the approach in terms of pedons emphasized the existence of autonomous "soil individuals" rather than soil interconnectedness.

In the 1990s, it became evident that the SESCPF program of national soil mapping did not advance as quickly as expected: in the mid-1990s, 27 years after its implementation, only 9 million hectares (i.e., 16% of the total area of continental

France) had been mapped at the 1:100,000 scale, because of a lack of budget and resources. SESCPF soil maps were sometimes deemed too costly, time-consuming, and difficult to use. Soil scientists who were not familiar with the nomenclature and classification of soils found them difficult to understand:

> [Relevant soil properties] are not contained in soil type names ... I cannot do anything with such a map. Anyone who is not an expert in soil maps cannot do anything with it.
>
> Julie, a soil physicist

An increasing number of soil scientists started to consider that field-based descriptions of soil pedogenesis were not "objective" enough as they stemmed from potentially arbitrary field-based judgments (see, for instance, Fauck et al. 1979). This shift in understanding soil maps' "objectivity" departed from pedologists' views that soil maps should reflect, as accurately as possible, their own academic efforts and struggles to adequately describe and name the formation mechanisms of local soils (pedogenesis); instead, new criteria of objectivity were progressively taking precedence over field-based descriptions of soil types, relying on the use of quantitative data and measurements of the type used by statisticians.

From Soil Surveying to Soil Monitoring

In 1992, the French soil classification system inspired by Aubert and Duchaufour's work was replaced by a new Pedological Framework that began to change how soils were conceptualized and mapped. This new framework unsettled the idea of bounded soils that was at the core of the former classification system by emphasizing the notion that "soils are not discrete entities: they form a three-dimensional continuum across the earth's surface" (Selcer 2015: 184). Claude, who was coordinator of the Pedological Framework, told us:

> In the new conception, what we call "soil" is an observation at a given point of a continuous soil cover. And we cannot consider that this observation refers to an area. Initially, in every country soil classifications were inspired by zoology and botany: but soil is completely different. There is no soil species so to speak ...

The new Pedological Framework initiated a shift toward a vision of soil as a global entity, i.e., the belowground part of our planetary environment. Furthermore, while the former classification placed much emphasis on characterizing the specific pedogenesis mechanisms that led to the formation of local soils in specific places, the new framework also granted a new focus to soil properties and functioning that could be approached through quantitative measurements of soil characteristics and components (pH, amount of carbon, nitrogen, etc.[3]).

A new national network of soil monitoring called RMQS,[4] which is still working today, was set up at the start of the 2000s, further contributing to shifting the attention from issues of soil classification and taxonomy toward monitoring soil properties—thus leading to a focus on what soils contain and what they do, rather than which "type" they belong to. RMQS introduced a grid of 2,240 sampling points covering the whole of France, i.e., one sampling point for each 16 × 16 km quadrat (including cultivated, forest, mountain, and urban soils). Soil was regularly extracted and analyzed at every point of RMQS in order to measure and monitor the changes in a range of soil properties. The first RMQS campaign produced 2 million pieces of data quantifying and describing soil properties for each of the 2,240 points of the network. Overall, the new soil mapping infrastructure tended to conceive of soils in a more reductionist manner (as soil was reduced to a range of quantitative variables that were both surveyed over space and monitored over time) but also as being much more connected to human activities that influence soil properties, such as carbon and nitrogen content, pH, and pollutants, than the SESCPF soil types were.

While SESCPF maps had emphasized the distinction between various soil types in local places, the Pedological Framework and RMQS tended to make various local soils commensurable and comparable from the point of view of their composition and functioning (for instance, their carbon or nitrogen content). The focus on making soils commensurable and comparable is clear from RMQS's systematic and standardized sampling strategy to collect and analyze soil pieces at the various points in the network. Soil samples were no longer extracted according to soil horizons (i.e., soil layers) visually identified by soil scientists; instead, they were extracted at a standard depth fixed in RMQS guidelines. Samples were extracted with standard tools, as close as possible to the theoretical point defined by the grid. Several samples were extracted at each place and at each depth and were then mixed in order to obtain an average sample.

Soil analyses and measurements were represented on maps called cartograms that provided managers and decision-makers with new tools for soil policy. Cartograms did not represent delimited areas corresponding to various types of soil; instead, they depicted a representation of the spatial distribution of a given property of soil across the country. On cartograms, the various soil types constituted the background while points represented the values of the specific soil property being mapped (such as, for instance, the amount of copper in topsoil).

Cartograms thus materialized the spatial surveillance of the various properties of soil and their evolution over time, i.e., the national soil *panopticon* introduced by the RMQS, in the Foucauldian sense of the term (Foucault [1975] 1995). They provided a central vantage point from which soil components and properties were observed over time.[5] Such maps allowed, for instance, the French government to provide the average level of soil pollution at the European or international level. To further the future-oriented dimension of the new mapping and monitoring infrastructures, a new Soil Conservatory—a soil archive dedicated to conserving soil samples for further potential analysis—was also instituted. As explained by Dominique Arrouays, a former head of InfoSol, the Soil Conservatory aimed at not only "keeping the memory of soil's past states" but also answering "questions that [were] likely to arise in the future" (Arrouays et al. 2003: 247).

The new set of mapping and monitoring infrastructures thus tended to no longer view soil as a local and national resource for long-term land-use planning but rather reconfigure it as an evolving national and European environmental resource. At the beginning of the 2000s, the framing of soil as a European environmental resource was also at work in the project of a new European Framework Directive on soil launched in 2006 on the model of the EU Water Framework Directive—which eventually failed to materialize (Fournil et al. 2018).

In 2000, the former SESCPF was split into a soil research lab and a new research support unit called InfoSol, in charge of soil mapping and monitoring. InfoSol continued to produce traditional soil maps alongside cartograms. InfoSol's various products were used by different organizations and groups: while governmental bodies and scientists increasingly turned to cartograms and data for the national, statistical values they provided regarding soil properties, local organizations, notably agricultural groups, continued to favor "conventional" soil maps and particularly the maps representing soils' agronomic potential that were derived from them.

Mapping Soils from the Sky

From the mid-1990s, soil mapping increasingly relied on the rise of digital techniques. Digital soil mapping uses the increasing amounts and varieties of environmental data (i.e., topography, climate, and geology data) that have been made available by the development of remote sensing techniques, satellite imagery, geographic information systems, and modeling techniques over the last two decades. Progress in computing science has also made it possible to store and process those data at ever-increasing speeds, and at lower cost. Digital soil mapping works by modeling the correlations between environmental data and field-based soil observations and measurements in order to predict soil characteristics and properties anywhere around the globe. Computer scientists and statisticians seek to formalize the statistical correlations between soil properties and their environmental conditions—thus making it possible to "guess" soil properties without physically measuring them in the field (Voltz et al. 2018). Sylvain, a team leader at InfoSol, emphasized that relying on the 2,240 data points provided by RMQS and using satellite data and digital models, he was able to "predict soil carbon at 90-meter intervals."

Digital soil mapping further fostered a vision of a global and continuous "soil cover" with varying properties, amenable to anticipatory strategies aimed at managing and securing a range of "soil services." Most digital maps are close to RMQS's cartograms: they do not represent separate local soil areas corresponding to various soil formation histories and structures; instead, each pixel represents the local value of a quantitative property of soil, such as organic carbon content, soil pH, or soil grain size. When new data are produced, modelers can re-run their models to revise the map: digital soil maps can thus be gradually improved following the continuous advances in soil information and environmental data.

In a context where the soil mapping community had long been striving to gain more support and users, digital soil mapping offered new opportunities to soil cartographers. Many of them still consider those new techniques a true "mapping revolution" (Hartemink et al. 2010), as they allow for a shift from a naturalistic enterprise of describing and classifying local soils to a new form of data-driven, computer-based, prediction-oriented soil science. According to Dominique Arrouays, who was head of InfoSol from 2000 to 2011, the constitution of this "emerging global soil information system" would "ultimately help contend with food security, global climate change, and other wide-reaching environmental and economic issues across the globe" (Arrouays et al. 2014: xi, 13). Soil monitoring and digital mapping were not only meant to help decision-makers and land-use planners regarding the agricultural potential of soils but, more broadly, to help assess and enhance the various "services" rendered by soil to society, including plant production as well as water purification, carbon regulation, and biodiversity maintenance (Arrouays et al. 2003). Digital soil mapping thus provided soil scientists with new opportunities to develop powerful promises and expectations in the field of global change adaptation and food security, relying on the reconceptualization of soil as a global provider of ecological services that can be conserved, managed, and enhanced by using information and expertise derived from the new infrastructures of soil monitoring and digital mapping.

Importantly, the rise of digital soil mapping techniques was linked to new agendas and initiatives of soil mapping at the global, planetary scale, including the international project GlobalSoilMap, in which InfoSol was a leading institute through the role of Dominique Arrouays as Science Officer since 2012.[6] The GlobalSoilMap project, which is still very much active today, aims to map the planet's soil at a very detailed scale following a 90 × 90 m grid—resonating with the utopia of "an 'unconscionable' map at the same size as the empire itself" (Borges 1964, quoted in Edney 1997: 1). Julie, a soil physicist, explained the objectives of the GlobalSoilMap in the following terms:

> Anywhere on the emerged part of the planet, GlobalSoilMap will not tell you: this is a ranker soil, this is a clay soil … instead, it will tell you: between 0 and 5 centimeters deep there is this percentage of clay, this rate of porosity, this amount of carbon … We provide a new representation of soil that provides soil properties in any place.

Considering soil as "one of the top priorities for the global environmental policy agenda," the GlobalSoilMap project aims to develop instrumental information and tools for "scientific communities from climate and environmental modeling to decision making and sustainable resources management" (Arrouays et al. 2018: 5).

Initiatives and projects such as GlobalSoilMap contributed to reconfiguring soil as the underground part of the "global environment" understood as an object of scientific monitoring, big data analysis, and modeling aimed at informing global environmental governance. Miller accounted for the implementation of "impressive new technoscientific capabilities for data collection and analysis on global scales" (2015: 284) in the wake of the Second World War, thus making possible "the modeling and visualization of global systems and processes" (2015: 279; see also Elichirigoity 1999). Miller emphasized how big data infrastructures were both embedded in and contributing to emerging sociotechnical imaginaries of globalism, including imaginaries of a global climate and a global environment. The reimagining of soil as the underground part of the global environment to be monitored and managed further extends the imaginaries of globalism connected to environmental big data and new global organizations of environmental governance (such as, for instance, the IPCC—Intergovernmental Panel on Climate Change—and IPBES—Intergovernmental Platform on Biodiversity and Ecosystem Services). Critics of this rising connection between environmental big data and global environmental governance emphasized how the notion of a "global environment" was remote from any situated observation and experience of local places and environments— thus tending to "sacrifice local and heterogeneous living forms to the grandiose ideal of global [environment]" (Devictor and Bensaude-Vincent 2016: 11; see also Jasanoff 2010). Instead, the "global environment" combines a notion of a finite and fragile global system with an overrated confidence in the capacity of Earth system science modeling and big data development to understand and ultimately manage this system (Turnhout et al. 2016), as environmental big data and modeling are part of the "daunting task [that] lies ahead for scientists and engineers to guide society towards environmentally sustainable management during the era of the Anthropocene" (Crutzen 2002, quoted in Bonneuil 2015: 23). They also pointed out that refining environmental monitoring systems to collect ever larger volumes of data on ongoing environmental deterioration would amount to little more than "rearranging the chairs on the Titanic to get a better view" (Braverman 2017).

The development of digital soil mapping clearly aims to make soil and soil science part of the global environment narrative connecting big data infrastructures and modeling with anticipatory strategies to secure the biosphere and humankind against environmental degradation. Distancing itself from the scholarly agendas of understanding local *pedogenesis* mechanisms, digital soil mapping tends instead to affirm soil cartography's contribution to the "green stewardship" of the global environment in a time of climate change. We found, for instance, that digital soil mapping specialists tended to conceive of their work as being useful for providing soil-related big data to feed ever more integrated Earth system models, as explained by Alexandre, a statistician at InfoSol:

> Climate scientists use a 1 km by 1 km grid … we should provide them with homogeneous soil data, following their grid, in order for them to cross-analyze them with climate data.

This statement is telling of a certain vision of which type of soil knowledge "matters," i.e., a type of knowledge likely to make soil science part of the environmental expertise provided to policymakers for global environmental management purposes.

In the final section, we suggest that not all soil researchers hold the same visions of the types of soil knowledge and soil mapping that matter, and we unpack controversies and criticisms within soil science regarding digital mapping agendas.

Losing Ground?

Far from merely representing the soil "out there" with greater accuracy or objectivity, digital infrastructures of soil mapping contributed to shifting visions of what soils are, as well as of who soil experts are and what sort of soil knowledge matters—as summarized by Pierre, a pedologist at InfoSol, who remarked that, "it [has become] easier to justify hiring a technician in charge of databases than a soil scientist." The rise of digital soil mapping techniques indeed contributed to enacting a vision from above, a "non-terrestrial" approach to soil (Arènes et al. 2018), remote from the ways in which field experts make sense of soils in specific places. Satellites, drones, radars, and sensors are able to produce vast sets of measurements without having to dig into the soil, on much broader scales and with a much higher frequency than soil scientists in the field. Remote-sensing measurements of soils' colors, capacities to reflect light, and other physical characteristics, when adequately processed and interpreted by computer scientists, provide information on soil uses and even on certain mechanisms of soil formation and weathering. We found that a number of pedologists feared that digital soil mapping might reduce the resources allocated to fieldwork and more generally the need for field-based expertise. Recently, InfoSol members have indeed been asking for training in geostatistics, statistical software (such as R), and big data rather than in pedology. Already a number of decisions related to RMQS sampling were made by statisticians; pedologists merely had to apply them in the field: "We carry out the extraction at this point because it's where . . . statistics says it's where it should be done" (Pierre, a pedologist involved in RMQS). We found that recent decisions at InfoSol revolved around orientating fieldwork toward testing, confirming, and improving digital models—meaning that soil fieldwork would increasingly be carried out in order to meet the needs of modelers instead of those of pedologists, who would tend to be reduced to the role of "invisible" field technicians.

We found that this new division of soil mapping work was intensely discussed and sometimes resented by a number of pedologists trained in field research, who argued that digital mapping techniques do not necessarily allow for developing adequate understandings of soils. To one of them, "digital mapping cannot go without field observation—even though some people tend quite quickly to dispense with soil scientists and make maps that do not make any sense." This is why, he added, statisticians and modelers need to "keep their feet planted on the ground." Some recent publications in high-ranking soil science journals have also argued that "delivering a result every 100 m makes no sense given the inadequate soil density information that we have" (Hempel et al. 2013: 12); in order to make sense, computer techniques and results should be accompanied by a much larger amount of field-based soil information (Baveye et al. 2018).

According to certain soil scientists skeptical of digital soil mapping, the focus on computer modeling and predicting not only hinders a "real understanding of soil," it also risks producing absurd results "remote from any real soil knowledge", including creating "fake soils", as pointed out by a computer modeler at InfoSol (see also Rossiter 2018):

> Digital mapping often predicts properties one by one and for a given depth, which means that we miss two things: first, it is precisely the correlations between various soil properties that allow models to represent real soils . . . and if you predict those properties in an isolated manner, at some point, you can get a combination of properties that does not exist in nature.

Pedologists in particular criticized the use of data-mining methodologies by computer scientists, i.e., statistical methodologies that seek to try and find correlations between soil data and various available environment data sets. To Sylvain, a pedologist and team leader at InfoSol, this may lead to "crazy" results without any grounding in the reality of the field:

> Some colleagues think, "What if I tried to cross-analyze this data with climate data? Maybe that would give me a better prediction," and they do it. So we start hunting out data in order to add it to our stuff . . . and you can cross-analyze soil data with any kind of crazy criteria and maybe it will work!

Science historian Perrin Selcer observed that "the material characteristics that make soil such a vivid symbol of local identity—its boundless variability—made it particularly resistant to the standardization necessary to achieve the view from above" (2015: 184). Here we do not only argue that soil variability may resist the standardization involved in the data-fication of soil: following certain critiques made by pedologists, our key point is that digital soil mapping tends to disassemble soil as an object of study and concern into a range of variables and functional properties of the "global environment" that may no longer have any direct relation to soil as a reality in the field. For instance, a soil scientist at INRA explained that digital soil mapping tends to disassemble and dissect soil into a range of quantitative values—at odds with field experts' systemic approach to local soils as wholes:

> When I was a young researcher in soil science, we were finding pedologists a bit boring because they were obsessed with soil types and classification . . . but on the other hand, they had a naturalist and systemic vision of soil as an object . . . We are now doing very nice soil maps with remote sensing techniques, spatial databases; but this is not the same thing as the knowledge brought by pedology, by someone who is able to identify soil areas' shapes on the paper and to integrate the slope, parent material, vegetation cover into that determination . . .

Pioneering Russian soil scientist Dokuchaev in the late eighteenth century made the seminal observation that soil was an "independent natural-historical body . . . which made a soil science possible" because it enabled "the synthetic study of soil morphology" (Selcer 2015: 184). As any organized body, soil "could be dissected to understand the relations of parts to the whole" (2015: 185). While digital mapping techniques still dissect soil into a range of components, the whole to which soil components are related has shifted from the situated soil under study to the global earth system. The ultimate goal of digital soil mapping is no longer to study soil for itself but instead to describe the various underground properties and services of soil as the underground part of the "global environment"—sacrificing the heterogeneity and specificities of land and soil as they can be observed and experienced in favor of the production of big soil data as the dominant strategy for anticipating and securing global environmental governance and adaptation in a rapidly changing world.

Conclusion

Soils in cartograms and digital maps are no longer the same soils as in "conventional" soil maps: from a bounded object, a variety of stable "soil individuals," soil has been reconceptualized as a global, continuous cover and dissected into a range of functional properties to be monitored over time. While conventional soil mapping was grounded in painstaking fieldwork, soil information systems and digital soil mapping have greatly strengthened the predominance of statisticians and computer scientists over field experts—contributing to soil science shifting from field-based natural science technologies toward big data technologies that are typically in use in Earth system science. Of course "conventional" maps of soil have not disappeared, and digital soil mapping also includes attempts to predict soil types relying on digital computer and modeling. However, there is no doubt there is an increasing interest from both academic communities and decision-makers in soil property monitoring and computer modeling and prediction, in particular in relation to growing hopes and expectations around bio-geo-engineering, including the use of soils as carbon sinks in climate mitigation policies (Kon Kam King et al. 2018; Granjou and Salazar 2019).

On the one hand, these transformations can be read as an ecologization of soil knowledge: while conventional maps constituted soils mostly as agricultural resources, soils have been progressively reconfigured as environmental and ecological resources central to water and climate regulation and biodiversity conservation. On the other hand, our findings suggest how the shift from soil surveying to soil monitoring also resulted in further extending the technoscientific, imperialist dream of an all-encompassing ecological surveillance of the globe into the underground. Soils have been made into a new component of the ever more integrative initiatives of Earth system expertise and forecasting. The rise of digital soil mapping pertains to the technoscientific big-data vision of producing an ever increasing amount of environmental data as the best option to "manage" the environmental crisis. This trend also echoes with the recent emergence of the "critical zone" science community, which brings together soil scientists, hydrologists, geomorphologists, and hydrologists in order to monitor and study the thin layer situated between the bedrock and the canopy (including soil) as being "critical" to all life on Earth. One of the critical zone scientists, interviewed in *Libération*, one of the largest French daily newspapers, explained his conviction that we need to monitor the environment with a much higher frequency than has been done up until now: "sampling and analyzing a river once a week is like listening to a Beethoven symphony by sampling one note every minute."[7]

By reconfiguring soil as the underground part of the global environment, the rise of digital soil mapping continues the broader move, started after the Second World War, by which climate and then biodiversity have been made global environmental objects. Yet compared with the making of climate and biodiversity into abstract and global objects of environmental monitoring and governance, the globalization of soil through digital soil maps also raises some specific issues related to the place-based character of soils. Soils, being inherently situated and local, ground us in our sense of being "there." As digital soil maps no longer seek to link geographical and historical patterns with specific places but rather to achieve an information system on the underground infrastructure of the global environment, they paradoxically contribute to reinforcing the problematic "absence" of soil from our view, everyday experience, and sense of care (Puig de la Bellacasa, 2014).

Notes

1   Soil scientists also relate the beginning of soil mapping in the United States and Russia with efforts to expand soil exploitation and agriculture in the eighteenth century (Hartemink 2016).
2   Although most pedologists are men, we did interview a few female pedologists.
3   These are classical soil properties in soil science, providing information about soils' agronomic value and helping assess soils' hydrological and climatic role.
4   Réseau de Mesures de la Qualité des Sols.
5   Foucault was inspired by Jeremy Bentham's panopticon, which he proposed in the eighteenth century for prisons, insane asylums, schools, hospitals, and factories. Bentham's panopticon was a circular building with an observation tower in the center of an open space surrounded by an outer wall. This structure would allow guards to continually see inside each cell from their vantage point in a high central tower, unseen by the prisoners. Constant observation acted as a control mechanism because the awareness of being constantly surveilled is internalized.
6   The GlobalSoilMap project has been supported in particular by France, Australia, the United States, China, and international organizations (the World Bank, the FAO, and private sponsors such as the Bill and Melinda Gates Foundation and the Alliance for a Green Revolution in Africa), as well as by the International Union of Soil Sciences.
7   Jérôme Gaillardet, interviewed in *Libération*, June 30, 2016 [https://www.liberation.fr/debats/2016/06/30/une-zone-si-critique_1463172].

References

Arènes, A., B. Latour, and J. Gaillardet (2018), "Giving Depth to the Surface: An Exercise in the Gaia-graphy of Critical Zones," *The Anthropocene Review*, 5 (2): 120–35.

Arrouays, D., C. Jolivet, L. Boulonne, G. Bodineau, C. Ratié, N. Saby et al. (2003), "Le Réseau de Mesures de la Qualité des Sols (RMQS) de France," *Étude et Gestion des Sols*, 4 (10): 241–50.

Arrouays, D., N. McKenzie, J. Hempel, A. Richer de Forges, and A. B. McBratney, eds. (2014), *GlobalSoilMap: Basis of the Global Spatial Soil Information System*, London: CRC Press.

Arrouays, D., A. Richer-de-Forges, A. McBratney, A. Hartemink, B. Minasny, I. Savin et al. (2018), "The GlobalSoilMap Project: Past, Present, Future, and National Examples from France," *Dokuchaev Soil Bulletin*, 95: 3–22.

Baveye, P. C., J. Berthelin, D. Tessier, and G. Lemaire (2018), "The '4 per 1000' Initiative: A Credibility Issue for the Soil Science Community?," *Geoderma*, 309: 118–23.

Bonneuil, C. (2015), "The Geological Turn: Narratives of the Anthropocene," in C. Hamilton, F. Gemenne, and C. Bonneuil (eds.), *The Anthropocene and the Global Environmental Crisis: Rethinking Modernity in a New Epoch*, 17–31, London: Routledge.

Braun, B. and S. J. Whatmore (2010), "The Stuff of Politics: An Introduction," in B. Braun and S. J. Whatmore (eds.), *Political Matter: Technoscience, Democracy, and Public Life*, ix–xl, Minneapolis, MN: University of Minnesota Press.

Braverman, I. (2017), "*Bleached!* Managing Coral Catastrophe," *Futures*, 92: 12–28.

Cosgrove, D., ed. (1999), *Mappings*, London: Reaktion Books.

Devictor, V. and B. Bensaude-Vincent (2016), "From Ecological Records to Big Data: The Invention of Global Biodiversity," *History and Philosophy of the Life Sciences*, 38 (4): art. 13 [https://doi.org/10.1007/s40656-016-0113-2].

Edney, M. (1997), *Mapping an Empire: The Geographical Construction of British India, 1765–1843*, Chicago, IL: University of Chicago Press.

Elichirigoity, F. (1999), *Planet Management: Limits to Growth, Computer Simulation, and the Emergence of Global Spaces*, Evanston, IL: Northwestern University Press.

Engel-Di Mauro, S. (2020), "Learning Dialectics to Grow Better Soils Knowledge, not Bigger Crops: A Materialist Dialectics and Relationality for Soil Science," *Capitalism Nature Socialism*, 31 (1): 52–69.

Fauck, R., M. Lamouroux, A. Perraud, P. Quantin, P. Roederer, J. Viellefon et al. (1979), *Projet de classification des sols*, Paris: Services scientifiques centraux de l'ORSTOM.

Foucault M. ([1975] 1995), *Discipline and Punish: The Birth of the Prison*, New York: Penguin Random House.

Fournil J., J. Kon Kam King, L. Cécillon, and C. Granjou (2018), "Le sol: Enquête sur les mécanismes de (non) émergence d'un problème public environnemental," *VertigO*, 18 (2) [https://doi.org/10.4000/vertigo.20433].

Granjou, C. and J. Salazar (2019), "The Stuff of Soil: Below-ground Agency in the Making of Future Climates," *Nature and Culture*, 14 (1): 39–60.

Hartemink, A. E. (2016), "The Definition of Soil Since the Early 1800s," *Advances in Agronomy*, 137: 73–126.

Hartemink, A. E. and A. McBratney (2008), "A Soil Science Renaissance," *Geoderma*, 148 (2): 123–29.

Hartemink, A. E., J. Hempel, P. Lagacherie, A. McBratney, N. McKenzie, R. A. MacMillan et al. (2010), "*GlobalSoilMap.net*—A New Digital Soil Map of the World," in J. L. Boettinger, D. W. Howell, A. C. Moore, A. E. Hartemink, and S. Kienast-Brown (eds.), *Digital Soil Mapping: Bridging Research, Environmental Application, and Operation*, 423–28, Dordrecht: Springer.

Hempel, J. W., A. B. McBratney, N. J. McKenzie, A. E. Hartemink, R. MacMillan, P. Lagacherie et al. (2013), "Vers une cartographie numérique des propriétés des sols du monde: Le programme GlobalSoilMap," *Étude et Gestion des Sols*, 20 (1): 7–14.

Jacob, C. (1992), *L'empire des cartes: Approche théorique de la cartographie à travers l'histoire*, Paris: Albin Michel.

Jamagne, M. (1977), "Le service d'étude des sols et de la carte pédologique de France de l'INRA," *Génie Rural*.

Jasanoff, S. (2010), "A New Climate for Society," *Theory, Culture & Society*, 27 (2/3): 233–53.

Kon Kam King, J., C. Granjou, J. Fournil, and L. Cecillon (2018), "Soil Sciences and the French 4 per 1000 Initiative—The Promises of Underground Carbon," *Energy Research & Social Science*, 45: 144–52.

Latour, B. (1999), "Circulating Reference: Sampling the Soil in the Amazon Forest," in *Pandora's Hope: Essays on the Reality of Science Studies*, 24–79, Cambridge, MA: Harvard University Press.

Meulemans, G. (2018), "Des hommes qui creusent: Suivre le sol en pédologie," in L. Mariani and C. Plancke (eds.), *(D')écrire les affects: Perspectives et enjeux anthropologiques*, 299–325, Paris: Petra.

Miller, C. A. (2015), "Globalizing Security: Science and the Transformation of Contemporary Political Imagination," in S. Jasanoff and S.-H. Kim (eds.), *Dreamscapes of Modernity: Sociotechnical Imaginaries and the Fabrication of Power*, 277–99, Chicago, IL: University of Chicago Press.

Puig de la Bellacasa, M. (2014), "Encountering Bioinfrastructure: Ecological Struggles and the Sciences of Soil," *Social Epistemology*, 28 (1): 26–40.

Rossiter, D. G. (2018), "Past, Present & Future of Information Technology in Pedometrics," *Geoderma*, 324: 131–37.

Selcer, P. (2015), "Fabricating Unity: The FAO-UNESCO Soil Map of the World," *Historical Social Research/Historische Sozialforschung*, 40 (2): 174–201.

Star, S. L. (1999), "The Ethnography of Infrastructure," *American Behavioral Scientist*, 43 (3): 377–91.

Turnbull, D. (1989), *Maps are Territories: Science is an Atlas; A Portfolio of Exhibits*, Geelong, VIC: Deakin University Press.

Turnhout, E., A. Dewulf, and M. Hulme (2016), "What Does Policy-Relevant Global Environmental Knowledge Do? The Cases of Climate and Biodiversity," *Current Opinion in Environmental Sustainability*, 18: 65–72.

Voltz, M., D. Arrouays, A. Bispo, P. Lagacherie, B. Laroche, B. Lemercier et al. (2018), *La cartographie des sols en France: État des lieux et perspectives*, Paris: INRA.

4

Soils and Commodification

Salvatore Engel-Di Mauro and Levi Van Sant

Introduction

Selling soils is now part of everyday fare. Or, at least, soil is what is claimed to be sold. The deed is often spread out for us as displays of tidy bags of topsoil or peat for gardens or landscaping. One even hears talk of importing soil, as if soils were detachable from the landscapes where they form. Officially, for instance, the USDA recognizes soil as movable, and includes all sorts of organic materials in this framing (except peat).[1] All sorts of commercial activities thrive on soil even when soils are not sold directly, in the form of farmland, overburden, or excavation waste in mining and building ventures. Some even go so far as to assert that "[h]istorically, land and soils have mostly been treated as private property" (Bartkowski et al. 2018: 1; see also Pascual et al. 2015). And since soils are said to be in a state of degradation worldwide (FAO 2015), much fanfare has accompanied the turning of soils into an object of governance, supposedly as management of (mostly) private property. This understanding provides a framework of government-based decision-making about soil use that is widely promoted within the European Union and the United Nations. The framework forms part of the instigation of such lofty ideals as the "circular economy" and the "bioeconomy" (European Commission 2018; Juerges and Hansjürgens 2018). For instance, under such a scheme, agro-mining promises new riches through the use of hyper-accumulator plants to extract metals in highly polluted soils. Polluting could never have been more useful, at least for those reaping the profits (van der Ent et al. 2015). These policies are far from mere fantasies. They are being translated into action. In the case of the soil bank of New York City, for example, soil removal becomes a recycling program—the circular economy in full splendor (Egendorf et al. 2018; Walsh et al. 2018).

These projects are part of a future that claims to conserve or protect soils. Yet this wonderful world, where profit-making is perfectly compatible with ecological reality, seems eerily similar to something witnessed before. It is like an attempt to update or "rebrand" what used to be touted as "ecological modernization" or, prior to that, "sustainable development"—with the fundamental contradiction between actually existing ecosystems (and soils) and actually existing capitalism left essentially intact. In many ways, the above-described initiatives are diverse ways in which soils are treated as if they were commodities. In this chapter, we argue that soil commodification is a self-contradictory process that enables ecological destruction, fundamentally constraining (and sometimes prohibiting) soil conservation or protection.

But can soils even be commodities in a capitalist sense? This depends in some ways on what is considered to qualify as soil within a capitalist system. Typically, soil is collapsed into the concept of land or vice versa, even as the selling of soil is separated from land sale and in spite of physical land features that are manifestly not soil, such as dunes, rock outcrops, and much else. Such incoherence emerges not out of any characteristics specific to the non-human world but out of capitalist attempts to objectify "soil" and "land." To make sense of such patent incoherence in capitalist understandings of soil, we deem it useful to distinguish between the commodification of soil as land and of soil itself.

Definitions abound regarding soil, even within the conventional scientific communities dedicated to the study of soils. It is not the intention here to list and describe the multiple ways in which soils are defined, a topic that has already been taken up elsewhere (Engel-Di Mauro 2014). The details of the multifarious and contradictory valuations within a capitalist system remain firmly entrenched within a unifying notion of value as that which is marketable (exchange value). Since the commodification process implies a specifically capitalist society, the discussion here is limited to conventional notions of soil as a medium made up of altered and bound mineral and organic materials, with variable characteristics and permutations, and amenable to growing crops or, in less restrictive understandings, to sustaining ecosystems. The broadly contrasting views of soil as object of economic exploitation and as component of ecosystems will not be investigated here, but it is important to consider that within scientific communities, there have always been (usually unwitting) dissenters even in the very conceptualization of soil, just as within capitalist societies there have always been dissenters from market reductionism generally. In exploring the relationship between soils and commodification, we must nevertheless draw from dissenting perspectives largely external to soil science as a result of a lack of any articulation of critiques of capitalism among soil scientists.

Regardless, it could even be questionable whether soils can make it as a commodity, as will be discussed below. This is because soils are not detachable from the ecosystems of which they are part in ways that single organisms are, and because soils entail interacting and mutually dependent mineral and organic substances and organisms that literally fall apart when removed from context. Yet, if soils can be *treated* as commodities, which they undoubtedly are, the prospects for soil conservation or protection may be fatally undermined in the process of commodification (the making of something or someone into a commodity, an item whose worth is determined by the degree to which it can be marketed, sold, purchased). For it would mean conserving or protecting something only as long as it is commercially viable, or profitable, to do so. One might therefore hope that soils will never be really made into commodities. Even if soils somehow slipped, due to their very nature, from the commodification process, the consequence would be their worthlessness within a capitalist society. In capitalist logic, there is no exit from profit-contingent worth (not in the environmental economists' sense) other than indifference toward soils. Both are processes that lead to partial or total soil destruction. Thus, in the end, soil conservation or protection ends up not being about soils in themselves at all, but about how capitalism conditions relationships to soils.

Commodities and Commodification

Before even beginning a discussion on soil as commodity, it is helpful to gain some clarity about what commodities are and/or imply. There are, we believe, sufficiently compelling reasons to deny any legitimacy to conventional understandings pivoting on marginal utility based on individual preferences or choices. In the same manner, we regard as equally contestable Ricardian-Smithian assumptions about values being tied to human labor. These are exercises in reductionism and tautology, as pointed out by many over more than a century, including Marx regarding the labor theory of value[2] (Postone 1996; Guerrien 2003). We find it much more convincing and analytically effective to grasp commodities as having the dual and contradictory values of use and exchange and as first and foremost products of social relations and struggles. The process of commodification is hardly accounted for or even recognizable by appealing to human labor quantities, since, as Marx made amply clear throughout his critiques of the capitalist mode of production, the issue is the extraction of surplus labor to capitalists' collective benefit. Commodification is among the essential conduits to this end (Marx [1857–58] 1963, [1867] 1992).

Likewise, individual or consumer choice cannot be the basis of commodification, since individual preferences only count once something or someone is turned into a commodity, that is, prior to any possibility of market sale. This is another reason to look to other social processes when it comes to commodities and therefore value. Commodification, rampant and taken for granted worldwide, is a valuation process that is peculiar to capitalist societies. There are many kinds of ways in which something or someone is turned into an item with exchange-value (i.e., potentially sellable), but a commodity can only have exchange-value if it first has a use-value. Use-value may precede capitalist practices or preexist capitalist relations or be enforced by them, such as technological innovations for which markets must be created through economic coercion or inculcation via marketing or educational apparatuses. Given the nature of commodification and commodities, we find any application of classical (labor-input) and neoclassical (marginalist consumerist) notions of value irrelevant to soils, as discussed below. It is most unfortunate that these two frameworks continue to predominate in both conventional and alternative discussions when it comes to soils (see, for example, Baveye et al. 2016; Bartkowski et al. 2018).

One may therefore need to start from rather elementary questions to grasp the full consequences of treating a biophysical process as if it were a commodity. This is what defines most societies today, which are pervaded by capitalist practices and under capitalist hegemony. An investigation into any process of commodification necessitates a discussion of the meaning of the term commodity. As with soils, there is a range of definitions for commodity, albeit a much more restricted one. However, conventional notions of commodities have little analytical utility when attempts are made to explain how soils are valued in capitalist ("free-market") terms. This is because of their reductionist and tautological nature.

In mainstream economics, commodities are fungible (i.e., interchangeable or, more specifically, tradable in a capitalist market) goods or services, whose value is determined by market forces, which in turn determine whether a good or service is a commodity

(Bigger and Robertson 2017). Fungibility is a reductionism, especially in ecological terms (Burkett 1999). There is in this notion the pretense that anything or anyone can have equal value. With respect to soil, one would be led to believe by this kind of economistic approach that soil could be conceivably equivalent to one or more earthworms, depending on the values for such "goods" established by those with the power to sell and purchase. Or perhaps soils are now just "services," given the prevailing parlance of ecosystem services (Kosoy and Corbera 2010; Peterson et al. 2010).

At the same time, since commodity market value (expressed as price) is the very basis of fungibility, one enters rapidly into an exercise in tautology. That is, commodities have value because they are interchangeable and commodity interchangeability is due to commodities having the same market value (or price). Translated into soil terms, soil has a price because it is tradable (fungible) and soil is tradable because it has a price. This now common-sense conceptualization of biophysical phenomena (such as land) has been imposed, as many have pointed out, through centuries of blood and gore involved in wresting people away from their means of survival (Blaikie 1985; Mrozowski 1999; Prudham 2007; van der Ploeg 2010) and from their understandings of their place firmly within (not outside of) nature. This is how it can even be conceivable to ascribe prices to soil, where the relative value or worthlessness of soil is ultimately contingent on what is deemed profitable by those with the greatest economic leverage—a tiny minority of humanity.

Commodification and the Rest of Nature

Much has been written on the commodification of "nature" (e.g., McAfee 1999; Liverman 2004; Smith 2007; Bermejo 2014; Emel 2017; Gunderson 2017; Huber 2017; Bryant 2018), but the matter of soils seems largely excluded so far from such critical analyses. Since their emergence, capitalist relations are premised on appropriating— usually by force or implicit threats of force and with crucial state assistance (or as part of statecraft)—bits of the environment or ecosystems, or whatever can be derived from them. This is also the basis of how private property is established and enforced (everything else historically follows, as one cannot eat or drink or be clothed or sheltered by the circuitry behind financial transactions). Land is therefore a primary component in the process of forging private property (Prudham 2015). But capitalist relations are not about hoarding bits of the Earth but about accumulating capital. Capital is value in motion, going cyclically from production to commodity to money forms. Commodities sit squarely within this constant transformation process and are valued only insofar as they can be sold (turned into monetary form) so that they can be useful for capital accumulation. Yet, for commodities to be sold, they must also be useful, and not to just anyone, but specifically to those who have purchasing power (or be associated with those having such economic means on their behalf, be it a household, cooperative, state organ, etc.). Commodities in capitalist contexts are by and large useful specifically for human beings in possession of money forms of capital (Marx [1867] 1992).

Castree (2003) has critically summarized various approaches to the relationship between commodification and the rest of nature. He provides a succinct overview of

Marxist perspectives that sees the process as involving privatization, alienability, individuation, abstraction, reductionist valuation, and displacement. The making or forcing of property (exclusionary access) over bits of nature is, in this light, a precondition of commodification, as pointed out above (Labban 2008: 39–40). However, alienability is another facet of commodities that may or may not entail ownership, but it is a prerequisite for exchangeability (see also Musto 2010). For something or someone to be treated as exchangeable, though, there has to be a process of individuation, that is, the possibility for separability and decontextualization (for an example involving soils and biochar, see Leach et al. 2012). An object needs to be understood as sufficiently homogeneous to be replaceable with an equivalent (functional and spatial). This is the process of abstraction, which is evident each time we receive wages for our labor. Concrete labor is thereby made into an abstract form, which can be equated with all other concrete instances of labor. To illustrate, fixing a toilet and ploughing are all equalized through the wage. Abstraction makes for a peculiar form of valuation in that it is reduced to the quantitative (abstracted) dimension of human labor, as discussed above (this is really why, ultimately, the activities of other beings cannot be made to count in a capitalist system). In turn, valuation conforms to suitability or potential for making profits (exchange-value), regardless of usefulness (use-value). Finally, the social relations that are behind commodities and commodification are displaced to the commodities themselves. This is the specific kind of fetishism Marx argued is typical of capitalist society (e.g., Marx [1876] 1978, critiquing social democrats for conflating natural wealth with what is socially produced). Hence, in capitalist logic, values can be derived from ecosystem services. The ecosystem, not the social relations that chalk up what is valuable, is deemed the source of value (perhaps even price, to the zealous). Even more obvious is when geological strata are given magical price-determining and even war-making powers in the discourse on the economics of, and conflicts over, mineral and fossil fuel resources.

As Neil Smith (2008) pointed out, nature is a contradictory notion in capitalist practices and ideologies. It is at once internal (capitalism as human nature, natural capital, etc.) and external (exploitable otherness). Hence, soil is external insofar as it is a non-valued condition of production, free for the taking or exploiting. It is literally worth nothing unless it forms the precondition for power conferred by means of land ownership. Soil in itself, within capitalism, cannot be valued because "it is not the product of human labor, and hence it is not reproducible" (Labban 2008: 40). When soil disappears, through erosion, it is not part of any capitalist calculation until erosion hampers production and so profitability. This is one way to understand the consequences of the Dust Bowl and the interventions that succeeded it, including valuation systems (Baveye et al. 2016) and the Soil Conservation Service. At such moments, capitalist value is ascribed to soil as a cost of production (often borne by state institutions; that is, socialized) and thereby internalized, though never completely, within capitalist calculation. In this relationship to nature as external and internal, commodification can be direct or indirect, by proxy (Castree 2003: 285–86). Extracting and selling topsoil would be a direct form, while land valuation (based on expected soil productivity) for taxation or sale is a potential proxy form of, or a precursor to, soil commodification. Another example of proxy or indirect commodification would be the various prices ascribed to soil by scientists in the absence of any marketability, such as estimates of the economic loss related to soil erosion (e.g., Pimentel et al. 1995). Yet such exercises should make it clear that specifically capitalist relations are the ultimate source of pricing, including what is deigned to be commodified and the manner in which commodification is carried out.

Therefore, soils cannot be commodities, but social relations may change in such a way as to compel people to treat soils as if they were commodities. While soils cannot become commodities, as in fact nothing (and especially no one) can, the commodification process is necessarily affected by the rest of nature, since society is always part of an ecosystem. However, to state the obvious, it is not the rest of nature that imparts objects with the qualities of commodities, and certainly not with the very idea of commodity. Commodities refer to specific kinds of social relations, not to anything external to society. This does not mean, for example, that soils will not be altered as a consequence of being treated like commodities. They manifestly are altered whenever they are planted and pumped with fertilizers so as to maximize profitable crop yield. At the same time, it is not possible to do whatever one wants with soil when it is treated as a commodity. A soil cannot be driven or swum in, to give a couple of admittedly absurd examples. More subtly, soils cannot be expected to be mere nutrient containers for crops or to contain or retain endlessly circulating amounts of plant-available nutrients. But just because soils affect the commodification process as a result of their nature, it does not follow that soils themselves are part of the commodification process. Commodification, or the commodity designation process, is entirely social, yet always in relation to the rest of nature. One does not sell soil to elephants or to clay particles suspended in air. One does not establish exclusive possession of soil by guarding against trespassing ants or calling the police on squirrels invading one's land as private property. Nor does one bring such squirrels to trial for infringing property laws. One does not manufacture soil by paying wages to earthworms (though capitalism does depend on the privatization of these "gifts" of nature to enable profit). And yet it is everyday expression to talk of commodification as if the commodified had anything to do with it. This is the sleight of hand Marx called fetishism, which masks the social arrangements that determine whether something or someone is a commodity. It cannot be sufficiently stressed that social relations and struggles determine the worth of the rest of nature, including soils. Capital sees nature in particular ways because it sees society as well in particular ways. Capitalists appreciate and use soil (and science) insofar as it deepens their pockets and does not contradict their social status (Robertson 2006: 369).

Soils and Commodification

The relationship between commodification and soils is complicated by the fact that soils are highly varying products of organisms (including us) interacting with each other and with physical materials (minerals, organic matter, water, air). The complication manifests itself in the multiple and shifting definitions of soils across social contexts, where soil can be the upper portion where most rooting takes place, or a prescribed depth; masses of organic materials in varying stages of decomposition (e.g., peat);

movable dirt; or just whatever facilitates plant growth for human consumption. Hence, what is commodified when one speaks of soil commodification depends on how one understands soils, which is also related to social position. But because soils are really interactions and manifold processes, as soon as one pays more attention it should become apparent that it is only as reasonable to treat soil as a homogeneous or static unit as it is a forest or river. So, what exactly is going to be appropriated and sold, if soils are to be regarded as commodities? Is it the organisms, and if so, which? Is it the water and air that traverse soils or that are trapped therein? Is it the mineral matrix or parts thereof? Is it the organic material or the processes that make it happen? And to what depth is soil commodifiable—to that of crop rooting potential only, or deeper? Such matters seem not to be considered, just as in discussions over "soil governance" most of the world is excluded from a decision-making process that takes a very narrow, bourgeois view of soils as conducive for profits (which is essentially the subtext of food services in ecosystem services, since people are largely forced to buy food). Or, when there is enough courage to admit other perspectives, the issue becomes one of aesthetic pleasure and cultural importance to some vague, context-free human subject. It is in any case necessary to pretend that soils are changeless and controllable in order to think that one can really own soil as such so as to participate in production relations for market exchange and capital accumulation. It is a collective delusion common to capitalist societies.

Even if one were to agree that soils can be thought of as commodities, they have a dual value in capitalist systems. First and foremost, soils are useful directly or indirectly to most people living mainly off of terrestrial ecosystems, in that soils enable most food, fiber, and construction material to be produced, among other benefits. In a capitalist system, soils have a value due to their usefulness (use-value). The uses may differ widely, but for soils to be a commodity, the prerequisite is that they be useful. However, there is no necessary linkage between soils and their value as commodities. The linkage has to be socially made and enforced. Soils will only have value for exchange if they are useful (or made to be) and are owned by someone (i.e., to the extent to which social institutions can enforce ownership of soil) so that they can be sold to other people. In general, then, converting soils into marketable items implies usefulness for people (few, some, many, or all), exclusive appropriation (private property, hence institutions with the monopoly of violence to enforce private property), and valuation (e.g., pricing) based on capital accumulation criteria (if it is not profitable, soil will be devalued or, if soil cannot be sold, it will have no value). Fortunately, this is not what actually happens in society regarding soils, as many people do not reduce soil to the status of commodity. However, the predominant value system is capitalist, and hence there are tendencies and pressures to commodify even soils (just as with water, land, forests, and even people).

The commodification process is consequently ongoing and arguably impossible to complete without, ideologically, collapsing that which is produced in the rest of nature into that which is socially produced (see also Marx [1876] 1978), and without, in practice, destroying that which sustains us. This is because, as stated earlier, soils are sets of interactions among organisms and physical materials and processes that take many different forms and have highly variable qualities, including formation times.

The object of commodification is always much larger than, and too dynamic to be captured by, the commodification process. Soil is much larger because society is only a small (even if very significant) fraction of an ecosystem, including soil ecosystems, which are composed of myriad species. Soil also precedes human existence and can form largely without human intervention. Soils are also much too dynamic to be encompassed by commodification because they are constituted by many different interacting beings and processes. In other words, when one sells soils, it is unclear, ultimately, whether it is an entire soil, a physical or chemical portion of soil, future developments in soil formation (as soil undergoes change), fragments or the entirety of soil ecosystems, etc. Generally, this is not even recognized as a problem because there is no concern about soils as soils when they are turned into commodities. The concern is over soil as conduit for the making or extracting and selling of something else, be it crops, building material, topsoil, metals, or other forms of matter that can be appropriated and sold.

Another reason for the impossibility of full commodification is due to the prevailingly destructive character of capitalist uses of soils. Hence, soil's high variability (in part reflected in multiple ways to define what soils are)—in how it is constituted and in how long it takes to form—means that the commodification process is an exercise in infinite regression. It is like pricing something that constantly changes in character both within and beyond human control, disaggregating (e.g., soil erosion), reconstituting (e.g., downslope additions of eroded material), and even disappearing (e.g., soil removal). Soil commodification also expresses itself differently in different social contexts. Where people have been effectively removed from access to the means of survival (including land), alienation from soil tends to be rife. Any attempt to return to farming or to appreciate and work soil becomes a way of countering alienation, and implicitly capitalist outlooks. In most of the world, however, people still interact directly with soils to gain a livelihood (which is not necessarily capitalist in character).

The reason this even needs to be stated at all is because the commodification of soils involves not only alienation and privatization processes but also an ideological form specific to capitalism, which is commodity fetishism. For example, soils can become magically endowed with the power of valuing or even selling themselves to us. This strange world of soil self-valuation is essentially what lies under the concept of soil productivity. The construct masks the fact that it is people who determine what ought to be produced out of soils and how such products should be valued. Concepts like soil productivity in fact precede by decades the increasingly fashionable ecosystem service construct, where one pretends that ecosystems provide services to us, rather than acknowledging that people are involved in the valuation of, and access to, such means of survival or wellbeing. By switching soils from productive functionality (for industrial farming) to servicing entities, soils are effectively treated as self-selling service providers. Therefore, it is surprising to find treatment of such new terms as ecosystem services as in any way novel relative to the nature of the commodification process. The issue is, rather, one of an intensification of commodification.

One is typically informed that soils form over thousands of years, if not longer. Actually, "soils" are increasingly produced industrially or otherwise (e.g., constructed technosols) over a span of years or faster, especially in urban settings and to replace soils lost through mining (Scalenghe and Ferraris 2009). What is more, as alluded to in the beginning, potting mixes are often equated with soil. Burgeoning systems of soilless cultivation (Schwarz 1994) are thereby making a mockery of the typical (narrow) understanding of soils as a medium for plant growth. For soil becomes superfluous when replaceable with sludge, rockwool, composts, peat, or other mined and/or manufactured materials (Asaduzzaman et al. 2015; Barrett et al. 2016), at least for containerized or greenhouse food production. As this superfluity is not possible without massive population decline (e.g., cereal cropping and arboriculture require much larger spaces and well-developed, deeper soils), soils remain as important as ever, even for vegetable cultivation. But containerized plant growth can also involve transfers of soil into containers, as apparently commonly practiced for thousands of years (Raviv and Lieth 2008). There is a very short slippage from "native" to "commercial" topsoil when topsoil can be removed and put up for sale. In vain does one endeavor to push for topsoil conservation if topsoil becomes more lucrative when mined or manufactured. As soon as topsoil is made to be understood as a commodity, all differences among soils melt into market exchangeability and monetary calculation and thereby into the worth of human labor, which ultimately subtends capitalist relations (unless one believes that wages or rents are paid to soils).

The problem, in a wider ecological sense, is how to distinguish soils from soilless media if usefulness for capital accumulation is the main, if not the only, criterion. Appealing to a notion of soils' multiple ecosystem services (Legaz et al. 2017; Bartkowski et al. 2018) is an evasive maneuver, because ecosystem services refer to benefits to society. Worse, such notions are promulgated without consideration for immense social inequalities (who benefits or who is really most serviced by such ecosystem services?). Soil scientists have also been most unhelpful in this regard, even while acknowledging historically shifting scientific definitions of soils. Within the very core of the scientific mainstream, soil has long been reduced to its marketable food productivity potential and more recently to marketable ecosystem services. There is utter disinterest in confronting and resisting the capitalist relations within which soil science is immersed. The result is a set of contradictions that tend to foster soil destruction and that are resolvable not by studying or protecting soils but by changing society.

On the one hand, there is recognition that soils are important to humanity as a whole (universalization). This is a central pillar to discussions, or rather, petitions, to introduce soil protection norms and enforce them. On the other hand, when it comes to identifying stakeholders, the vast majority of humanity disappears in conformity with the exclusive club of landowners ("farmers"), policy-makers, and like persons of power and prestige, or those under their yoke, like tenant farmers.

On the one hand, scientists admit that definitions of soils and the criteria constituting sustainable management shift over time. On the other hand, the wider social relations (especially relations of power) that shape the treatment and definition of soils are virtually ignored, since scientists are expected (or pressured) to be politically neutral, all the while making inescapably political arguments about human impacts on and protecting soils. One goes with the current, and when the current is capitalist, the rest follows. Hence, in good bourgeois fashion, many soil scientists insist on treating humanity as if separate from or inexorably destructive of soil formation and development, which perhaps says more about soil scientists than humanity generally.

On the one hand, soils are understood as intrinsically characterized by irreplaceability (it takes thousands of years to form, etc.), interconnectivity with other parts of geosystems (water, air, aboveground ecosystems, etc.), contiguity and enormous variability, interlinked layers (horizons), and multiple-scaled organic–inorganic complexes (from molecular, chemically reactive bonding to visible clumps of bound material), as Hartemink (2016) has ably summarized. On the other hand, there is even an insistence on finding the elementary, separable, individual soil unit like the pedon, unwittingly conforming to bourgeois notions about society (see Engel-Di Mauro 2020). There is a pretense that soils' status is coextensive with benefits to humans, or, worse, that soils exist for the sake of a generic humanity (as embedded in the notions of soil quality, soil health, and soil ecosystem services). At times, some even pretend that soils are essentially replaceable (for a fuller discussion, see Engel-Di Mauro 2014).

A study of the multiple meanings (and uses) of soils would be fascinating in itself, but it would not allow us to specify that which exists independent of ourselves and to which we relate. For this reason, we emphasize the ecological, rather than the cultural, and the ecological as including society but being also beyond it. This is important in identifying what commodification does to the relationship between people and soils. Hence, soils are underground ecosystems and part of even larger aboveground ecosystems that include us. As ecosystems, soils are constituted by interacting organisms (both soil-dwelling and not) and their physical habitats in a highly variable mix of mineral and organic substances traversed by water and air. A main way of differentiating soils from other relatively loose material that makes up land (or the bottom of water bodies) is to note the interdependent layers (horizons) formed out of ecological and physical interactions and the binding of mineral and organic substances at the molecular level. This is at least one way to understand soils as much greater than the sum of social uses and definitions of them.

In other words, conflating soil with potting mix or a soilless media presents ambiguities with substantial social and ecological repercussions. Within a capitalist system, the social implication is that soil can be subsumed under society, as if produced by people, whose labor can be purchased to make soils for sale. Soil becomes a mobile and fungible commodity. Ecologically and relative to environmental policy, soils can be expendable if they can be supplied in sufficient quantities to replace destroyed or used-up soils. And, to carry this to another logical conclusion, spilling soil from a pot could constitute soil erosion. Although rarely done in the sciences, such conflation of soils with non-soils is exactly what happens when soils are treated as movable or replaceable. More broadly, this is an always-lurking potential danger, hardly recognized by soil scientists, whenever formulating classification systems in a society where market exchangeability reigns supreme. Theoretically, taking US soil taxonomy as a basis, one could create a Churchville silt loam in one part of New York State to replace another that is being destroyed elsewhere, just as Robertson (2000) has eloquently shown in the case of wetland mitigation banking. One wetland can be the same as another when attributes are limited (or made up; Robertson 2006) to what can conform to capitalist prerogatives and when the point of life is to facilitate the endless accumulation of capital.

Implications for Soil Conservation

Soil commodification is a contradictory process that creates conditions for the further undermining of soils and for misidentifying the causes of soil destruction. The contradiction is evident whenever farmers remove soil to sell as "topsoil" while valuing their land according to the properties of the soil being in part removed. The first process, the commodification of soils *per se*, involves the development of a relationship to soils as detachable, transferable (physically transportable), and replaceable. For this to occur, soil must be severed from its ecological and landscape context, as well as social context when it comes to capitalist relations. In itself, this is a process common to many different societies for tens of thousands of years. Earth mounds, terracing, hanging gardens, pottery, and many other activities have involved the removal of soil (Baveye et al. 2016). What is novel in capitalist society is turning this long-standing relationship to soil into the production of a commodity for capital accumulation and thereby the alienation of soil from its socioecological context.

The commodification of soils is therefore underlain by or produces a tension between two understandings of soil that are essentially incompatible. One is soil as part of an ecosystem or a landscape or land. The other is soil as a collection of context-independent aggregated particles (mineral and organic) whose main purpose is as substrate for plant growth or other reductionist understandings—that is, the notion that soil can be manufactured (e.g., potting mix) and placed anywhere to provide a means to stabilize a surface with plant cover or to grow crops or other such activities whose objective is to provide for human needs and/or marketability.

This is how, arguably, soil removal and soil manufacturing have intensified. Soils are mined for "topsoil" (or for minerals, as in bauxite, or potentially for metals, as in agromining) or removed as sellable peat (wetland soils) or as waste that has recently begun to be revalued. Potting soils or mixes and "organic soil" (e.g., humus from composted materials) are increasingly manufactured as part of an industrialization of soil production. All these developments share the objective of exchanging "soil" for money as part of the endless accumulation of capital. And with an endless accumulation of capital comes a potentially endless appetite for soil that is impossible to fulfill. Soils are finite, and manufactured soils, though viable for some purposes, cannot replace centuries or millennia of soil formation, development, and coevolution with landscapes and organisms. The second process includes but is not coextensive with soils and implies soils as part of a larger set of processes, whether ecosystems (e.g., habitats, substrate, soil as ecosystems) or landscapes (e.g., stabilized surface, biomantle, overburden). Consequently, the value of soil is contingent on the initial alienation and commodification of land more broadly. Once land is commodified, it may or may not be ascribed value according to prevailing soil characteristics, if the plot of land features soils at all. Beaches, for instance, do not necessarily contain soils.

Given the above, the notion of soil conservation beckons a redirection of one's focus to the social relations spawning the conditions for and content of conservation. The conditions for conservation have been long compromised in many places by the removal of people from the land and by the imposition of capitalist logic, where soils are alienable, even expendable. In most places, however, such conditions remain, thanks to ongoing bitter struggles against expulsion from the ecological sources of sustenance, including soils. Where most people are excluded or historically alienated from soils, additional efforts are necessary to convince people of the importance of soils and of protecting them from destruction. The obstacle becomes even greater when institutions recognize only a very narrow band of stakeholders on the basis of property or government office. People are effectively being asked to have a stake in something over which they have virtually no political say and from which they gain no income. The process of mass social exclusion, where most people are forced to rely on wages to live, is instead taken as the starting point of conservation. One can wonder stubbornly, as many scientists do, why most of society is uninterested in what sustains it, until it is realized that the problem is not to be found between society and soils, but *within* society *in relation to* soils.

Where people continue to struggle over retaining access to land, on the other hand, the stakes are very clear. The matter becomes not one of protecting soils *per se* but rather one of protecting communities from the ravages of capitalist encroachment so as to conserve soils much more broadly than the immediate sites of struggle. As Blaikie (1985) and others pointed out decades ago, it is a recurring conceit that soils are destroyed merely by poor management on-site. To avoid poor soil management, it is necessary to grasp how communities are interlinked regionally and globally, whether by means of historical coercion into farming more erodible soils or under economic strain to maximize yield no matter the impact on soils. In the case of, say, communities under pressure to abandon land for conservation purposes, one may be swapping potential soil erosion in one area for the certitude of soil destruction elsewhere through urban expansion related to forced mass migration.

The content of soil conservation is as questionable as the conditions for conservation are contingent. This is for the same underlying reasons of a context where soils are commodified and thereby made exchangeable. One challenge is conserving something whose worth is made coextensive with market price. The practice of putting price tags on the environment has been intensifying and uncritically accepted, including by most scientists (e.g., Pimentel et al. 1995; Bartkowski et al. 2018). To accept pricing schemes (capitalist value) is to accept soil erosion when it is more profitable than soil conservation. This troubling aspect of the capitalist commodity is linked to the delineation of what constitutes a soil. If topsoil for potting mixes is also soil, it follows that one should protect potting soil as much as soil that is part of land or in an original ecological context. The irony is that industrially produced soils become equivalent to— and potentially as valuable as, or even more so than—soils created through natural processes. Destruction and conservation converge and melt into each other, in line with capital accumulation prerogatives, where commodities must be exchangeable, and thereby indistinguishable beyond profitability and monetary calculation. Profits from removing soils are the same as profits from conserving soils, under capitalist lenses.

Another challenge extends from the conditions of conservation outlined above in places where most must seek wages to live. In such cases, one is supposed to protect not only an object whose meaning is reduced to marketability and thereby alienable (if not alien anyway), but also a set of social relations that dramatically forecloses the possible uses of soils, and often prohibits one's ability to access, know, work with, and care for soils at all. Ultimately, protecting soils can only promote ecologically sustainable futures if the issues of soil and land commodification are confronted and overcome.

Notes

1   According to the USDA, soil is any "loose surface material of the earth in which plants grow" and "in most cases consisting of disintegrated rock with mixture of organic material." Such material, when transported, also falls under USDA regulatory jurisdiction as soil. This can include "topsoil, forest litter, wood or plant compost, humus, and earthworm castings" (https://www.ehs.ucsb.edu/files/docs/hw/import-soil. pdf). It should be little wonder that formal definitions of soil suffer from underlying contradictions due to diverse political aims, often ensconced in scientific garb, and exacerbated by statecraft and fractious capitalist practices.
2   That there are still those who insist that Marx came up with the labor theory of value attests to a widespread ignorance of original texts, if not to cynical manipulation by detractors who have little else to contribute save justifications for the capitalist status quo of the day. After all, Marx specified even in the title of the first volume of *Capital* that his was a critique of political economy, which includes the labor theory of value.

References

Asaduzzaman, M., M. Saifullah, A. K. M. S. R. Mollick, M. M. Hossain, G. M. A. Halim, and T. Asao (2015), "Influence of Soilless Culture Substrate on Improvement of Yield and Produce Quality of Horticultural Crops," in M. Asaduzzaman (ed.), *Soilless Culture: Use of Substrates for the Production of Quality Horticultural Crops*, 1–32, London: InTechOpen.

Barrett, G. E., P. D. Alexander, J. S. Robinson, and N. C. Bragg (2016), "Achieving Environmentally Sustainable Growing Media for Soilless Plant Cultivation Systems—A Review," *Scientia Horticulturae*, 212: 220–34.

Bartkowski, B., B. Hansjürgens, S. Möckel, and S. Bartke (2018), "Institutional Economics of Agricultural Soil Ecosystem Services," *Sustainability*, 10: 2447 [https://doi. org/10.3390/su10072447].

Baveye, P. C., J. Baveye, and J. Gowdy (2016), "Soil 'Ecosystem' Services and Natural Capital: Critical Appraisal of Research on Uncertain Ground," *Frontiers in Environmental Science*, 4: 41 [https://doi.org/10.3389/fenvs.2016.00041].

Bermejo, R. (2014), "The Commodification of Nature and Its Consequences," in *Handbook for a Sustainable Economy*, 19–33, Dordrecht: Springer.

Bigger, P. and M. Robertson (2017), "Value is Simple. Valuation is Complex," *Capitalism Nature Socialism*, 28 (1): 68–77.

Blaikie, P. (1985), *The Political Economy of Soil Erosion in Developing Countries*, Harlow: Longman.

Bryant, G. (2018), "Nature as Accumulation Strategy? Finance, Nature, and Value in Carbon Markets," *Annals of the American Association of Geographers*, 108 (3): 605–19.

Burkett, P. (1999), *Marx and Nature: A Red and Green Perspective*, New York: St. Martin's Press.

Castree, N. (2003), "Commodifying What Nature?," *Progress in Human Geography*, 27 (3): 273–97.

Egendorf, S. P., Z. Cheng, M. Deeb, V. Flores, A. Paltseva, D. Walsh et al. (2018), "Constructed Soils for Mitigating Lead (Pb) Exposure and Promoting Urban Community Gardening: The New York City Clean Soil Bank Pilot Study," *Landscape and Urban Planning*, 175: 184–94.

Emel, J. (2017), "Valuing the Earth and Each Other," *Capitalism Nature Socialism*, 28 (1): 62–67.

Engel-Di Mauro, S. (2014), *Ecology, Soils, and the Left: An Ecosocial Approach*, New York: Palgrave Macmillan.

Engel-Di Mauro, S. (2020), "Learning Dialectics to Grow Better Soils Knowledge, not Bigger Crops: A Materialist Dialectics and Relationality for Soil Science," *Capitalism Nature Socialism*, 31 (1): 52–69.

European Commission (2018), "What is the Bioeconomy?" [https://ec.europa.eu/research/bioeconomy/index.cfm].

Food and Agriculture Organization (FAO) (2015), *Status of the World's Soil Resources: Main Report*, Rome: FAO and Intergovernmental Technical Panel on Soils.

Guerrien, B. (2003), "Marchandisation et théorie économique," *Actuel Marx*, 2003/2 (34): 121–32.

Gunderson, R. (2017), "Commodification of Nature," in D. Richardson, N. Castree, M. F. Goodchild, A. Kobayashi, W. Liu, and R. A. Marston (eds.), *International Encyclopedia of Geography: People, the Earth, Environment and Technology*, Oxford: Wiley-Blackwell [https://doi.org/10.1002/9781118786352.wbieg0332].

Hartemink, A. E. (2016), "The Definition of Soil Since the Early 1800s," in D. L. Sparks (ed.), *Advances in Agronomy*, Vol. 137, 73–126, London: Academic Press.

Huber, M. T. (2017), "Value, Nature, and Labor: A Defense of Marx," *Capitalism Nature Socialism*, 28 (1): 39–52.

Juerges, N. and B. Hansjürgens (2018), "Soil Governance in the Transition Towards a Sustainable Bioeconomy—A Review," *Journal of Cleaner Production*, 170: 1628–39.

Kosoy, N. and E. Corbera (2010), "Payments for Ecosystem Services as Commodity Fetishism," *Ecological Economics*, 69 (6): 1228–36.

Labban, M. (2008), *Space, Oil and Capital*, New York: Routledge.

Leach, M., J. Fairhead, and J. Fraser (2012), "Green Grabs and Biochar: Revaluing African Soils and Farming in the New Carbon Economy," *Journal of Peasant Studies*, 39 (2): 285–307.

Legaz, B. Vidal, D. Maia De Souza, R. F. M. Teixeira, A. Antón, B. Putman, and S. Sala (2017), "Soil Quality, Properties, and Functions in Life Cycle Assessment: An Evaluation of Models," *Journal of Cleaner Production*, 140: 502–15.

Liverman, D. (2004), "Who Governs, at What Scale and at What Price? Geography, Environmental Governance, and the Commodification of Nature," *Annals of the Association of American Geographers*, 94 (4): 734–38.

Marx, K. ([1857–58] 1973), *Grundriße*, trans. M. Nicolaus, New York: Vintage.

Marx, K. ([1867] 1992), *Capital: A Critical Analysis of Capitalist Production*, Vol. 1, trans. S. Moore and E. Aveling, New York: International Publishers.

Marx, K. ([1876] 1978), "Critique of the Gotha Program," in R. C. Tucker (ed.), *The Marx-Engels Reader*, 2nd edition, 525–41, New York: W. W. Norton.

McAfee, K. (1999), "Selling Nature to Save It? Biodiversity and Green Developmentalism," *Environment and Planning D: Society and Space*, 17 (2): 133–54.

Mrozowski, S. A. (1999), "Colonization and the Commodification of Nature," *International Journal of Historical Archaeology*, 3 (e): 153–66.

Musto, M. (2010), "Revisiting Marx's Concept of Alienation," *Socialism and Democracy*, 24 (3): 79–101.

Pascual, U., M. Termansen, K. Hedlund, L. Brussaard, J. H. Faber, S. Foudi et al. (2015), "On the Value of Soil Biodiversity and Ecosystem Services," *Ecosystem Services*, 15: 11–18.

Peterson, M. J., D. M. Hall, A. M. Feldpausch-Parker, and T. R. Peterson (2010), "Obscuring Ecosystem Function with Application of the Ecosystem Services Concept," *Conservation Biology*, 24 (1): 113–19.

Pimentel, D., C. Harvey, P. Resosudarmo, K. Sinclair, D. Kurz, M. McNair et al. (1995), "Environmental and Economic Costs of Soil Erosion and Conservation Benefits," *Science*, 267 (5201): 1117–23.

Postone, M. (1996), *Time, Labor, and Social Domination: A Reinterpretation of Marx's Critical Theory*, Cambridge: Cambridge University Press.

Prudham, S. (2007), "The Fictions of Autonomous Invention: Accumulation by Dispossession, Commodification, and Life Patents in Canada," *Antipode*, 39 (3): 406–29.

Prudham, S. (2015), "Property and Commodification," in T. Perreault, G. Bridge, and J. McCarthy (eds.), *Handbook of Political Ecology*, 430–45, New York: Routledge.

Raviv, M. and J. H. Lieth (2008), "Significance of Soilless Culture in Agriculture," in M. Raviv and J. H. Lieth (eds.), *Soilless Culture: Theory and Practice*, 1–12, Amsterdam: Elsevier.

Robertson, M. (2000), "No Net Loss: Wetland Restoration and the Incomplete Capitalization of Nature," *Antipode*, 32 (4): 463–93.

Robertson, M. (2006), "The Nature that Capital Can See: Science, State, and Market in the Commodification of Ecosystem Services," *Environment and Planning D: Society and Space*, 24 (3): 367–87.

Scalenghe, R. and S. Ferraris (2009), "The First Forty Years of a Technosol," *Pedosphere*, 19 (1): 40–52.

Schwarz, M. (1994), *Soilless Culture Management*, Berlin: Springer-Verlag.

Smith, N. (2007), "Nature as Accumulation Strategy," *Socialist Register 2007: Coming to Terms with Nature*, 43: 19–36.

Smith, N. (2008), *Uneven Development: Nature, Capital, and the Production of Space*, 3rd edition, Athens, GA: University of Georgia Press.

van der Ent, A., A. J. M. Baker, R. D. Reeves, R. L. Chaney, C. W. N. Anderson, J. A. Meech et al. (2015), "Agromining: Farming for Metals in the Future?," *Environmental Science & Technology*, 49 (8): 4773–80.

van der Ploeg, J. D. (2010), "The Peasantries of the Twenty-first Century: The Commoditisation Debate Revisited," *Journal of Peasant Studies*, 37 (1): 1–30.

Walsh, D., K. Glass, S. Morris, H. Zhang, I. McRae, N. Anderson et al. (2018), "Sediment Exchange to Mitigate Pollutant Exposure in Urban Soil," *Journal of Environmental Management*, 214: 354–61.

5

Knowing Earth, Knowing Soil: Epistemological Work and the Political Aesthetics of Regenerative Agriculture

Matthew Kearnes and Lauren Rickards

Introduction

Soil carbon sequestration and regenerative agriculture have emerged as technologies of eco-social optimism. In the face of the dire warnings of "peak nitrate" and "peak phosphorus" on the one hand and climate change on the other, soil's capacity to store carbon, reverse climate change, regenerate itself, and breathe life into agricultural landscapes has been presented as something of a revelation (Kearnes and Rickards 2017; Kon Kam King et al. 2018; Granjou and Salazar 2019). Marshaled as a response to a raft of contemporary sociopolitical and environmental problems, the retention and long-term sequestration of soil carbon and the promise of regenerative agriculture encode soil and farming with political atmospherics that are simultaneously speculative and hopeful (Krzywoszynska 2019a). At the same time, the management of soil carbon concentrations is increasingly being depicted in technoscientific terms. In this guise, soil carbon sequestration is cast as an earthly technology, overlain by the technics of remote visualization, greenhouse gas accounting, and scenario modeling. Soil carbon sequestration is heralded as one of a number of strategies for directly manipulating environmental and climatic systems in response to global warming, what Tim Flannery evocatively terms "third-way" technologies designed to "recreate, enhance or restore the processes that created the balance of greenhouse gases which existed prior to human interference, with the aim of drawing carbon, at scale, out of Earth's atmosphere and/or oceans" (2015: 151). Agricultural soil carbon sequestration simultaneously features as a core rationale for the emergent paradigm of "smart farming," which harnesses environmental sensing technologies and automated management systems to enable more efficient, sustainable, and profitable farm outcomes and related market opportunities (Rossel and Bouma 2016). This quintessentially modernist take on carbon sequestration and agriculture is imbued with extremely different language and images to that of "alternative" regenerative agriculture, but shares with it a promissory logic and similarly high hopes for a brighter future.

This reimagining of soil as a varied site of promissory and speculative investment is characterized by a bricolage of calculative and aesthetic sensibilities. A series of overlapping ethical and epistemological claims are invoked in the representation of soil carbon sequestration and regenerative agriculture as alternatives to, and accommodated within, the infrastructures of mechanized and industrial farming. In the opening passages of his major work on the connections between agricultural and environmental ethics, Paul Thompson (2016) engages in a brief discussion of what he terms the "spirit of the soil." Reviewing pagan, Greek, and Christian understandings, Thompson suggests that a "modern agronomic view of soil" has resulted in a "depersonalized, lifeless concept of soil [that] predominates." For Thompson, "those who reject" this view, in the manner of those committed to the restoration and regeneration of soil, have "been inclined toward mystical, animistic, or spiritualistic speculation, and have invented an alternative metaphysic of soil that ... presents the spirit of the soil as a neglected life force to be called forth by ritual and incantation" (2016: 18–19). For Thompson, this rejection is set in the context of the foundational alliance, forged throughout the nineteenth and twentieth centuries, between mechanized farming and the disciplines of soil science (Engel-Di Mauro 2014), the political mobilization and appropriation of agronomic expertise, and the consequent representation of alternative and regenerative agriculture as "unscientific."

However, contemporary interest in soil carbon sequestration troubles this dichotomy. It remains the case that much regenerative agriculture draws for sustenance on a wellspring of cultural and theological sensibilities and has emerged in the context of challenges to established modes of scientific authority (Wynne 1996; Bijker et al. 2009) by new modes of social and political expertise. Yet, at the same time, regenerative agricultural practices are characterized by hybrid epistemological strategies. Proponents of regenerative agriculture do not so much reject agronomic visions of soil productivity as much as they attempt to forge an accommodation of regenerative farming practices within the epistemologies of contemporary soil science. These attempts to epistemologically and institutionally legitimate regenerative agriculture deploy established frameworks of agronomic expertise, notably the political demonstration of specific practices and calculative work designed to establish both the potential and permanence of terrestrial carbon storage. More than a one-way adaptation, however, this accommodation involves attempts to widen the frame of what generally counts as "scientific" evidence by advocating for the inclusion of more systemic understandings of landscape function and aesthetic representations and embodied experiences of soil health. For example, in their work on developing interdisciplinary mixed-methods techniques for mapping soil carbon farming, Brockett et al. seek to "open up the soil carbon mapping process with the intention of revealing implicit assumptions within current agri-environmental research and policy" whilst at the same time deploying "interdisciplinary mapping processes to work with natural and social scientific, place-based and experiential knowledge of upland soil management" (2019: 193). This project, and the quasi-calculative work designed to realize the promise of regenerative agriculture, evokes Cochoy's (2008) notion of *qualculation*. Alongside calculative efforts to produce quantitative assessments of sequestration potential and permanence are efforts to recognize the aesthetic, moral, and spiritual *qualities* of regenerated soil.

In her work on practices of soil care, Puig de la Bellacasa (2015) captures something of the hybrid knowledge-work engaged in regenerative agriculture. She argues that while soil regeneration practice is based in "moves away from productionism towards conceptions of soil as living and correlated practices of involvement with soil," these practices are "not disentangled from technoscientific time ... but [are] committed to making alternative ontologies from within" (2015: 706–7). In a similar sense, Krzywoszynska notes the fracturing of contemporary systems of agronomic expertise, which she casts as a move "beyond unidirectional knowledge exchange" and the emergence of "more participatory, social learning and co-production frameworks" (2019b: 161). One outcome of such fracturing and hybridity is that agronomy is now fundamentally "contested" (Sumberg et al. 2013) and "political" (Sumberg et al. 2014).

In the following sections, we explore this line of analysis by examining the kinds of *ethical and aesthetic improvisations* entailed in the construction of soil as an earthly savior, and the project of simultaneously regenerating landscapes and securing carbon underground. As we will argue, in this complex contact zone between matters of fact and matters of concern, we see a web of aesthetic and ethical sensibilities at play. As Paterson and Stripple (2012) remind us, the "ethical contestation" of carbon sequestration projects is central to the making of "virtuous carbon" and good soil. We conclude by suggesting that by "going to ground," land-based carbon sequestration raises the prospect of addressing not just technoscientific challenges but ethical questions of "good," while lacking a means of resolving them. In place of a universalizing notion of virtue, we argue that what is emerging is an improvised form of land aesthetic, cobbled together in multispecies contact zones and storied landscapes.

The Magic of Mimicry

Despite the earthly origins of anthropogenic climate change—driven by the transformation of fossilized carbon and underpinned by the historical development of what Nigel Clark (2015) describes as the "fiery arts" of pyrotechnology—it is striking that international climate policy has proceeded by way of a series of distinctly un-earthly and extraterrestrial abstractions. Calculative, abstracted figures of atmospheric concentrations of CO_2—presented in parts per million as 350 ppm/400 ppm/450 ppm—or the threshold mean temperature calculations (1.5°C/2°C) have become the default aesthetic registers through which global warming is represented. At the same time, infrastructures and techniques of carbon accounting have been designed to abstract certain forms of terrestrial and atmospheric carbon into commensurable units of exchange (while bracketing out less amenable forms of carbon and other greenhouse gases; see Wedderburn-Bisshop and Rickards 2018). In this context, recent work has begun to make important moves in demonstrating the performative qualities of carbon accounting, making important moves toward materializing accounts of carbon abstraction (Kuch 2015; Lovell 2015). As Bulkeley argues, the "work of calculation and commensuration of carbon ... requires that they are seen not only as *abstractions* but also as forms of *material intervention* in the configuration of governmental assemblages" (2016: 161, emphasis added). Nevertheless, despite this emphasis on the materiality of carbon accounting, until relatively recently soil has remained curiously absent from the political aesthetics of climate change. One likely reason is that, compared with Whitington's (2016) depiction of carbon as a "metric of the *human*," attending to the promissory logics of *soil carbon* and the rise of land regeneration and soil carbon sequestration as an emergent horizon of climate politics requires engaging with the more-than-human, earthly, and terrestrial entanglements of carbon.

Given the relative neglect of soil in climate change discourses, 2015 was a significant year in the political life of soils, where it emerged as a figure of both concern and hope. World Soil Day, a culmination of events marking the International Year of Soils (IYS 2015), was celebrated on December 5, 2015, at the headquarters of the Food and Agriculture Organization (FAO) of the United Nations in Rome, and in a series of national events around the world. The theme for the Day was "soils—a solid ground for life." Images of soil degradation and desertification that "continue to pose serious challenges to the sustainable development of all countries, in particular developing countries" (UNGA 2012, para. 205), were contrasted with an optimism that "good land management" will contribute to "economic growth," "sustainable agriculture and food security," "women's empowerment," and "addressing climate change" (UNGA 2014: 2). It is a framing that illustrates how, in the midst of the seemingly inexorable degradation of soils, soil management is increasingly being enrolled in a range of humanitarian, political, and environmental projects.

The relationship between soils and climate change also featured prominently in the 2015 Paris COP21 climate meetings. Broadly celebrated as a significant step toward decisive climate action—whether as a parable of the power of diplomacy over political intransigence or evidence of a new, more mature understanding of the stakes climate change poses, as Latour (2018) suggests—the Paris COP21 agreements also signaled a shift in emphasis in international climate policy. Earlier commitments to "stabilize greenhouse gas concentration in the atmosphere at a level that would prevent dangerous anthropogenic interference with the climate system" (Conference of the Parties 2009, Art. 1) were reframed in the Paris agreement, to "achiev[ing] a balance between anthropogenic emissions by sources and removals by sinks of greenhouse gases in the second half of this century, on the basis of equity, and in the context of sustainable development and efforts to eradicate poverty" (Conference of the Parties 2015, Art 4.1).[1] In the context of what has been regarded as an "emission-centric" model of climate governance—what Gwyn Prins and Steve Rayner (2007) characterized as "an exclusive preoccupation with [the] mitigation" of CO_2—and the broad perception that agriculture and land use had been "left out" of international climate thinking, the Paris agreements represented something of a success for the activists striving to get soil, carbon farming, and "negative-emission" technologies onto the international "climate agenda." Indeed, in the weeks leading up to the Paris talks a host of US and international environmental groups and NGOs—the Center for Food Safety, Regeneration International, and Soil4Climate—had collaborated in the release of the 4 per 1000 Initiative by the French Ministry of Agriculture, a program designed to "demonstrate that agriculture, and in particular agricultural soils, can play a crucial role where food security and climate change are concerned" through a commitment to an "annual growth rate of 0.4% in the soil carbon stocks . . . in the first 30–40 cm of soil."[2]

A striking feature of commentary that followed the Paris climate talks was the open acknowledgment that the majority of climate models and scenarios that predict a better than 50% chance of stabilizing global mean temperatures to 2°C above pre-industrial levels "assume the successful and large-scale uptake of negative-emission technologies" (Anderson 2015: 899), many of which are based on the direct removal of greenhouse gases from the atmosphere and their sequestration and long-term burial underground—in soils and agricultural systems. Subtending the congratulatory tone that surrounded the Paris climate meeting were more critical analyses that characterized both the 1.5°C/2°C target and the renewed reliance on technologies designed to directly remove carbon from the atmosphere—including the envisaged scaling up of soil carbon sequestration and regenerative agriculture—as a kind of collective delusion (Nordhaus 2018). This analysis reflects both a normative assessment of negative-emission technologies as a kind of moral hazard—an "unjust and high-stakes gamble" (Anderson and Peters 2016: 183)—and concern for the pragmatics of seeking to technologically optimize what Granjou and Salazar term the "situated, heterogeneous, and volatile dynamics of carbon within soils" (2019: 39). In a series of editorial commentaries, Rayner (2016), Kruger and colleagues (2016), and Buck (2018) capture much of this more critical discussion by characterizing the reliance of climate models on negative-emission technologies, and the assumed permanence of soil carbon sequestration, as "magical thinking."

In this guise, the association between soil carbon sequestration, regenerative agriculture, and magic functions as a way of designating the fantastical quality of climate scenarios and the tacit assumptions that underpin projections of reversing climate change through the large-scale deployment of negative-emission techniques. What is apparent, however, is the ways in which the magical quality of soil carbon sequestration is not *mere* trickery. Rather, integral to notions of regenerative agriculture is a mode of imitation, or biomimicry, akin to Frazer's (1925) notion of "sympathetic magic." For example, the explanatory text accompanying the 4 per 1000 Initiative speaks of photosynthesis as "nature's own system for pulling excess carbon out of the air and sequestering it in the soil,"[3] whilst the broader field of research devoted to soil carbon sequestration, regenerative agriculture, and negative emissions is overlain by notions of biomimesis, the imitation and optimization of biochemical processes.

Integral to Frazer's theory of magic—and its later development by Mauss ([1972] 2001) and Taussig (1993)—is a distinction between imitative resemblance and material contact. For example, Frazer distinguishes between a "Law of Similarity" whereby "like produces like, or that an effect resembles its cause" and a "Law of Contact or Contagion" where "things which have once been in contact with each other continue to act on each other at a distance after the physical contact has been severed" (1925: 11). In invoking a kind of biological imitation, the magical thinking that underpins soil carbon sequestration and regenerative agriculture—particularly in the promissory guise of the negative-emission potential of these techniques—seemingly troubles this dualism between the ideational and the material. Indeed, in their discussion of regenerative agriculture, as embodied in the writing of Wes Jackson and the Land Institute, Johnson and Goldstein (2015) distinguish two prominent forms of biomimicry. The first is a common form of biological imitation, based on Janine Benyus's (1997) seminal work, that seeks to take "inspiration in specific plants or isolated characteristics of discrete nonhuman 'innovators'" (Johnson and Goldstein 2015: 393). In contrast, the second form of biomimicry, which is evident in regenerative agriculture, is seemingly closer to Frazer's "Law of Contact": is forged through a "collaborative, distributed project [that] serves as an invitation to continually recombine with other forms of life, other ecologies, and other systems of knowledge production" (2015: 393). In this sense, the magic at work in this second form of biomimicry—and in the practice of regenerative agriculture—is of an altogether material form. As Weszkalnys suggests, magic "depends on the objects it commands—but the force of these objects is engendered in their practical association with other things, human and nonhuman" (2013: 277). The magic of soil carbon sequestration and regenerative agriculture in the context of anthropogenic climate change—which appears as an ever-present potentiality—is not simply a matter of delusion or trickery. Rather, it is the contingent, often-physical assemblage of technoscientific, biochemical, and geo-aesthetic forces in visualizing and producing alternative climatic futures.

The Political Aesthetics of Soil Carbon

Alongside developments in international climate policy that have shaped the emergence of negative emission techniques, a burgeoning genre of popular writing on regenerative agriculture and carbon farming presents soil carbon sequestration in redemptive, restorative, and even soteriological terms. To paraphrase the many works in this developing genre, soil *will save us*, principally by reversing climate change.[4] In this literature—which draws on other recent "naturalist" trends such as green consumerism, "paleo" dieting, functional fitness, "natural capital," and circular economies—"regenerative agriculture" is infused with the capacity to rediscover neglected assets and recover a lost agrarian idyll. At the core of its redemptive claim is the promise of transforming the broad-acre "industrial food complex" into authentic, productive, and sustainable agricultural landscapes.

Numerous narratives now depict soil carbon sequestration, regenerative land-management practices, and negative-emission technologies as possessing an almost mystical power to "reverse climate change." However, it is important to note that soil did not simply emerge as a heroic climate savior *after* COP21. Soil has long been invested with redemptive promise, as organic and agrarian farming movements, for instance, demonstrate (see Matless 2001; Lowe 2015). In addition, the notion of balancing the emissions of greenhouse gases against the sequestration of carbon by terrestrial sinks has constituted a central, albeit highly contested, component of long-range climate scenarios and projected emissions trajectories. In this sense, the political and policy enthusiasm for land-based carbon sequestration techniques is underpinned by a set of structural transformations in global climate modeling that represent a further way in which the subsurface has been rendered legible and manageable. The general circulation models originally developed in the 1970s have been progressively augmented with data on terrestrial and ocean carbon cycling and geochemical processes to produce complex earth system models (Dahan 2010). Incorporated into integrated assessment models

(IAMs) and IPCC emission scenarios, projections of the possible replenishing of terrestrial sinks are increasingly central to the core political objectives of global climate policy (Anderson 2015). At the same time, a shift in scenario modeling techniques adopted for the fifth assessment report of the IPCC (AR5)—that preceded the Paris climate meeting—replaced the former reliance on "plausible" emission scenarios with a primary focus on a single physical metric: radiative forcing (Beck and Mahony 2018). This technical shift and the accompanying primary focus on concentrations of atmospheric greenhouse gases, rather than emission scenarios *per se*, had the effect of revealing the tacit, yet hitherto unacknowledged, role that soil—and the promise of sequestering significant quantities of carbon in soil—had played in international climate modeling.

Popular and social science literatures have been quick to pick up on and amplify this shift. An example is the recently released documentary film *2040* and accompanying website and handbook. Part-manifesto, part-lifestyle guide, it is presented as a form of "fact-based dreaming" that draws on calculations conducted for the Project Drawdown initiative.[5] Led by Australian filmmaker Damon Gameau, it presents a compelling vision of a wholesale shift in agricultural production in order to return carbon to the soil, enhance soil health, and support farm productivity and resilience, with each seen as mutually beneficial to the other. The project's handbook neatly combines these calculative claims with familiar and evocative imagery and a vernacular narrative of the magnificence, beauty, and wonder of soil. The "soil ecosystem needs to be lavished with praise," Gameau effuses in a discussion of the "unknown universe" of soil; it "provides plants with nutrients . . ., casually helps reverse global warming by storing carbon, and, while juggling these civilisation-saving traits, it also plays a pivotal role in buffering us from the short-term climate pain that awaits us" (Gameau 2019: 106).

The emergence of a political aesthetic characterized by the soteriological promise of soil carbon sequestration and regenerative agriculture is accompanied by an analogous shift in the visualization of climate change. Alongside sublime and apocalyptic images of melting ice sheets, stranded polar bears (Yusoff 2010), and the images of a burning world that characterize what Schneider (2016) terms the "climate cosmograms of the Anthropocene," soil has come to represent the twin operation of two interrelated scalar logics. Visualizations of planetary biomass operate as a kind of proxy for the promissory logic of soil carbon sequestration and the reversal of global warming, while a more localized, practical, and "down-to-earth" imagery evokes restored landscapes as visions of eco-social hope in times of climatic grief. In place of what they term the "totalizing [and] disabling . . . global synopticism" of climate maps and imagery, Schneider and Walsh suggest that in recent years, and particularly after COP21, there has been "a push to 'downscale' global climate knowledge to the local level to empower communities" (2019: 1). They go on to suggest that this project of "downscaling" global climate imagery is being undertaken in ways that seek to render global circulation models at more granular—commonly regional— scales, whilst translating relevant climatic, geochemical, and ecological data and visualizations into platforms usable by communities and land managers. While these tools "are created with the goal of relating *global* knowledge to *local* situations and thereby empowering communities to take climate action" (Schneider and Walsh 2019: 2, emphasis in original), they continue to bear the traces of what Edwards (2010) terms "infrastructural globalism" and the territorial logics of nation-state investments in tools designed to measure, incentivize, and in some cases pay for the remediation of landscapes and the enhancement of soil organic carbon levels. The association of soil carbon with the local and even micro scale illustrates such traces of globalism, in that "seeing" once-atmospheric carbon in a handful of soil requires an imagination shaped by a certain degree of reductionism, abstraction, and universalism.

Facts on the Ground

Much of the literature on carbon sequestration practices is premised on the notion that *good* farming will restore landscapes, lock carbon in the soil, and enhance the resilience of farming communities and the people and systems that rely on their products. At work here is a narrative shift not only about climate change—from a despairing to more hopeful register—but about agriculture in the context of climate change. More specifically, there is a shift from narratives of agriculture as a climate change villain and victim—as both a significant contributor to and uniquely vulnerable to climatic changes (Rickards et al. 2017)—toward a newer, more positive narrative that presents a certain type of regenerative agriculture as a climate change savior. The FAO has gone so far as to flag its support for agroecology, which is not only an area of agricultural science and policy but also a practice and (often oppositional) social movement (Wezel et al. 2009; Giraldo and Rosset 2018). Calling for the "scaling up" of agroecology to help address the ambitions of the sustainable development goals (SGDs), the FAO notes that "agroecology embraces the spirit of the 2030 Agenda," is "key to transforming food and agricultural systems," and is supported by "growing scientific evidence *and* local experiences" (2018: 1, emphasis added).[6]

As we described above, the entwined calculative and aesthetic logics of agricultural soil carbon sequestration are evident here. The modernization and professionalization of agriculture has long relied on agronomic expertise and agricultural extension characterized by efforts to "show farmers the numbers" (Rickards 2006). Accompanying the development of policy architectures and payment systems designed to incentivize soil carbon retention have been allied efforts to produce theoretical models of existing soil carbon stocks and sequestration potential. Research programs at both international and national scales have functioned to transform national carbon reservoirs into objects for international carbon markets (Lövbrand and Stripple 2006). Concurrent efforts to produce "facts on the ground" work to substantiate the promissory logics of carbon faming and regenerative agriculture and reinforce the theoretical models that underpin global climate scenarios. They utilize a hybrid set of verification methodologies. On the one hand, a set of practice-based verification models focuses specifically on individual land users and entails systems of self-assessment or regulated methodologies for ensuring sequestration "integrity" (Higgins et al. 2015). On the other hand, the standardization and automation of soil carbon sampling methodologies, particularly through the use of remote sensing imagery, propels a political logic abstracted from both the territorial and terrestrial entanglements of soil carbon in landscapes.

In this sense, the hybrid knowledge work engaged to substantiate the promise of carbon farming mirrors the overlapping roles that scientific knowledge plays in contemporary agricultural practice. Farmers have been taught to become scientifically literate not only as a means to produce improved farming practices, but as a good in itself: underpinned by a notion of the redemptive value of science (Nally and Taylor 2015). However, agricultural science has struggled to prove itself as a "proper" science and academic discipline, one that is pure and experimental, not "merely" descriptive and localized (Richards 1983). Some would argue that it has never fully succeeded in this endeavor and that this is one reason why it is now among the most vulnerable to both climate change and a lack of "new blood": new young farmers wanting to join the profession/occupation. Imagined as rational, economic agents, the latter are presumed to need numerical proof before engaging in innovative practices, even as representations of agriculture concurrently try to leverage its more qualitative, aesthetic appeal. A World Bank report, for example, argues that not only can African agriculture be made profitable and competitive with the addition of digital and other technologies, this success can in turn help attract young people ("agripreneurs") to agriculture as an exciting, attractive career option (Brooks et al. 2013).[7]

Ongoing insecurities about agriculture help explain why popular, often populist, genres of writing about the climatic promise of soil and regenerative farming are presented in rationalist, quantifiable terms. At the same time they evoke the eco-spirituality and agrarian political sensibilities of Berry and Leopold and longer histories of colonial and Christian traditions of land stewardship (Hodge 2007; Lowe 2015). As an area of research and government programming, agricultural soil carbon sequestration has an uneasy relationship with this literature, where enthusiastic accounts of the practical potential of sequestration are interpreted as naïve and dangerously populist. Soil carbon policies are thus redolent with claims to scientific authority, including calculations of the potential carbon sequestration benefits and water-holding capacity and the biodiversity co-benefits, as well as cost–benefit analysis of their application to nascent markets.

Positioned awkwardly between calculation and more qualitative knowledge is the key agricultural practice of "demonstration." Since the early colonial era, "demonstration farms" have been used by agricultural scientists and improvers to bridge abstract scientific principles and the lived experience and local knowledges of farmers (Nally and Taylor 2015). There are arguably two main reasons for this. First, pedagogically, there is a strong sense in agricultural education and extension that farmers learn better—or according to some, can only learn—through embodied training and experiential learning rather than didactic teaching of the sort associated with normal scientific instruction (Stone 2016). Thus demonstration farms are valued as a learning space. The ideal of mimicry notably reappears here. While the mimicry of interest described earlier was how to replicate nature, the ideal relation here is one of emulation between farmers and scientists, and between leading, science-trained farmers (such as those leading demonstration farms) and the mass of other farmers to whom new practices are continually being directed (Nally and Taylor 2015). The second related role of demonstration is to offer proof of the practical utility—"research impact," in today's parlance—of the scientific knowledge involved. In other words, the value of demonstration farms feeds back into the world of science.

In his genealogy of the term "demonstration," Andrew Barry (2001) argues that alongside the now commonplace notion of the "demonstrator as a political actor" (as in a protestor), the figure of the demonstrator was someone engaged in making public scientific claims. "To be in the presence of a demonstration," Barry concludes, "was a matter of *witnessing* a technical practice" (2001: 177, emphasis in original). Demonstration is, in this sense, both personal and material. The task of embodying "facts on the ground" in regenerative agriculture can be seen to be operating in this fashion. Numerous demonstration farms (including those of leading, inspirational farmers) provide "a gathering ground" for farmers, where their presence and impressions help to verify the realness and facticity of the improved, regenerative approaches on offer. In doing so, they help enable the related information and principles to travel to other ground through what Latour terms the "small anthropological mysteries" in which "the earth becomes a sign, takes on a geometrical form, becomes the carrier of a numbered code, and will soon be defined by a color" (1999: 47, 49)—whilst at the same time manifesting an altogether more embodied and material factuality "on the ground." Moreover, by translating the message of regenerative agriculture from science to practical farming, the farmers involved help provide cultural legitimacy to the science of regenerative agriculture, in keeping with the sort of move that de Wit and Iles (2016) argue is especially needed in agroecology given the precarity of its acceptance in mainstream agricultural science circles. As they note, what agroecology and regenerative agriculture also enjoy—which conventional agriculture increasingly does not—is a wider social legitimacy enabled by the performance of its perceived virtue.

Demonstrating Virtue

Besides conventional scientific and agrarian narratives about agriculture, *regenerative* agriculture is also characterized by what Lave et al. (2010) call the "simple kindergarten logic" of (landscape) restoration projects. As they put it: "Ecological restoration is predicated on the idea that humans can undo past anthropogenic environmental harm." They note that "the intuitive appeal of this vision of humans as positive environmental actors has made restoration a driving force of the American environmental movement" (2010: 678), helping it evolve from a grassroots social movement to become a central pillar of much contemporary environmental thinking and practice.

A central challenge that confronts landscape restoration projects—particularly as they are increasingly enrolled as a tool of climate policy and carbon sequestration— is the relationship between above and belowground worlds. More specifically, the challenge is how to read the land (the aboveground world) for signs of the condition of the belowground world, notably the carbon content of soil. It is useful to follow here Stuart Elden's (2013) provocation to examine the "verticality" of contemporary climate capitalism. As he argues, the systems designed to incentivize—and in some cases pay for—ecosystem and climatic services literally go all the way down. In climate change practice and discourse, the subterranean world is increasingly being rendered transparent by the complex of geospatial imagery and speculative political and financial investment (Kearnes and Rickards 2017). At the same time, in carbon farming a series of aboveground indicators are taken as proxies for the soil health and carbon richness below. Data on bird life, grass growth, water flow, and vegetation quality and diversity—together with direct soil sampling—are often taken as diverse proxy indicators of the health of the land and soil.

The ideal of healthy soil and land represents a powerful social norm and aesthetic (Matless 2001). Across the literature on carbon farming the interplay between above- and belowground is posed in the language of virtue, redolent with the values and cultural aesthetics of "good land" and "good soil." In one sense, this call toward good land has an obvious normative intent, reflecting the long-standing deployment of agricultural extension in a project designed to morally improve farmers as much as scientifically improve farming (Rickards 2006). It is "good grazing"—and by extension "good farmers"—who are presented as restoring "bad" land and "poor soil." At the same time, the notion of virtue that is at play here—of virtuous farming and what Matthew Paterson and Johannes Stripple term "virtuous carbon" (2012)—appears as both a commonplace and vaguely ill-defined. There is no agreement on what constitutes "good soil," or good land. Is good soil "innately good," for example, or just "good for the climate"? Is good soil simply functionally good, when measured for its carbon sequestration and storing capacity?

In her work on what she calls "geomorphic aesthetics"—the prehistoric traditions of cave painting and the use of pigments drawn from earth and soil—Kathryn Yusoff argues that these aesthetic practices offer a vantage point for conceptualizing the human as a "geologic subject," and "offer a passage into thinking a mixed inheritance that might help conceptualize a more ecologically excessive notion of subjectivity in the Anthropocene" (2015: 384). In the worlds of carbon farming, and the compositional economies that shape the political promise of these techniques for effecting significant changes in atmospheric CO_2 concentrations, these geomorphic aesthetic sensibilities—of working with land, with grass, and with soil—appear in the altogether more moral terminology of landscape restoration and agricultural regeneration. This is a language drawn from traditions of landscape care and stewardship, that speak of the need to create a kind of order and harmony between humans, cows, and grass, and the soil underfoot and the unseen microbes and insects that are (sometimes) willing accomplices in this task. However, as Thom van Dooren (2014) insists, eco-care is often messy, and often violent, and as Maria Puig de la Bellacasa (2015) insists, caring for soil entails making time for the entangled more-than-human relationality of soil. A recent profile of an Australian regenerative and carbon famer published by the Australian Broadcasting Corporation (ABC), for example, marveled at the epistemological bricolage and aesthetic improvisation characteristic of this form of landscape care. "Colin still uses a very low rate of fertilizer and occasionally uses a herbicide, but the studies done on his property clearly showed that he has achieved great environmental outcome," the profile effused. "As we go for a drive down the paddock, the place looks amazing, sheep happily grazing: there's grass everywhere, in the middle of a drought" (ABC Radio National 2019).

What we see here is that the invocation of the goodness of soil and land falls between the twin poles of traditional reasoning in environmental ethics: those of instrumental and intrinsic values. What instead emerges in the proto-ethical spaces of carbon farming are the virtues of working *with* land, soil, and earth. That is to say, following James Proctor, the virtues of good land, and good soil—with all of their indeterminacy—emerge from working with an earth that is "already a moral place" (1999: 151), from a landscape aesthetic overlain by an agrarian invocation of a *working* harmony with the land. That carbon farming operates in a morally contested context is constitutive of, rather than antithetical to, the construction of *qualculative* knowledge that seeks to produce a verifiable accounting of soil sequestration, whilst at the same time qualifying this enumeration with aesthetic visions of restored landscapes.

Conclusion: Down to Earth

Writing in the aftermath of the Paris climate talks, Latour (2018) argues that COP21 symbolized the emergence of a new "attractor" for society: a hazily imagined world characterized not by the dominant science-based logic of the Global (exemplified by climate change science and its "view from nowhere"), *or* by the resistive logic of the Local (epitomized by some ecological and agrarian traditions seeking to retreat into the local), or even by the Out-of-this-World logic of orienting toward and escaping to another planet. Instead, it is characterized by an alternative orientation, a nascent Terrestrial logic "bound to the earth and to land" and also "*a way of worlding*" (2018: 54, emphasis in original). Latour argues that at the heart of this new orientation are the physical changes and rediscovered agency of the E/earth itself, and a resurgent but reoriented science, one that abandons the pretense of viewing the world (the Globe) disinterestedly from a distance to instead grasp "the same structures from *up close,* as *internal* to the collectivities and *sensitive* to human actions, to which they *react* swiftly" (2018: 67). This requires transcending the conventional, hard-won "bifurcation between the real—external, objective, and knowable—and the inside—unreal, subjective, and unknowable" (2018: 70–71). The Terrestrial offers a way of escaping the "phony war" between the non-existent Global and Local. It simultaneously engages "two complementary movements that modernization has made contradictory: *attaching oneself* to the soil on the one hand, and *becoming attached to the world* on the other" (2018: 91–92). Soil carbon sequestration offers a striking example of the sort of ambiguous but crucial move that Latour detects is emerging as a social response to the conundrums climate change poses. While Latour does not discuss it *per se,* regenerative agriculture and terrestrial carbon sequestration represent a key area for future social science research into the shifting materiality and political aesthetics of climate change.

Following Latour's lead, we might conclude that climate change is being—somewhat paradoxically—terrestrialized, that is, being brought "back to earth" through a series of sociotechnical infrastructures designed to attend to both the materiality and geographies of carbon. Where carbon is, and where it might be—that is, moving carbon from the atmosphere (back) to the earth—has become one of the preeminent tasks of contemporary climate policy. While the implicit political stakes of this move toward broad policy commitments that aim to achieve negative emissions through carbon removal and sequestration technologies, rather than through aggressive cuts to emissions, remain significant in shaping the uptake of these techniques, it is also important to keep in mind that a return to earth, and a return to the terrestrial, is not a return to some kind of foundational grounding. Though framed in the terms of regenerative agriculture practice the projects of carbon farming are as consumed with the challenge of creating a new earth as they are with restoring an old one. Commitments to negative emissions—of the sort that shape much of the political outfall of the recent COP21 and IPCC AR5 statements—are thoroughly enmeshed in the infrastructures of climate modeling and scenario development, framed by a series of grand projects of commensuration. The project, in other words, is to transform atmospheric carbon into biological and geological carbon.

If, as Wynne (2010) argues, climate science constitutes a *strange* political art, the epistemological terrain of contemporary carbon farming seems equally quixotic. As Earth is itself being committed to multiple and overlapping forms of anthropogenic transformation and is also being mobilized to combat and even reverse these changes—in some cases, literally using fire to fight fire and earth to fight earth (Clark 2012) under the guise of geoengineering and negative emissions—these earth technics are made legible through new forms of political aesthetics that are manifest in carbon landscapes. In this chapter, we have attempted to demonstrate that in the worlds of carbon sequestration being deployed along the carbon frontier, a form of ethical and aesthetic improvisation is at work. This is about recognizing that the emergent task of negotiating the E/earth demands an appreciation that it is *already* moral, *already* storied. To complement the commendable impulse to assess these techniques and strategies for both their technical feasibility and their political meanings, this chapter begins to examine how we might dwell with these techniques as technologies of earth-writing, to probe what earthly narratives they make possible and those that they proscribe. While a critical impulse would likely produce a more ambivalent "stance on the growing expectations of storing more carbon into soils" and insist on a "consideration of the situated, heterogeneous, and volatile dynamics of carbon within soils" (Granjou and Salazar 2019: 39), not to mention the intense politics of land (e.g., land-grabbing) involved in the terrestrial carbon sequestration project (e.g., Lyons and Westoby 2014), the argument we have developed here might be read as a call to recognize—and indeed value—the necessarily hybrid epistemological work needed to craft an altogether more terrestrial and earthly land ethic in the context of climatic change.

Acknowledgments

The research that underpins this chapter was enabled by funding from the Australian Research Council (award number FT130101302). We also acknowledge a research collaboration grant provided by the School of Humanities and Languages, UNSW.

Notes

1 This shift in emphasis from "stabilization" of GHG concentrations to notions of balancing emissions against sinks was accompanied by a broader shift in the institutional arrangement that underpinned the Paris Agreement. In place of the model of decarbonization targets and timetables epitomized by the Kyoto Protocol and the UNFCC, the Paris Agreement was premised on a more distributed system of "intended nationally determined contributions" (INDCs) prepared and submitted by individual governments.
2 http://4p1000.org/understand
3 https://regenerationinternational.org/4p1000/. See also Kon Kam King et al. (2018).
4 Here we include titles such as *The Soil Will Save Us: How Scientists, Farmers, and Foodies are Healing the Soil to Save the Planet* (Ohlson 2014), *Cows Save the Planet: And Other Improbable Ways of Restoring Soil to Heal the Earth* (Schwartz 2013), *Grass, Soil, Hope: A Journey Through Carbon Country* (White 2014), *Defending Beef: The Case for Sustainable Meat Production* (Niman 2014), *Drawdown: The Most Comprehensive Plan Ever Proposed to Reverse Global Warming* (Hawken 2017) and Michael Pollan's (2007) *The Omnivore's Dilemma: A Natural History of Four Meals*.
5 Project Drawdown is itself a multi-platform initiative designed to "review, analyse, and identify the most viable global climate solutions, and share these findings with the world." See www.drawdown.org/
6 See also www.fao.org/agroecology
7 For insightful critiques of the neoliberal "agripreneur" discourse see Ripoll et al. (2017) and Mwaura (2017).

References

ABC Radio National (2019), "A Revolution in the Paddocks—Regenerative Farming" [https://www.abc.net.au/radionational/programs/earshot/a-revolution-in-the-paddocks/11211088; accessed June 22, 2019].

Anderson, K. (2015), "Duality in Climate Science," *Nature Geoscience*, 8 (12): 898–900.

Anderson, K. and G. Peters (2016), "The Trouble with Negative Emissions," *Science*, 354 (6309): 182–83.

Barry, A. (2001), *Political Machines: Governing a Technological Society*, London: Athlone Press.

Beck, S. and M. Mahony (2018), "The Politics of Anticipation: The IPCC and the Negative Emissions Technologies Experience," *Global Sustainability*, 1: e8 [https://doi.org/10.1017/sus.2018.7].

Benyus, J. (1997), *Biomimicry: Innovation Inspired by Nature*, New York: William Morrow.

Bijker, W. E., R. Bal, and R. Hendriks (2009), *The Paradox of Scientific Authority: The Role of Scientific Advice in Democracies*, Cambridge, MA: MIT Press.

Brockett, B. F. T., A. L. Browne, A. Beanland, M. G. Whitfield, N. Watson, G. A. Blackburn et al. (2019), "Guiding Carbon Farming Using Interdisciplinary Mixed Methods Mapping," *People and Nature*, 1 (2): 191–203.

Brooks, K., S. Zorya, A. Gautam, and A. Goyal (2013), *Agriculture as a Sector of Opportunity for Young People in Africa*, Policy Research Working Paper 6473, The World Bank.

Buck, H. J. (2018), "The Need for Carbon Removal," *Jacobin*, July 24 [https://www.jacobinmag.com/2018/07/carbon-removal-geoengineering-global-warming].

Bulkeley, H. (2016), *Accomplishing Climate Governance*, New York: Cambridge University Press.

Clark, N. (2012), "Rock, Life, Fire: Speculative Geophysics and the Anthropocene," *Oxford Literary Review*, 34 (2): 259–76.

Clark, N. (2015), "Fiery Arts: Pyrotechnology and the Political Aesthetics of the Anthropocene," *GeoHumanities*, 1 (2): 1–19.

Cochoy, F. (2008), "Calculation, Qualculation, Calqulation: Shopping Cart Arithmetic, Equipped Cognition and the Clustered Consumer," *Marketing Theory*, 8 (1): 15–44.

Conference of the Parties (2009), *Copenhagen Accord*, FCCC/CP/2009/L.7, Copenhagen: United Nations Climate Change Conference.

Conference of the Parties (2015), *Adoption of the Paris Agreement*, FCCC/CP/2015/L.9/Rev.1, United Nations Framework Convention on Climate Change.

Dahan, A. (2010), "Putting the Earth System in a Numerical Box? The Evolution from Climate Modeling Toward Global Change," *Studies in History and Philosophy of Science B: Studies in History and Philosophy of Modern Physics*, 41 (3): 282–92.

de Wit, M. M. and A. Iles (2016), "Toward Thick Legitimacy: Creating a Web of Legitimacy for Agroecology," *Elementa: Science of the Anthropocene*, 4: 000115 [http://doi.org/10.12952/journal.elementa.000115].

Edwards, P. N. (2010), *A Vast Machine: Computer Models, Climate Data, and the Politics of Global Warming*, Cambridge, MA: MIT Press.

Elden, S. (2013), "Secure the Volume: Vertical Geopolitics and the Depth of Power," *Political Geography*, 34: 35–51.

Engel-Di Mauro, S. (2014), *Ecology, Soils, and the Left: An Ecosocial Approach*, New York: Palgrave Macmillan.

FAO (2018), *Scaling up Agroecology Initiative: Transforming Food and Agricultural Systems in Support of the SDGs. A proposal prepared for the International Symposium on Agroecology, 3–5 April 2018*, 19049EN/1/04.18, Rome: FAO.

Flannery, T. (2015), *Atmosphere of Hope: Searching for Solutions to the Climate Crisis*, Melbourne: Text Publishing.

Frazer, J. G. (1925), *The Golden Bough: A Study in Magic and Religion*, abridged edition, New York: Macmillan.

Gameau, D. (2019), *2040: A Handbook for the Regeneration Based on the Documentary 2040*, Sydney: Pan Macmillan Australia.

Giraldo, O. F. and P. M. Rosset (2018), "Agroecology as a Territory in Dispute: Between Institutionality and Social Movements, *Journal of Peasant Studies*, 45 (3): 545–64.

Granjou, C. and J. F. Salazar (2019), "The Stuff of Soil: Belowground Agency in the Making of Future Climates," *Nature and Culture*, 14 (1): 39–60.

Hawken, P., ed. (2017), *Drawdown: The Most Comprehensive Plan Ever Proposed to Reverse Global Warming*, New York: Penguin.

Higgins, V., J. Dibden, and C. Cocklin (2015), "Private Agri-food Governance and Greenhouse Gas Abatement: Constructing a Corporate Carbon Economy," *Geoforum*, 66: 75–84.

Hodge, J. M. (2007), *Triumph of the Expert: Agrarian Doctrines of Development and the Legacies of British Colonialism*, Athens, OH: Ohio University Press.

Johnson, E. R. and J. Goldstein (2015), "Biomimetic Futures: Life, Death, and the Enclosure of a More-Than-Human Intellect," *Annals of the Association of American Geographers*, 105 (2): 387–96.

Kearnes, M. and L. Rickards (2017), "Earthly Graves for Environmental Futures: Techno-burial Practices," *Futures*, 92: 48–58.

Kon Kam King, J., C. Granjou, J. Fournil, and L. Cecillon (2018), "Soil Sciences and the French 4 per 1000 Initiative—The Promises of Underground Carbon," *Energy Research & Social Science*, 45: 144–52.

Kruger, T., O. Geden, and S. Rayner (2016), "Abandon Hype in Climate Models," *The Guardian*, April 26.

Krzywoszynska, A. (2019a), "Caring for Soil Life in the Anthropocene: The Role of Attentiveness in More-Than-Human Ethics," *Transactions of the Institute of British Geographers*, 44 (4): 661–75.

Krzywoszynska, A. (2019b), "Making Knowledge and Meaning in Communities of Practice: What Role May Science Play? The Case of Sustainable Soil Management in England," *Soil Use and Management*, 35 (1): 160–68.

Kuch, D. (2015), *The Rise and Fall of Carbon Emissions Trading*, New York: Palgrave Macmillan.

Latour, B. (1999), *Pandora's Hope: Essays on the Reality of Science Studies*, Cambridge, MA: Harvard University Press.

Latour, B. (2018), *Down to Earth: Politics in the New Climatic Regime*, Cambridge: Polity Press.

Lave, R., M. Doyle, and M. Robertson (2010), "Privatizing Stream Restoration in the US," *Social Studies of Science*, 40 (5): 677–703.

Lövbrand, E. and J. Stripple (2006), "The Climate as Political Space: On the Territorialisation of the Global Carbon Cycle," *Review of International Studies*, 32 (2): 217–35.

Lovell, H. (2015), *The Making of Low Carbon Economies*, London: Routledge.

Lowe, K. M. (2015), *Baptized with the Soil: Christian Agrarians and the Crusade for Rural America*, Oxford: Oxford University Press.

Lyons, K. and P. Westoby (2014), "Carbon Colonialism and the New Land Grab: Plantation Forestry in Uganda and its Livelihood Impacts," *Journal of Rural Studies*, 36: 13–21.

Matless, D. (2001), "Bodies Made of Grass Made of Earth Made of Bodies: Organicism, Diet and National Health in Mid-Twentieth-Century England," *Journal of Historical Geography*, 27 (3): 355–76.

Mauss, M. ([1972] 2001), *A General Theory of Magic*, London: Routledge.

Mwaura, G. M. (2017), "Just Farming? Neoliberal Subjectivities and Agricultural Livelihoods Among Educated Youth in Kenya," *Development and Change*, 48 (6): 1310–35.

Nally, D. and S. Taylor (2015), "The Politics of Self-Help: The Rockefeller Foundation, Philanthropy and the 'Long' Green Revolution," *Political Geography*, 49: 51–63.

Niman, N. H. (2014), *Defending Beef: The Case for Sustainable Meat Production*, White River Junction, VT: Chelsea Green.

Nordhaus, T. (2018), "The Two-Degree Delusion: The Dangers of an Unrealistic Climate Change Target," *Foreign Affairs*, February 8.

Ohlson, K. (2014), *The Soil Will Save Us: How Scientists, Farmers, and Foodies are Healing the Soil to Save the Planet*, New York: Rodale.

Paterson, M. and J. Stripple (2012), "Virtuous Carbon," *Environmental Politics*, 21 (4): 563–82.

Pollan, M. (2007), *The Omnivore's Dilemma: A Natural History of Four Meals*, London: Penguin.

Prins, G. and S. Rayner (2007), "Time to Ditch Kyoto," *Nature*, 449 (7165): 973–75.

Proctor, J. (1999), "A Moral Earth: Facts and Values in Global Environmental Change," in J. D. Proctor and D. M. Smith (eds.), *Geography and Ethics: Journeys in a Moral Terrain*, 149–62, New York: Routledge.

Puig de la Bellacasa, M. (2015), "Making Time for Soil: Technoscientific Futurity and the Pace of Care," *Social Studies of Science*, 45 (5): 691–716.

Rayner, S. (2016), "What Might Evans-Pritchard Have Made of Two Degrees?," *Anthropology Today*, 32 (4): 1–2.

Richards, S. (1983), "'Masters of Arts and Bachelors of Barley': The Struggle for Agricultural Education in Mid-Nineteenth-Century Britain," *History of Education*, 12 (3): 161–75.

Rickards, L. (2006), "Capable, Enlightened and Masculine: Constructing English Agriculturalist Ideals in Formal Agricultural Education, 1845–2003," DPhil thesis, University of Oxford.

Rickards, L., T. Neale, and M. Kearnes (2017), "Australia's National Climate: Learning to Adapt?," *Geographical Research*, 55 (4): 469–76.

Ripoll, S., J. Andersson, L. Badstue, M. Büttner, J. Chamberlin, O. Erenstein et al. (2017), "Rural Transformation, Cereals and Youth in Africa: What Role for International Agricultural Research?," *Outlook on Agriculture*, 46 (3): 168–77.

Rossel, R. A. V. and J. Bouma (2016), "Soil Sensing: A New Paradigm for Agriculture," *Agricultural Systems*, 148: 71–74.

Schneider, B. (2016), "Burning Worlds of Cartography: A Critical Approach to Climate Cosmograms of the Anthropocene," *Geo: Geography and Environment*, 3 (2): e00027 [https://doi.org/10.1002/geo2.27].

Schneider, B. and L. Walsh (2019), "The Politics of Zoom: Problems with Downscaling Climate Visualizations," *Geo: Geography and Environment*, 6 (1): e00070 [https://doi.org/10.1002/geo2.70].

Schwartz, J. D. (2013), *Cows Save the Planet: And Other Improbable Ways of Restoring Soil to Heal the Earth*, White River Junction, VT: Chelsea Green.

Stone, G. D. (2016), "Towards a General Theory of Agricultural Knowledge Production: Environmental, Social, and Didactic Learning," *Culture, Agriculture, Food and Environment*, 38 (1): 5–17.

Sumberg, J., J. Thompson, and P. Woodhouse (2013), "Why Agronomy in the Developing World Has Become Contentious," *Agriculture & Human Values*, 30 (1): 71–83.

Sumberg, J., J. Thompson, and P. Woodhouse (2014), "Political Agronomy," in P. B. Thompson and D. M. Kaplan (eds.), *Encyclopedia of Food and Agricultural Ethics*, 1502–8, Dordrecht: Springer Netherlands.

Taussig, M. (1993), *Mimesis and Alterity: A Particular History of the Senses*, London: Routledge.

Thompson, P. B. (2016), *The Spirit of the Soil: Agriculture and Environmental Ethics*, New York: Routledge.

United Nations General Assembly (UNGA) (2012), *The Future We Want: Resolution Adopted by the General Assembly on 27 July 2012*, A/RES/66/288, United Nations.

United Nations General Assembly (UNGA) (2014), *Resolution Adopted by the General Assembly on 20 December 2013: 68/232. World Soil Day and International Year of Soils*, A/RES/68/232, United Nations.

van Dooren, T. (2014), *Flight Ways: Life and Loss at the Edge of Extinction*, New York: Columbia University Press.

Wedderburn-Bisshop, G. and L. Rickards (2018), "Livestock's Near-Term Climate Impact and Mitigation Policy Implications," in D. Bogueva, D. Marinova, and T. Raphaely (eds.), *Handbook of Research on Social Marketing and Its Influence on Animal Origin Food Product Consumption*, 37–57, Hershey, PA: IGI Global.

Weszkalnys, G. (2013), "Oil's Magic: Contestation and Materiality," in S. Strauss, S. Rupp, and T. Love (eds.), *Cultures of Energy: Power, Practices, Technologies*, 267–83, Abingdon: Left Coast Press/Routledge.

Wezel, A., S. Bellon, T. Doré, C. Francis, D. Vallod, and C. David (2009), "Agroecology as a Science, a Movement and a Practice: A Review," *Agronomy for Sustainable Development*, 29 (4): 503–15.

White, C. (2014), *Grass, Soil, Hope: A Journey Through Carbon Country*, White River Junction, VT: Chelsea Green.

Whitington, J. (2016), "Carbon as a Metric of the Human," *PoLAR: Political and Legal Anthropology Review*, 39 (1): 46–63.

Wynne, B. (1996), "May the Sheep Safely Graze? A Reflexive View of the Expert–Lay Knowledge Divide," in S. M. Lash, B. Szerszynski, and B. Wynne (eds.), *Risk, Environment and Modernity: Towards a New Ecology*, 44–83, London: Sage.

Wynne, B. (2010), "Strange Weather, Again: Climate Science as Political Art," *Theory, Culture & Society*, 27 (2/3): 289–305.

Yusoff, K. (2010), "Biopolitical Economies and the Political Aesthetics of Climate Change," *Theory, Culture & Society*, 27 (2/3): 73–99.

Yusoff, K. (2015), "Geologic Subjects: Nonhuman Origins, Geomorphic Aesthetics and the Art of Becoming Inhuman," *Cultural Geographies*, 22 (3): 383–407.

6

To Know, To Dwell, To Care: Towards an Actionable, Place-based Knowledge of Soils

Anna Krzywoszynska with Steve Banwart and David Blacker

Introduction: Elements of a Place-based Knowledge of Soils

What *is* a soil? What we know about soils informs how we act on them, and how we act on them informs what we know about them. In most arenas associated with the modernization project, the production of knowledge about soils has come to be dominated by particular natural sciences. This has been especially felt in the context of modern agriculture, where scientific framings of soils as inert repositories for chemical fertility have become embedded into agronomic practice.[1] Such chemical agronomic soil knowledges have served to support ecologically and socially destructive forms of land use in agriculture by underpinning particular forms of soil-related action (Krzywoszynska 2020). In the face of the ecological crisis of soils (FAO 2015), the future of soils and humans calls for new forms of actionable soil knowledge which would enable the much-needed practical ethic of soil care (Puig de la Bellacasa 2015; Krzywoszynska 2019a), and which would contribute to sustainable and just socioecologies.

In this chapter, we argue that a focus on place is a fruitful way forward for building such socioecologically sustainable soil knowledges. We suggest that current dominant modes of knowing soils in modern agriculture encourage both a shallow approach to soils as surfaces and a universalist approach to soils that negates their place specificity and connectedness. We, the authors of this chapter, come from different backgrounds, but we meet in the soil. What unites us is a concern with places—with landscapes, with fields, with mountains. What also unites us is a belief that we can make these places better—more healthy, vibrant, and full of life—by knowing them better. We believe in the world-changing power of knowledgeable action and actionable knowledge. And we believe that soils are a crucial matter in relation to which knowledgeable action and actionable knowledge need to be better developed. This chapter is thus a transdisciplinary dialogue between a social scientist (Anna Krzywoszynska), a natural scientist (Steve Banwart), and an arable farmer (David Blacker). At times, disruptions are needed so that our conceptual horizons and capacities for action extend—and so that new ethical relations become possible, thinkable. This is the benefit of transdisciplinary dialogues, events which can shake up ontological foundations so that new vistas can emerge (Holmes et al. 2018). While this chapter was conceived of and written by Anna, its content is underpinned by a series of conversations between the three authors about the Critical Zone. The final text was approved by the whole authorial team.

The relevance of place to the building of better soil knowledges can be illustrated by thinking through two recent science fiction films, which take an interestingly contrasting approach to the future of humans and humus. The first is Christopher Nolan's *Interstellar* (2014), in which humans seek to abandon Earth, which has become uninhabitable due to a crop-destroying and atmosphere-altering phenomenon. The main character, Cooper (Matthew McConaughey), a pilot by training, disparages the farming he has had to take up in the effort to feed an increasingly desperate population: "It's like we've forgotten who we are. Explorers, pioneers, not caretakers ... we used to look up in the sky and wonder at our place in the stars. Now we just look down and worry about our place in the dirt." In the narrative of the film, humanity's survival relies on overcoming a "dirty" nature as an obstacle to the fulfillment of its true potential, which lies in the stars. Soil, as the hateful "dirt" of the farmer's field, as the dust which physically chokes and kills the characters, and finally as Earth, the doomed and dying planet, comes to symbolize an entrapment that humanity has to overcome. All technoscientific effort is directed toward the purpose of lifting people off the Earth in giant spaceships, the insides of which, pointedly, reproduce the aspirational non-place of American suburbia. Looking down and seeking to make "a place in the dirt" is contrasted with looking up to space as an arena of boundless possibility. In the words of Cooper, "We're not meant to save the world. We're meant to leave it."

An unexpected response to this vision of non-place comes in the form of Andrew Stanton's animated film *WALL-E* (2012).[2] WALL-E, the main protagonist, is one of an army of robots tasked with "cleaning up" the Earth, which has been turned into one big garbage landfill. Humanity's escape from a trashed Earth has been successfully achieved, but the success seems a pyrrhic victory as people lead untroubled but boring and meaningless lives on a never-ending space cruise. In this film, knowledge of place-making is *reclaimed* by humans, and becomes a tool for the rediscovery of the beauty, delight, and meaning that comes from embracing "dirt." In attempting to care for a seedling recovered by WALL-E from Earth, the space cruise's captain uses the on-board AI system to educate himself about the needs of plants. From that call to care for another living being, he starts to use the AI to learn about humanity's Earthly and earthy history, and to retrain himself and others in the delights of cultivation. In the final scenes of the film, the cruise returns to Earth and the seedling is planted in Earth's soil. As the credits roll past, a new future of re-inhabitation of Earth and the earth is illustrated through activities of farming, fishing, and playing in beautiful living landscapes. In *WALL-E*, humanity is only fulfilled through its connection to soil, and knowledge is only meaningful when it is used to support the development of this connection.

These two films illustrate distinct pathways for the use of and development of soil knowledge. In *Interstellar*, technoscientific knowledge is used to separate humans from their planetary home; a small group of scientists single-handedly saves humanity by freeing it from the tyranny of "place." In contrast, in *WALL-E* knowledge and technoscience are mobilized by humans to enrich their connection with places and to support them in developing a practical ethic of care in which places and their inhabitants become lively, fulfilled, and vibrant. We'd like to argue that these two films enact the kind of contemporarily pertinent questions around what kind of knowledge we want to pursue in relation to soils.

Soil scientists continue to express surprise at the fact that the growing stock of knowledge about soils is not translating into real-world action as the health of soils globally continues to deteriorate (Koch et al. 2013; FAO 2015). This issue is still often framed as a failure of science communication, of failed technoscientific leadership (e.g., Bouma 2009, 2015). In this chapter, we wish to explore a different direction, one which starts from those who engage with soils in practice—such as farmers—as both users and producers of soil knowledge (Krzywoszynska 2019b). We suggest that to develop truly actionable knowledge of soils (beyond the science communication paradigm), we need to start with places as socioecological webs of relations that involve soils and their humans, humans and their soils. Human beings are placelings, Escobar (2001) suggests: culturally and phenomenologically, our lives are rooted in and shaped by the places in which we dwell. From a knowledge perspective, this place-dwelling and place-making nature of human beings points toward the importance of embodied and localized experiences in knowledge production, the interrelation between embodiment and enmindment explored by Ingold (2000). This knowledge- and world-making process has a further ethical dimension, as it is by bringing new elements of the world into our field of attention, into our knowledge, that we can develop ethical and caring relations with them (Krzywoszynska 2019a). Making knowledge about places and developing care for those places, and all the elements that contribute to the making of those places, therefore, go hand in hand. A place-based knowledge of soils starts with the soil-dwellers, and takes their embodied and purposeful activities as a point of departure for developing greater practical and ethical attentiveness to soils.

What might a place-based knowledge of soils look like? In this chapter, we argue that crucial elements of place-based soil knowledge are depth and connectivity. We have all developed an interest in soil depth and connectivity in our separate arenas of expertise and experimentation. As a natural scientist researching the Critical Zone, Steve focuses on soils as the key layer in which many of the life-supporting processes on our planet occur. His work, however, typically excludes or simplifies the human agency in changes to this vital layer. For Anna, human agency is of primary interest. In her research on the adoption of sustainable soil management methods in England, she was struck by the dominance of scientific narratives and framings of soils amongst farmers, whose vernacular and embodied knowledge of soils was, in contrast, weakly developed.[3] This dominance of scientific framings, and by extension scientific institutions as the primary speakers *for* soils, means that other ways of making sense of soils—of making soils *meaningful as part of dwelling*—were not being sufficiently explored.[4] David, who participated in Anna's research, has been using a variety of tools and methods to explore soils in the context of his fields. For him, the importance of soil depth and connectivity are both empirical and conceptual findings, and are reconfiguring his farming practice. Through shared conversations, we have all come to relate to and use the concept of the Critical Zone in new ways in our work.

This chapter has two main objectives. First, by introducing a perspective on soils offered by the Critical Zone framing, and by exploring soil depth and connectivity in the context of real arable fields, we wish to disrupt the "surface" perspective on soils that dominates in many disciplines, including applied agronomy.[5] Secondly, we illustrate the benefits of transdisciplinary dialogues between soil-dweller and scientist perspectives for developing actionable knowledge about soils *and* in transforming scientific perspectives on soils. Rooting our conversation about soils in a particular place, we illustrate the relevance of developing place-specific research methods for exploring soils as part of dwelling, methods that blend scientific insights with phenomenological and embodied experiential knowledge. While soil sciences have made significant advances in showing that non-scientific forms of soil knowledge are valuable and viable (especially in ethnopedology; see, for example, Barrera-Bassols and Zinck 2003; Richelle et al. 2018), soil knowledge continues to be largely communicated rather than jointly developed. We instead call for a place-based approach to soils as a pathway to developing actionable soil knowledge.

Thinking soils through the Critical Zone: Depth and connectivity

Much of our thinking about soils focuses on soils as a surface. This surface perspective dominates in many academic disciplines as well as in non-academic soil engagements. When considering land-use changes, and their consequences for societies and ecosystems, we tend to focus on the surface processes, or, lately, those occurring in the atmosphere. But to understand how our actions affect and fit into a specific place, we need to move beyond this surface perspective and think through the connectivity of different processes that constitute a place. This vertical integration is the advance of the Critical Zone science—an interdisciplinary effort to understand the processes occurring in the thin layer of our planet that sustains life. The Critical Zone is a narrow band extending from the top of the tree canopy to the bottom of drinking water aquifers. The Critical Zone is Earth's livability; it is the difference between Earth and the other planets. The science of the Critical Zone seeks to understand the interactions between physical, chemical, and biological mechanisms that enable this unique life-supporting environment to emerge and continue to exist (see, for example, Banwart et al. 2013).

Critical Zone science is primarily a planetary science. And as a planet, the Earth has largely developed without people, and it will continue to function whether people are present on it or not. As far as the Critical Zone is concerned, macro-life such as human beings doesn't count for very much at all (at least not until the past few thousand years), as most of the show is run by microbial life—it is microbial activity that we are utterly dependent on for the planet's livability (Hird 2010). Humans are also irrelevant to the plant's slow pulse, to its tectonic movements. From the Critical Zone perspective, humanity is an event, like a meteor strike—profound, but brief.

As a result, humanity does not really figure in Critical Zone inquiries. However, Critical Zone science does occur in specific places. These "Critical Zone Observatories" are located in locales either with very little human habitation or with specific types of

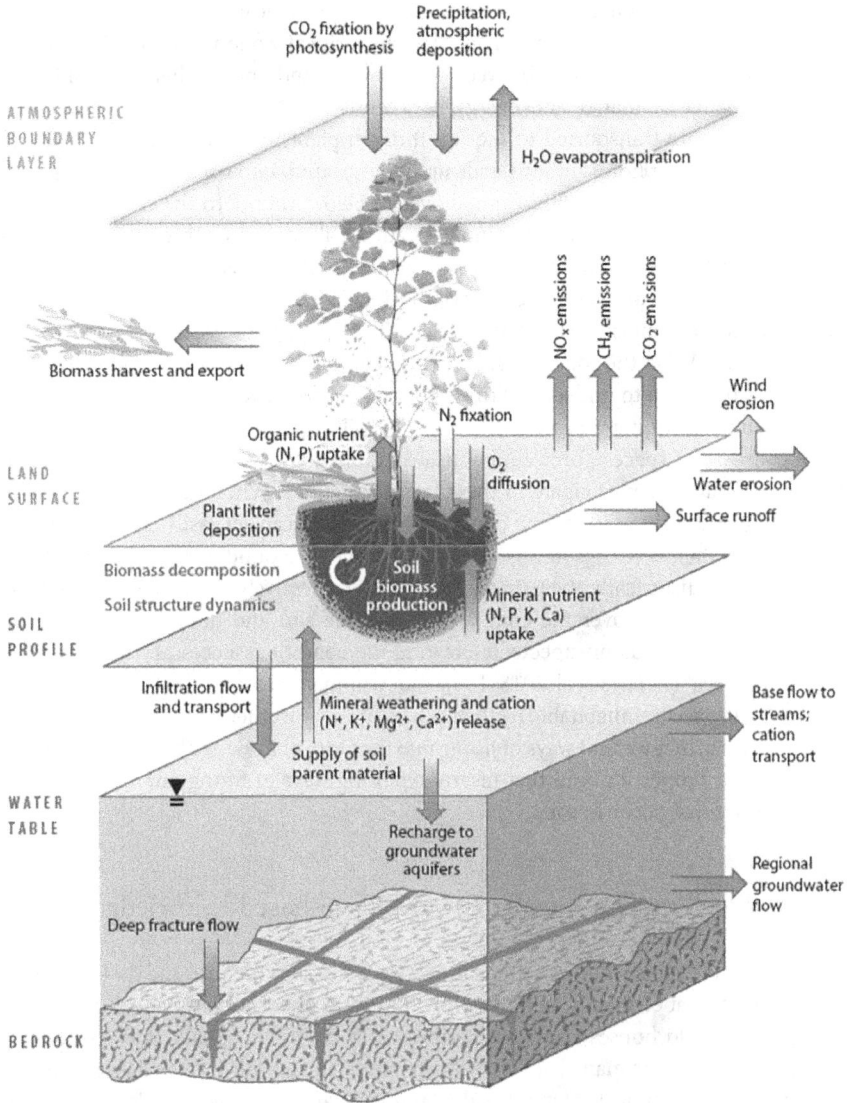

Figure 6.1 The Critical Zone. Diagram by Steven Banwart.

human habitation, so that relations between physical processes can be better studied. In the analysis of the Critical Zone Observatories, humanity is seen as part of the stocks and flows of matter and energy occurring in and flowing through particular places (see figure 6.1). Processes such as biomass harvest and export (e.g., agriculture), surface runoff (e.g., tillage-induced erosion), CO_2 emissions (e.g., from burning peat), and others imply human activity, as humans can be part of these processes, especially in land-use-intensive forms such as agriculture.

Soils are foundational for the functioning of the Critical Zone as a life-support system. They dominate the flows that make the Critical Zone work as a life habitat. Soils are the connective tissue between the aboveground and the belowground, and enable exchange of matter and energy between them. As vegetation captures solar energy, sugars are transported to the soil through plant roots; a fourth to a third of all energy fixed by photosynthesis ends up underground. Photosynthesis, understood vertically, is a huge energy flux from above- to belowground, to the roots and their fungal and bacterial microbiomes. Moreover, almost all rivers pass through soil, as does groundwater. Water's composition is thus imprinted by the soil, affected by its chemistry and structure, and carrying traces of even residual chemical pollution. Soils are also connected to the atmosphere; today, a quarter of anthropogenic greenhouse gases arise from land use. What the soils exhale has significant effects on the atmosphere and on weather patterns. So to understand the Critical Zone, whatever specific things we may want to know about it, we need to deal with the soil.

Soils are thus a space of profound transformations—and they are the space in which humans can and do participate in these transformations. While the atmosphere and the geology are fairly fixed in their composition, humans can act easily on the soil layer, and through their activities in this soil layer they can profoundly affect the rest of the Critical Zone. Historically, the Critical Zone "has progressively been engineered by life forms which learned over the eons how to use the sun and deep Earth energy to transform matter, thus unexpectedly creating the conditions necessary for other life forms to subsist" (Arènes et al. 2018: 130). Today, humans are transforming the Critical Zone into a space uninhabitable by themselves and many other forms of macro-life. It is crucial, then, that we find ways of *fitting into* the Critical Zone, without undermining its life-giving properties. And that means exploring ways of fitting our activities into the processes that occur in soils.

Dwelling and Caring: Toward Place-based Knowledge

Soil is not just the site of life-sustaining processes. Soil is also the land and the landscape; it is not only what enables humans to grow "food and fiber" but also what informs the way we live, build houses and communities, walk the earth, spend time. As Polanyi wrote, "[Land] invests man's [*sic*] life with stability; it is the site of his habitation; it is a condition of his physical safety; it is the landscape and the seasons" (Polanyi [1944] 2001: 187). Soils are not just ecological, geological, and biological entities; they are also social entities. They are not only what sustains our life; they are what makes our lives meaningful.

The Critical Zone's simplification of humanity to stocks and flows of matter and energy is utterly reductionist, but for this very reason incredibly powerful and important. It obliterates human exceptionalism and centrality, radically dissolving the boundary between human bodies and societies and their environments. All becomes matter and movement. This is a sobering message. At the same time, however, as a planetary science, the Critical Zone perspective adopts what Haraway (1988) criticized as the God's eye view, or "the view from nowhere." This perspective does not take into account the specificity of a human living in, experiencing, and exploring the Critical Zone as a particular place; it does not make space for human agency. In the Critical Zone analysis, humanity is "explained away" as a driver of or participant in particular processes. While this may produce knowledge about humanity as a generalized, universal construct, this way of analyzing place is not producing knowledge for *a human* seeking to act in and on their Critical Zone. As a result, the way that human participation in the Critical Zone is rendered "creates a cognitive dissonance since there is no commensurability between the lived experience of being situated in the [Critical Zone] and the image provided by the planetary view" (Arènes et al. 2018: 121).

A different knowledge-generation model, one which gets us closer to linking knowledge and action in places, comes from the dwelling perspective. Ingold (2000) suggests dwelling as a way of understanding humans as always already situated in and involved with the world around them, both its social and its material (nonhuman) aspects. For a human being already situated in the world, the task is not to build an image of that world, as if they were somehow external to it and looking from afar. Rather, the task is to build a view in it, inside it—so as to better understand one's own action within the world, as part of the world. Furthermore, through dwelling—living, working, interacting with a particular place and landscape—humans create relationships with places which are not only about use but also about meaning; the place dwells within us as we dwell within the place.

The dwelling perspective on knowledge production further connects with the role knowledge plays in giving rise to, shaping, and sustaining relations of care. As Fisher and Tronto argue, we can understand caring as "a species activity that includes everything that we do to maintain, continue, and repair our 'world' so that we can live in it as well as possible. That world includes our bodies, our selves, and our environment, all of which we seek to interweave in a complex, life-sustaining web" (1990: 40). Their conception of care draws together care for the individual self with the care for other human and nonhuman elements of the world. Puig de la Bellacasa further expands this notion of care as a socioecological practical ethic. She argues that as interdependency is the unavoidable fate of both humans and countless other beings, "there has to be some form of care going on somewhere in the substrate of their world for living to be possible" (2017: 5). This ontological condition of living as always part of a food web puts an obligation on human beings to care as part and parcel of living in an interdependent world.

Care, as Fisher and Tronto's definition suggests, is not only an ethic, but a practical ethic—care is an activity, a form of practice. It is therefore important to think through what caring means in practice—what good care demands of us as caretakers and as caregivers. As a practical activity aimed at improving someone or something's life/wellbeing, care implicates knowledge at various levels. As Fisher and Tronto (1990) indicate, in order to care for something, we must know what its needs are. That implies making decisions about what we consider to be the nature of the entity that we are caring for: "what soil is thought to be affects the ways in which we care for it, and vice versa" (Puig de la Bellacasa 2015: 692). In the delivery of care, we further need to be able to know what the effects of our actions are in order to assess how well we have responded to the needs of the thing we are caring for, and in order to further improve the caregiving process. This in turn means reaching a decision about the character of soils' needs, something that is currently hotly debated in relation to soil health.[6]

In relation to soil, following the obligation to care, then, presents us with a challenge of deciding what we consider the nature of soils to be, who is allowed to speak for and decide on the character of soils' nature, and who is expected to act on the satisfaction of soils' needs.[7] Such decisions are not innocent, but can be reflective of and indeed reproduce oppressive power relations when both the objects and subjects of care become foreclosed, and when care becomes a question of delivering a set list of objectives (Murphy 2015). This danger of foreclosing care can be counteracted by a commitment to care as a project of unsettling and challenging existing regimes through a commitment to those humans and nonhumans who are neglected, silenced, or hard to sense (Puig de la Bellacasa 2011; Gabrys 2017; Tironi and Rodríguez-Giralt 2017). This commitment to care as an ongoing project connects with the provisional and ongoing character of knowledge creation in processes of caring. Annemarie Mol, who wrote about the logic of care in the medical context, stresses that caregiving is characterized by both uncertainty and persistency. Unlike the dreams of technoscientific mastery where answers to complex questions are delivered by the pressing of a key, in the context of care knowledge is provisional and always in the process of being developed. As she writes, in the logic of care:

> facts and technologies are more fluid ... Control is not on offer. The world may well be adaptable and adjustable, but only up to a point. There are limits to what can be changed—but these limits are not obvious at the beginning. It is difficult to predict what may work and what will fail. Thus, the logic of care wants us to experiment carefully. Try, be attentive to what happens, adapt this, that or the other, and try again.
>
> Mol 2008: 53

Care is also urgent—if something is in need of care it means it is somehow broken. Such is the case with soils today. To care for soils, we cannot wait for perfect knowledge. If soils are in need of our care, we need to start delivering this care by the means available. At the same time, we must learn from our actions as we attempt to care so that we may become better caregivers. While scientific processes of knowledge creation—and so scientists and their research efforts—are important to this virtuous cycle of learning how to care, they are not sufficient. They lack the commitment to linking knowledge and action that comes from dwelling.

Approaching soils through the Critical Zone perspective encourages us to look at soils vertically rather than horizontally, appreciating the connectivity of soils within flows of matter and energy that support livability. The dwelling perspective helps us locate this connectivity in places as socioecological constructs. Theories of care developed by Fisher and Tronto, Puig de la Bellacasa, and Mol further indicate the forms knowledge-making should take so that better socioecological relations in places emerge. Retaining the connectivity of the Critical Zone approach, we can flip its perspective so that it centers not on a "no-place" of an idealized Earth Zone system, but on a human being. This human being is also not a universal and generalized "pattern of behavior," an idealized human whose intentionality and motivations we can fully map out so that they become a seamless and mechanistic part of the Earth System. Rather, what the dwelling and care perspectives suggest is that we need to focus on human perception, as "the primary condition of human existence is not 'knowing' the world from the outside, but rather 'being-in-the-world' through embodied engagement and experience" (West et al. 2018: 35). To support the emergence of relations of care for soils, we need to support situated dwellers in developing tools for a meaningful exploration of and action in their Critical Zones—empowering dwellers to become better dwellers. In the following sections, David's experiences of exploring and acting on his Critical Zone offer us some clues for how to proceed.

How Deep is a Farm? Transformative Knowledge on David's Farm

David grows arable crops in the "soulless clay" (his own words!) of the Vale of York. Over the years, David had noticed that more and more work with heavier and heavier machinery was needed to prepare his soils for planting. Instead of further intensifying the soil processing, he decided to change direction and stop disturbing his soils. This meant moving away from the conventional methods of ploughing and breaking up soils to suppress weeds and establish smooth seedbeds. Over the last few years, David has joined the growing community of farmers experimenting with sustainable soil management methods in England (Krzywoszynska 2019b). He is using a strip tillage system, in which only a narrow strip of soil is disturbed by machinery for seeding, while in the rest of the field the soils are not touched. Since starting with this new farming approach, David has become increasingly interested in other non-plough soil management practices, and in soil processes more widely. He has started to explore his fields and his soils in ways he had never done before, doing soil analysis, digging soil pits, and "noticing [everything] more than I ever would have done, just because I'm looking."[8]

David's exploration of his soils started, in line with good agronomic practice, by investigating his soils' crop nutrient levels through precision farming. The yield maps produced by his combine showed differences in yield between various areas in his fields, and David was curious to see if this variability could be linked with nutrient levels in the soil. He used GPS to map points on a one-hectare grid in his fields, where he sampled the soils for laboratory analysis.[9] On the basis of the sampling, he created specific nutrient spreading maps for his tractor, adjusting input levels to rectify the variability. It seemed that this process of sampling and adjusting allowed him to "get a grip" on soil nutrients, and to start acting on them for the benefit of his crop. Certainly, after a few years the soil nutrient maps showed a more uniform nutrient level in the fields.

Usually, soil samples only test the soil up to a depth of 15 cm. In David's nutrient-adjusted fields, within this shallow surface everything looked good: the soil nutrients and pH levels were optimal for his arable crops. However, David became interested in looking deeper. He used a small mechanical digger to make a deep soil pit, and took soil samples down the profile, inch by inch. The sample results taken vertically rather than horizontally produced alarming results (see Table 6.1). As he told Anna in an interview, looking at the results of in-depth soil analysis:

> You almost just want to give up! . . . My soil actually in this field, in this one place, is only as we would want it up to inch four. After inch four we are suddenly below where we would want to it to be for P [phosphorus], K [potassium], the lime [pH] has crashed, lime has crashed at an inch! So it's only the top three inches really that are any good . . . It just blows you away, doesn't it. A standard test [on the first three inches], that would tell you there's nothing wrong. [Looking at pH] you think, well happy days, there is nothing wrong there. And then you look at that, and you think Christ, well I'm planting my seed an inch deep, to start with, on the basis that roots are gonna grow down. There's only two inches of soil that's got everything as you'd like! And below that, it's all going to crap.

It is through this desire to look deeper into his soils that David made the striking discovery about the depth of his farm, and the shallowness of both his knowledge and the tools at his disposal to act on soils at depths not typically considered in agronomic practice. The tools he had for understanding and changing his soil were shown to act only superficially, in a very literal sense. For example, one of the key limiting factors for crop growth is pH, which is typically modified through the application of lime on the soil surface. However, David's in-depth analysis showed that these applications were failing to change the pH levels where they count the most, in the crop rooting zone. As David explained,

> You think you'll put lime on the top and it will percolate through the profile. That's what we're told and that's what we're, we've always understood as farmers. But you look at this and all the lime is hanging in the top two inches of soil. So how do you then rectify your pH issue down at five to six inches?

Table 6.1 David's in-depth soil analysis results

TEST	P	K	Mg	pH
NORMAL	2.6	2.3	2.7	6.6
INCH 1	3.2	2.7	2.8	7.0
INCH 2	3.0	2.3	2.8	6.9
INCH 3	2.8	2.3	3.0	6.6
INCH 4	2.1	2.1	2.9	6.2
INCH 5	1.7	1.8	2.7	6.0
INCH 6	1.5	1.7	2.7	6.0
INCH 7	1.4	1.4	2.6	6.0
INCH 8	1.7	1.7	2.1	6.0
INCH 9	1.5	1.3	2.6	6.0
INCH 10	1.1	1.3	2.8	6.2
INCH 11	0.7	1.2	2.9	6.4
INCH 12	0.6	1.1	2.9	6.4

As David's soil sampling experience illustrates, agronomic approaches to soil nutrition act only on the first few inches of soils. This shallow perspective is enabled and reproduced by the coupling of chemical nutrition as the primary source of plant fertilizer and the rooting characteristics of modern crop cultivars. Modern crop cultivars typically display shallow rooting systems (Waines and Ehdaie 2007), which are sufficient if most plant nutrition is applied on the soil surface. The application of chemical nutrients, combined with the power of farm machinery to travel across and physically transform the top layer of the soils, typically allows the farmers and the agronomists to ignore processes occurring underground, focusing all attention on the visible seed bed. Looking down and deep, understanding what is happening below this familiar surface layer and acting on it, is not part of normal practice. In many ways, modern farmers have been trained to ignore their soils rather than engage with them and learn from them. Creating actionable knowledge about their soils—knowledge that would enable better coexistence and sustainable co-dependence of humans and soil ecosystems—has not been supported.

While soil testing has proved to be a source of interesting, if frustrating, information for David, another indicator of soil processes has proven more useful and more satisfying—water. Managing water is a big part of David's farming, as his fields often suffer from waterlogging. Observing the behavior of water has allowed him to better understand the different processes which occur in his soils, and to act on them. First, he noticed that some of his fields, which in soil analysis showed a high silt content, were prone to "slumping." Slumping happens when fine silt particles separate under the impact of rainfall, plug up soil pores, and create a cling-film-like covering on the soil surface. This cuts off the soils from the atmosphere, suffocates some of the soil organisms and roots, and causes water to pool on the surface. David observed that the same soil type in areas under strip tillage, where straw residue was left on the surface, did not suffer from the same problem.

Following water also helped David understand the dynamics occurring in the deeper soil layers. To follow the movement of water through the soil, he used a homemade water infiltration test—a plastic barrel filled with blue-tinted water (see figure 6.2). The dye created a water infiltration pathway visible in the soil profile. Roots, earthworm holes, and fissures all helped the water infiltrate, until it hit soil compaction at around 15 inches. As the water hit the plough pan, it started to travel sideways, and David found the ink on the opposite side of the intersected trench, three feet away from the test area. This soil compaction meant that the roots of David's crops would also be travelling sideways rather than downwards, cut off from the deep water table and drying out during low rainfall, and suffering deep waterlogging in periods of heavy rain. Seeing the colored water seek out the fissures, roots, and earthworm channels and then suddenly stop on its downward journey gave David a new appreciation of the impact the plough pan was having in his fields. As he said:

You would have picked this up with a penetrometer.[10] If you would have dug down with a spade you would have seen the same with the spade; you would have felt the compaction pan. But with the visual effect of the ink infiltration test, it wouldn't have brought home how serious the problem was, and how restricting it was on water movement.

Figure 6.2 DIY water infiltration test. Photo by David Blacker.

Paying attention to water has given David a new understanding of soils, in terms of both their vertical architecture and soil–plant interactions. In recent years, David has turned to plants to address both the slumping and the compaction problem. He has been planting cover crops, that is, plants that do not produce a sellable product but are included in the crop rotation for the benefit of the soils. Cover crops are planted in the fields in the periods when they are not being used for growing cash crops, and the plant varieties are usually specifically chosen for particular soil-friendly characteristics. They can transform the soil structure through the activity of roots and provide food for the soil biota, whose increased activity can further lead to increasing soil organic matter. Higher levels of soil organic matter improve the soil structure, which is the long-term change David is hoping for. In the short term, having plant cover over slumping areas breaks up the impact of rain and prevents silt separation, while on the compacted land roots are doing their work in changing the soil structure at a depth inaccessible to machinery. Another important change David has undertaken as a result of his soil observations has been infrastructural: the installation of new drains to help move the water out of the fields more quickly. Watching the water gurgle away out of the fields in the drainage chamber, David said, "It's a great feeling. I've never had drains working like this before. It's quite addictive." Here, too, water movement is a good indicator of soil functions, and a satisfying one.

David's discovery of the shallowness of his farm was an empirical and a conceptual finding. He discovered the limitations of the tools at his disposal for understanding and acting on his soils as deep and interconnected. In the agronomic perspective on soils, the first 15 inches are all that counts. What the Critical Zone perspective can offer, in contrast, is a stress on the connectivity of soils with the rest of the environment/ ecosystem. David's experiences of following nutrients, water, and roots begin to make sense when thought of through a Critical Zone framework, which is why it made sense for him to engage with his co-authors around this concept.

Taking this further, we can say that what David's experiences make apparent is a process of losing his Critical Zone. His previous farming methods have caused it to shrink in a number of ways: different strata which should be interconnected and in constant process of exchange were instead being cut off from one another through, for example, silt or compaction. Such activities as planting cover crops can in turn be seen as a way of rebuilding and enlarging the Critical Zone, and as a result restoring livability. In the Critical Zone perspective, the soil is always already connected upward, through the plant, and toward the sun. The plant is the solar engine of the Critical Zone, capturing, transforming, and passing on the energy of the sun between strata. David's experience of using cover crops is in fact a form of capturing solar energy and harnessing it for soil transformation. Ancient solar energy, in the form of oil, driving machinery is replaced by new solar energy materialized as root growth.

What David's experiences further illustrate is the power of the human agent dwelling in the Critical Zone—not just as a user of processes which occur around her/ him, not just as a participant in the transformation of these processes, but as the maker or destroyer of the Critical Zone's interconnectivity. Especially through acting on soils, a dweller can affect all of the Critical Zone she/he inhabits. By polluting stocks such as groundwater or the atmosphere, as well as by blocking flows of matter and energy, humans shrink the Critical Zone. By reintroducing connectivity, they can heal it and restore these relations that are necessary for life. In situ learning about this connectivity requires a Critical Zone dweller to experiment to see which indicators and which tools make sense in that particular place. Through this experimentation, both the horizontal and vertical architecture of their Critical Zone can become both meaningful and actionable.

Concluding Remarks: Developing Tools for Actionable Knowledge to Support Better Dwelling

The example of David's exploration shows a way forward in terms of linking the Critical Zone perspective with place-specific activities of dwelling, that is, of knowledgeable action. The Critical Zone perspective allows us to acknowledge the impact that humans and their activities have on maintaining or destroying livability. In the social sciences, there is a growing critique of perspectives which separate humanity from the rest of nature, and which as a result explicitly or tacitly justify exploitative and destructive activities. Taking the Critical Zone perspective, we can see humanity as already *inside* nature, intermingled with and in the midst of all other chemical, biological, and geological processes. The Critical Zone perspective may allow us to talk about humanity not as a *user* of nature, but as part of nature in a very basic, material way. However, in thinking about the place of humanity in the Critical Zone, we must not be tempted to reduce humanity to stocks and flows, pretending that we could fully map out their intentionality and motivations in some way, so that they become a seamless and mechanistic part of the Earth System. Rather, as socially involved researchers who through their work seek to maintain the livability of our planet, we need to focus on developing tools that would make the Critical Zone accessible to the senses and sense-making of the irreducible and evolving human agent in the middle.

In his ongoing exploration, David seeks to understand the makeup of his Critical Zone. This means being able to observe and trace the stocks and flows within which he is situated as well as coming to know the boundary conditions, what is unchangeable in relation to his agency. Following water has enabled him to link his observations with his action in a meaningful way. By using cover crops, David also expanded his capacity to act within these boundary conditions. Cover crops thus became a way of amplifying his agency. There is a further role for scientific and research involvement here so that David's agency in terms of both observation and action can be enhanced, so that he and other explorers of the Critical Zone have a greater capacity to engage with and learn from place-specific processes to enhance their knowledge and action. That way the dwellers can become better dwellers, more responsive to their places, more connected, more relational.

Visibility and representation of inaccessible processes is key to this. David drew our attention to certain potential indicators, such as water, roots, and soil structure, and to his frustration with other indicators, such as soil analysis. This suggests an urgent need for more work on meaningful indicators—meaningful to their users, meaningful because they are connected to their own objectives and concerns. Further work on such indicators would enrich both the scientific and the dweller understandings of the Critical Zone as a sphere of action.

A further dimension of this future project of growing the Critical Zone through enhancing knowledgeable action is the relationship between better dwelling in and better care for the Critical Zone. As Krzywoszynska (2016) has argued elsewhere, place-specific and embodied knowledge is crucial to the delivery of care for nonhumans. The task for technosciences becomes not how to "explain" the Critical Zone to the dwellers but how to enhance their capacity for developing their own knowledge of it so that better care can emerge. Approaching soil knowledge creation from the dwelling perspective also highlights the importance of soil sense and of soil sensing. To engage with processes in soils we need to make them available to our senses; as David's example illustrates, this can be challenging due to the scales and temporalities of those processes. However, it is only through ongoing embodied engagement that we can start to make sense of soils in relation to our situated objectives. Making soils available to the human sensorium is crucial to enable virtuous cycles of learning and care.

Situating knowledge of the Critical Zone in the bodies of dwellers will be crucial to the process of "coming back to Earth," Latour's (2018) term for the urgent need to fit humanity back into the biogeochemical processes of our planet in a manner which is both socially and ecologically sustainable. This coming back to Earth is a process of re-habitation, of re-dwelling. "To find a way forward," Ingold writes, "we have to recognise that our humanity is neither something that comes with the territory, with our species-specific nature, nor an imagined condition that places the territory outside ourselves, but rather the ongoing process of our mutual and collective self-creation . . . The shape of the earth emerges . . . through our very practices of habitation. [With us] the earth is 'earthing'" (2011: 114). Embedding transdisciplinary efforts into the technosciences of soils in the Critical Zone, we believe, should play a central part in this rediscovering and re-habitation of our territories.

Notes

1   On the historical rise of the chemical conception of soils, see Marchesi (2020). On the rise of ecological perspectives on soil, see Puig de la Bellacasa (2014).
2   We thank Anne O'Brien for pointing out the significance of soil in *WALL-E* to us.
3   For a discussion of the epistemic rift between farmers and soils as related to the metabolic rift, see Schneider and McMichael (2010).
4   This situation can be interestingly compared with the joint epistemic and social authority of climate models as discussed by Hulme (2012), and their silencing of alternative ways of relating to the climate (Hulme 2011). To the best of our knowledge, a thorough historical account of the rise of the epistemic and social authority of soil science as the primary "speaker for" soils is currently lacking; however, interesting insights are offered by, for example, Sayre (2010) and Marchesi (2020).
5   For a critique of the surface perspective on urban soils, see Meulemans (2020).
6   For example, while Wood and Litterick (2017) claim that there is a broad agreement around what is meant by "soil health" in the natural sciences, the actual measurements of soil health are intensely contested (see, for example, Roper et al. 2017; Rinot et al. 2019). In relation to the care framework, this suggests that while there may be a consensus about what an "ideal" state of soil looks like (although I [Anna] would challenge that claim too), there is still no clarity around what the needs of soil are and how they can be best satisfied. Following Engel-Di Mauro (2014), we could argue this lack of clarity around soils' needs is due to the lack of reflexivity in the soil science community around the assumptions about desirable land use (and so the desirable social order) which underpin definitions of "soil quality" and indeed of "soil health."
7   As Hartemink's (2016) and Engel-Di Mauro's (2014) research indicates, the "nature" of soils is by no means a settled issue in the natural sciences.
8   The quotes in this paper come from interviews Anna undertook with David in 2017, and from a narrative about soil learning which David created and audio-recorded in February 2019, following a meeting with Steve and Anna to discuss the idea of Critical Zones. The structure of the section follows and elaborates the structure of this narrative.
9   It is worth noting that David was very aware of the huge simplification that soil analysis performs. "If I'm taking soil samples, you end up with a bag full of soil, and you send them to a lab, so that's 25 acres worth of soil, and they're only going to test a teaspoon . . . Are they really getting a representative sample in that teaspoon of soil that they're looking at?" David tries to make sure he at least replicates the error by

always using the same laboratory (as results for the same sample can differ between labs), and sampling the same areas at the same time of the year and in similar weather conditions.

10 A penetrometer is a device for measuring soil resistance, and so soil compaction.

References

Arènes, A., B. Latour, and J. Gaillardet (2018), "Giving Depth to the Surface: An Exercise in the Gaia-graphy of Critical Zones," *The Anthropocene Review*, 5 (2): 120–35.

Banwart, S., J. Chorover, J. Gaillardet, D. Sparks, T. White, S. Anderson et al. (2013), *Sustaining Earth's Critical Zone: Basic Science and Interdisciplinary Solutions for Global Challenges*, 48 pp., Sheffield: University of Sheffield.

Barrera-Bassols, N. and J. A. Zinck (2003), "Ethnopedology: A Worldwide View on the Soil Knowledge of Local People," *Geoderma*, 111 (3/4): 171–95.

Bouma, J. (2009), "Soils re Back on the Global Agenda: Now What?" *Geoderma*, 150 (1/2): 224–25.

Bouma, J. (2015), "Reaching Out from the Soil-Box in Pursuit of Soil Security," *Soil Science and Plant Nutrition*, 61 (4): 556–65.

Engel-Di Mauro, S. (2014), *Ecology, Soils, and the Left: An Ecosocial Approach*, New York: Palgrave Macmillan.

Escobar, A. (2001), "Culture Sits in Places: Reflections on Globalism and Subaltern Strategies of Localization," *Political Geography*, 20 (2): 139–74.

Fisher, B. and J. C. Tronto (1990), "Toward a Feminist Theory of Caring," in E. K. Abel and M. K. Nelson (eds.), *Circles of Care: Work and Identity in Women's Lives*, 35–63, Albany, NY: State University of New York Press.

Food and Agriculture Organization (FAO) (2015), *Status of the World's Soil Resources: Main Report*, Rome: FAO and Intergovernmental Technical Panel on Soils.

Gabrys, J. (2017), "Citizen Sensing, Air Pollution and Fracking: From 'Caring About Your Air' to Speculative Practices of Evidencing Harm," *Sociological Review*, 65 (2): 172–92.

Haraway, D. (1988), "Situated Knowledges: The Science Question in Feminism and the Privilege of Partial Perspective," *Feminist Studies*, 14 (3): 575–99.

Hartemink, A. E. (2016), "The Definition of Soil Since the Early 1800s," in D. L. Sparks (ed.), *Advances in Agronomy*, Vol. 137, 73–126, London: Academic Press.

Hird, M. J. (2010), "Indifferent Globality," *Theory, Culture & Society*, 27 (2/3): 54–72.

Holmes, H., N. Gregson, M. Watson, A. Buckley, P. Chiles, A. Krzywoszynska et al. (2018), "Interdisciplinarity in Transdisciplinary Projects: Circulating Knowledges, Practices and Effects," *disP—The Planning Review*, 54 (2): 77–93.

Hulme, M. (2011), "Reducing the Future to Climate: A Story of Climate Determinism and Reductionism," *Osiris*, 26 (1): 245–66.

Hulme, M. (2012), "How Climate Models Gain and Exercise Authority," in K. S. Hastrup and M. Skrydstrup (eds.), *The Social Life of Climate Change Models*, 30–44, London: Routledge.

Ingold, T. (2000), *The Perception of the Environment: Essays on Livelihood, Dwelling and Skill*, London: Routledge.

Ingold, T. (2011), *Being Alive: Essays on Movement, Knowledge and Description*, Abingdon: Routledge.

Koch, A., A. McBratney, M. Adams, D. Field, R. Hill, J. Crawford et al. (2013), "Soil Security: Solving the Global Soil Crisis," *Global Policy*, 4 (4): 434–41.

Krzywoszynska, A. (2016), "What Farmers Know: Experiential Knowledge and Care in Vine Growing," *Sociologia Ruralis*, 56 (2): 289–310.

Krzywoszynska, A. (2019a), "Caring for Soil Life in the Anthropocene: The Role of Attentiveness in More-Than-Human Ethics," *Transactions of the Institute of British Geographers*, 44 (4): 661–75.

Krzywoszynska, A. (2019b), "Making Knowledge and Meaning in Communities of Practice: What Role May Science Play? The Case of Sustainable Soil Management in England," *Soil Use and Management*, 35 (1): 160–68.

Krzywoszynska, A. (2020), "Nonhuman Labor and the Making of Resources: Making Soils a Resource through Microbial Labor," *Environmental Humanities*.

Latour, B. (2018), *Down to Earth: Politics in the New Climatic Regime*, Cambridge: Polity Press.

Marchesi, G. (2020), "Justus von Liebig Makes the World: Soil Properties and Social Change in the 19th Century," *Environmental Humanities*.

Meulemans, G. (2020), "Urban Pedogeneses: The Making of City Soils from Hard Surfacing to the Urban Soil Sciences," *Environmental Humanities*.

Mol, A. (2008), *The Logic of Care: Health and the Problem of Patient Choice*, Abingdon: Routledge.

Murphy, M. (2015), "Unsettling Care: Troubling Transnational Itineraries of Care in Feminist Health Practices," *Social Studies of Science*, 45 (5): 717–37.

Polanyi, K. ([1944] 2001), *The Great Transformation: The Political and Economic Origins of Our Time*, Boston, MA: Beacon Press.

Puig de la Bellacasa, M. (2011), "Matters of Care in Technoscience: Assembling Neglected Things," *Social Studies of Science*, 41 (1): 85–106.

Puig de la Bellacasa, M. (2014), "Encountering Bioinfrastructure: Ecological Struggles and the Sciences of Soil," *Social Epistemology*, 28 (1): 26–40.

Puig de la Bellacasa, M. (2015), "Making Time for Soil: Technoscientific Futurity and the Pace of Care," *Social Studies of Science*, 45 (5): 691–716.

Puig de la Bellacasa, M. (2017), *Matters of Care: Speculative Ethics in More than Human Worlds*, Minneapolis, MN: University of Minnesota Press.

Richelle, L., M. Visser, L. Bock, P. Walpole, F. Mialhe, G. Colinet et al. (2018), "Looking for a Dialogue Between Farmers and Scientific Soil Knowledge: Learnings from an Ethno-geomorphopedological Study in a Philippine's Upland Village," *Agroecology and Sustainable Food Systems*, 42 (1): 2–27.

Rinot, O., G. J. Levy, Y. Steinberger, T. Svoray, and G. Eshel (2019), "Soil Health Assessment: A Critical Review of Current Methodologies and a Proposed New Approach," *Science of the Total Environment*, 648: 1484–91.

Roper, W. R., D. L. Osmond, J. L. Heitman, M. G. Wagger, and S. C. Reberg-Horton (2017), "Soil Health Indicators Do Not Differentiate Among Agronomic Management Systems in North Carolina Soils," *Soil Science Society of America Journal*, 81 (4): 828–43.

Sayre, L. B. (2010), "The Pre-history of Soil Science: Jethro Tull, the Invention of the Seed Drill, and the Foundations of Modern Agriculture," *Physics and Chemistry of the Earth, Parts A/B/C*, 35 (15/18): 851–59.

Schneider, M. and P. McMichael (2010), "Deepening, and Repairing, the Metabolic Rift," *Journal of Peasant Studies*, 37 (3): 461–84.

Tironi, M. and I. Rodríguez-Giralt (2017), "Healing, Knowing, Enduring: Care and Politics in Damaged Worlds," *Sociological Review*, 65 (2): 89–109.

Waines, J. G. and B. Ehdaie (2007), "Domestication and Crop Physiology: Roots of Green-Revolution Wheat," *Annals of Botany*, 100 (5): 991–98.

West, S., L. J. Haider, V. Masterson, J. P. Enqvist, U. Svedin, and M. Tengö (2018), "Stewardship, Care and Relational Values," *Current Opinion in Environmental Sustainability*, 35: 30–38.

Wood, M. and A. M. Litterick (2017), "Soil Health—What Should the Doctor Order?," *Soil Use and Management*, 33 (2): 339–45.

7

Soiling Mars: "To Boldly Grow Where No Plant Has Grown Before"?

Filippo Bertoni

Introduction

At first sight, Mars does not seem like the best place in which to try to understand soil. In fact, the iconic red-ochre material covering the surface of the planet technically is not even soil: it is what geologists call *regolith*, a layer of loose superficial mineral deposits, devoid of organic matter. *Soil*, instead, is typically characterized by organic content and ongoing living processes. These are ostensibly unique to Earth and lacking on Mars, at least in the forms we know to expect. In a move that is only the latest instantiation of an ongoing imaginative traffic between Earth and outer space,[1] though, planetary scientists across the world have been using an extended functional definition of soils that allows consideration of terrestrial and martian soils as analogous. This move and its consequences for technosciences (and beyond) make martian soil a privileged vantage point to attend to how soil becomes grounded in the planet through changing entanglements of earth and Earth. This intimate and changing *materialsemiotic* relational field weaving the ground closer to outer space has recently attracted the attention of social scientists interested in the way these spheres transform each other and accompany changes in contemporary society and beyond.[2] Here, I follow this trend and consider the growing interest in off-Earth farming to explore the traffic between soil and planet. In particular, I present an ongoing experiment conducted at Wageningen University & Research (WUR), one of the world's leading centers for agricultural technosciences. Unlike many other experiments interested in off-Earth agriculture that tend to treat the soil merely as a material substrate for the delivery of nutrients, the one that occasions this essay centers on the soil as a lively ecosystem. It does so by experimenting with earthworms and other organisms in its test runs of future martian agriculture.

In what follows, the experiment offers an excuse and a tool to outline the way WUR scientists bring the soil and the planet closer together in their work. This relies on a functional and biogeochemical logic to account for how everything, from soil, to worms, to plants, and from heavy metals, to microbes, and all the way to the planet, and the cosmos, holds together. This cosmo-logic[3] is a powerful analytic that characterizes the way we understand both soil and planet today, as part of a larger and coherent whole, whose basic structure is clear to us, and perfectly quantifiable. The deep roots of this conceptual infrastructure—reaching all the way to the modern formulation of scientific approaches to soils in the nineteenth century—highlight how soils and planets as scientific objects share much of a common history. Unearthing this history, it becomes evident that scientific determinations of what counts as nature are not independent from their context. In fact, the post-war period and its articulation of science, society, and politics still inform contemporary biogeochemical understandings of earth and Earth. In particular, the alliance between the nascent ecosystems ecology, radioisotope research, and cybernetic control systems engineering that shaped the rise of US ecology and its growing hegemonic role in technosciences since the 1950s can still be traced in the biogeochemical logic at work in the WUR experiment. This analytic is pivotal to current dreams of off-Earth farming, as it forms the enduring backbone of current technosciences, especially in the so-called "new space age" and its constellations of knowledge formations, late capitalist society, and interplanetary dreams. Simultaneously, though, the silent hegemony of this biogeochemical framing of nature also informs the environmental critique of these promissory futures of endless interplanetary growth: the Anthropocene and its critical warning against the limits of planetary boundaries is often characterized by the same type of biogeochemical accounting. Such overrepresentation of a biogeochemical logic in thinking about the environment—and its alliance with Western neoliberal modernity and its imperialism—demands that we make space for other analytics, ones that might resist the unifying centripetal force of a coherent functionalist narrative.

To begin unearthing such an alternative, I pay closer attention to the practices of the WUR experiment and its technoscientific apparatus. Grounding this analysis in the materialsemiotic interrelation of theories and practices and some of its transformations over the course of the last century, I situate the specific soils, worms, and agricultures the experiment envisions. Rather than treating them as stable and already well-defined objects, soils and planets emerge from the experiment and the stories I recount as part of eventful practices and processes firmly rooted, among other things, in the concrete lives of earthworms. Simultaneously, these practices are never neat and clean, but always dirty and messy, carrying with them the stains of ongoing colonial and capitalist legacies of modern versions of the world, its past, its present, its future, and of our knowledge of it. Unlike the biogeochemical cosmo-logic, which easily overlooks these histories in its effort to make a universal and unitary cosmos, the approach I mobilize allows the slowing down of this compulsion to universalize. The logic of *soiling* I propose situates soils, worms, and planets in specific histories, making it easier to usher in different kinds of ethical questions, political futures, and *naturecultural* matters of concern. Soiling, then, opens our analysis up to much-needed alternative approaches to rethinking the articulation of technosciences and politics of nature that characterizes the Anthropocene, and that grounds—or, better, soils—current dreams of off-Earth agriculture. But, before I can attend to soiling, I introduce the WUR experiment I start from.

Marsworms?

Toward the end of 2017, a small experiment being conducted at Wageningen University, in the Dutch countryside, received much media attention, becoming a favorite of popular science magazines and websites. An article on space.com entitled "A 'Martian' First: Earthworms Born in Mock Mars Soil" was only one among many to report about the significance of the experiment:

> In what could be an important milestone for future farmers on Mars, two healthy baby worms were recently born in simulated Martian soil. The births took place in an experiment that is helping scientists understand how human settlers might one day grow crops on the Red Planet.

Involving growth experiments in soils meant to simulate martian conditions, the study weaves together terrestrial soil and outer space in its technoscientific research practices. The scientists working on the experiment can conveniently do this thanks to previous work in planetary sciences, which facilitated comparisons between Mars and Earth.[4] Indeed, as planetary and space sciences enjoyed a resurgence during the last decades, it became more common to talk of the loose surface deposits on Mars indifferently as regolith and as soil. In a paper making the case for closing "the long, annoying debate on the pedological nature of the planet's skin" (Certini and Ugolini 2013: 379), two soil scientists notice:

> In some papers focused on the investigation of Mars performed by the rovers Opportunity and Spirit, for example, it is significantly reported: The term soil is used here to denote *any loose, unconsolidated materials that can be distinguished from rocks, bedrock, or strongly cohesive sediments. No implication for the presence or absence of organic materials or living matter is intended* (Soderblom et al., 2004; Squyres et al., 2004a, 2004b).
>
> Certini and Ugolini 2013: 378–79, emphasis in the original

Bracketing off the question of the presence of life on Mars, this usage common among planetary scientists focuses on the material qualities of soil. These are easier to characterize and make comparisons between materials on Earth and on Mars much more handy. In fact, it was with the early robotic exploration of the Red Planet in the 1990s that the first Mars soil simulants were developed. These are terrestrial materials used to simulate the chemical and mechanical properties of martian regolith in a range of experiments and prototype tests. Mostly first developed by NASA and later commercially produced by other companies, these simulants are also what the WUR team used in their experiment as stand-ins for martian soil. Based on remote observation and on data from the landers, the simulants are defined by spectral readings and mechanico-technical properties derived from available data, since sample return missions from Mars are still waiting to be implemented. This physicochemical characterization of martian soil, then, is a first step for the experiment I describe here and for the commensurability it establishes between Mars and Earth, and between soil and planet. This first step is made easier by Mars soil simulants and their sieving through a chemical and physical framework, which is expanded to encompass everything—from a speck of dust to a planet.

To this analogical bridge between martian and terrestrial soil, the Wageningen group, led by Dr. Wieger Wamelink, adds a second step as they seek to explore a common *ecological* ground for their research. If terrestrial soil and martian regolith share the same basic makeup, and can be considered the same to the extent that their chemical and material properties can be made to match, then they should also allow for functionally similar ecosystems. It is in order to test this that the group introduced earthworms in their experiments with martian crops. As they put it on the webpage of their crowdfunding campaign:[5]

> Just growing crops is simply not enough. All non-eaten parts of the crops have to be returned to the soil and broken down so the nutrients will be released again for the next generation of crops. What we actually need is a small sustainable ecosystem that also is able to deal with the inhabitants [*sic*] poop and pee. A crucial part of the ecological chain is the earthworm. It will eat the organic matter, chew it to small parts and mix it with the soil. Bacteria can then break it down further. Worms also dig burrows and by doing so they aerate the soil and make it possible for water to enter the soil easily. All this is essential for an abundant crop harvest.

To ensure the success of future martian agriculture, the team says, it is necessary to prove the feasibility of a minimal sustainable soil ecosystem that would support the crops and the colonists. For this reason, they propose to add earthworms to their experimental systems, testing the growth, impact, and survival of the worms in different combinations of soil simulants, plants, and additional organic matter. The success of earthworms, according to the group, would pave the way to building sustainable agricultural ecosystems on Mars, and on Earth. While other organisms— like pollinators, fungi, and bacteria—are also included in the WUR ideal ecosystem, earthworms are the first in line for the experiment because of their function as soil *ecosystem engineers*. This term denotes "organisms that directly or indirectly modulate the availability of resources to other species, by causing physical state changes in biotic or abiotic materials. In so doing they modify, maintain and create habitats" (Jones et al. 1994: 373). Already noticed by Darwin—who dedicated much of his later years studying these common invertebrates—the role of earthworms is paramount to the formation of soil and its ongoing regeneration. For this reason, earthworms are now widely considered a key species, whose function in soils provides crucial "ecosystems services." Relying on this understanding of worms, the WUR experiment hinges the ecological function of earthworms on the biogeochemical structure made to stretch from terrestrial soils to martian ones, affording these invertebrates a special position at the forefront of the expansion of humanity through the colonization of Mars.

Grounding Biogeochemical Commensurability

But, how do the "lowly invertebrates" of Darwin's last monograph (1881) become the pioneers of off-planet human expansion? How do earthworms fit so snugly in the biogeochemical framework that grounds the analogy between Earth and Mars? The commensurability that ecological biogeochemistry establishes between soils and planets—and earthworms' role in it—has deep roots, which tie together soil sciences and planetary sciences. In fact, modern understandings of the soil and the planet were already vined together as they began to sprout, at the end of the nineteenth century. In this section and the following one, I briefly consider episodes in this shared genealogy of soil and planet to situate the cosmo-logic that also informs the practices of the WUR experiment. This, in turn, sheds new light on the kind of biogeochemical accountability that shapes current dreams of off-planet agriculture, and allows some of the tensions inherent to this cosmo-logic to surface.

Some of the roots of the modern approach to biogeochemistry can be traced to the fertile ground of post-reform tsarist Russia, and its unique combination of emerging scientific approaches and socioeconomic change. It is in the context of this historical effort to reform agriculture that Vasilii Vasil'evich Dokuchaev—often considered the father of modern soil science—shaped his approach to soil as a *natural body*. In the 1870s and 1880s, backed by the Imperial Free Economic Society and informed by its transdisciplinary intellectual fabric and its practical socioeconomic concerns, Dokuchaev joined this reformist effort by leading several expeditions to map, study, and classify soils throughout the Russian provinces.[6] In his work, he stressed the impossibility of tracing soil formation to only one factor. Instead, he suggested considering soil as a natural body, constantly interacting with other aspects of the environment, and with dynamic factors both biotic and abiotic. This early vision of soil was Dokuchaev's "answer to those who identified it with agricultural lands on the one hand, and those who saw in it a mere manifestation of underlying rock types on the other" (Evtuhov 2006: 130). Formed in collaboration with eminent chemists (like Mendeleev and Butlerov), geologists, biologists, statisticians, agronomists, meteorologists, and economists, but also farmers, reformers, and landowners, this notion challenged the primacy of any one, well-defined factor. Instead, it enabled Dokuchaev, and especially his student Vladimir Ivanovich Vernadskii, to develop a biogeochemical cosmo-logic that could allow them to describe the dynamic interactions of many different components, while opening up the complex interactions between living and non-living matter, as a way to appreciate their diversity and specificity.

Indeed, if the understanding of soil as a natural body is often considered pioneering in soil sciences, the work of Vernadskii had a similar import to Earth and planetary sciences. Expanding his mentor's understanding of soil to the whole surface of the planet, Vernadskii developed a biogeochemical formulation of the biosphere concept— fully described in his 1926 book *The Biosphere*. This notion characterizes the understanding of Earth as a complex system: Vernadskii "placed the biosphere within a cosmic framework powered by the Sun and reflected on the ways in which living matter (understood in its entirety) might influence the chemical and geological composition of inert elements in the atmosphere, lithosphere and hydrosphere" (Oldfield and Shaw 2013: 294). Accounting for the complex interactions between the biotic and the abiotic, biogeochemistry allows for understanding the entirety of the planet, and even of the universe, as a scalable set of physicochemical interactions, which are characterized by the movements and transformations of matter and energy. "In other words, [Vernadskii] established a framework for conceptualizing living matter in its entirety as a key entity making use of the Sun's energy with the potential to rework the inorganic/non-living environment" (Oldfield and Shaw 2013: 295).

Thanks to some fortunate personal circumstances,[7] the work of Vernadskii managed to reach the United States and profoundly influenced George Evelyn Hutchinson, a founding figure in ecology who taught at Yale University. It was through his and Lindeman's adaptation that, in the 1940s, such a biogeochemical framework converged in the young field of ecology.[8] In particular, Hutchinson and Lindeman "applied insights gained from the study of small-scale natural systems such as inland lakes to the global level, thereby supporting the view that the biosphere displayed similar characteristics to small-scale ecological systems and reinforcing the utility of the global conceptualization" (Oldfield and Shaw 2013: 299). But, while this reception of Vernadskii's work was instrumental to this early moment in US ecology, the field was still a marginal one by the end of the Second World War, with the biogeochemical approach mostly limited to aquatic ecology and aimed at better grasping the specific diversity of the components of simple freshwater models. It was the particular alignment of postwar technosciences, American society, and global geopolitics that placed a biogeochemical worldview in a hegemonic position, and placed the focus on the global and away from the particular.

Post-war Alliances

The changes brought about by the end of the Second World War profoundly influenced the scientific landscape and the understanding of the world it provided.[9] The war effort guaranteed a unique combination of industry and research, fitted to the structure of military hierarchy and secrecy. The Manhattan Project is perhaps the most iconic example of this change. Characterized by a new centrality of physics and engineering, a vast and secretive administrative structure dependent on military funding and control, a strong reliance on ideological narratives, and the collaboration of large numbers of researchers and technicians, the atomic bomb well represents the kind of Big Science that became the model for postwar research. These transformations were also crucial to the success of the biogeochemical cosmo-logic I am tracing here—which underwent a profound change in the second half of the twentieth century. But, if the urgency of developing atomic weapons was key to the success of physics, ecosystem ecology and its biogeochemical approach relied more on the retrofitting of that model to peacetime. As Angela Creager illustrates in her *Life Atomic* (2013), life sciences and biomedicine found their way to adapt to the postwar technoscientific landscape largely thanks to the Atomic Energy Commission (AEC), a civilian agency that was to develop peaceful uses of atomic energy—while also continuing atomic weapons production. Faced with mounting Cold War anxieties with atomic energy, the US government, by making radioisotopes readily available for scientific research, enrolled scientists to harness the power of the atom for peace. Creager documents the impact that the circulation of radioactive materials had on biochemists, physiologists, molecular biologists, physicians, and, importantly, ecologists: in these fields, radionucleotides were used to trace the movements and transformations of key molecules, mapping the circulation of matter and energy across cells, organisms, and environments.

This was especially formative for the ecosystem approach in ecology and its biogeochemical cosmo-logic: radiation ecology (as the application of radioactive materials to the study of ecosystems came to be called) was crucial to make ecologists' understanding of nature visible.[10] In addition, it provided them with the means to turn their discipline into a quantitative one, strengthening its predictive power and modeling ambitions[11] and forging important alliances with new funding streams—like those the AEC dedicated to the handling of nuclear waste and the study of the environmental impact of radioactivity, and later those made available by the International Biological Program (IBP).[12] The atomic bomb had tightened the relations between science and the military, so this alliance with nuclear physics and its politico-industrial complex was crucial to give shape to the biogeochemical view of nature. The translation of ecological approaches into the language of cybernetics—as exemplified by the systematization offered in Odum's 1953 textbook *Fundamentals of Ecology*—facilitated this alliance. Propelled forward by its role in the Second World War, cybernetics—or control systems engineering, as it became better known—had already influenced the vernacular of science policy and management thanks to its mathematical disposition and its visualization of circuits, systems, and cycles, which also lent themselves well to the characterization of the biogeochemical circuitry of ecosystems.[13] As Chunglin Kwa notes (1987), this cybernetic inflection of ecosystem ecology relied on a machinic metaphor, which—following Peter Taylor (1988)—was grounded in a widespread technocratic optimism. But this optimistic outlook, characteristic of the managerial upper echelons of US society, quickly encountered a vocal resistance. Surprisingly, though, as concerns with contamination and environmental pollution joined the fear of nuclear fallout, the cybernetic and nuclear biogeochemical vision of nature behind ecosystem ecology also became the main idiom for the countercultural environmental movement of the 1970s. Both environmentalists and technocrats were looking for ways to better manage the environment and its natural resources; both were concerned with the Club of Rome's report *The Limits to Growth* (Meadows et al. 1972) and its characterization of the planet as a finite system threatened by humans; and both looked at ecosystem ecology for answers. The feedback loop between ecology's popular success and its institutional fortunes encouraged the naturalization of its biogeochemical vision of nature, which gained growing support across extremely diverse and even opposite fields—and grew further away from the situatedness of the various components of ecosystems and more toward a functional schematics.

It is this version of the biogeochemical cosmo-logic of ecosystems that began to reach for the stars in those years. Reinforced by its cybernetic visualization of biogeochemical circuitry, ecology quickly became an important player in the development of submarines, atomic shelters, airplanes, and spaceships sped up by the Space Race. Imagining these confined spaces as closed systems, cabin ecology provided insights on how to manage them. In particular, starting in the late 1950s different groups concentrated their efforts on developing minimal self-sustaining ecosystems meant to help in the holistic task of providing life support in closed environments.[14] These efforts converged into what is currently called bioregenerative life-support systems (BLSS) research, stimulating transformations that influenced agriculture not only off-planet but also on Earth.[15] In fact, the ecological understanding of space reflected back on Earth, in a *mise en abyme* that understood space through Earth, but also Earth through space. As small, contained ecosystems like lakes had become models for the whole planet, and these in turn models for spaceships, the Earth began to be characterized as a spaceship itself, a move immortalized in Buckminster Fuller's 1968 cult classic *Operating Manual for Spaceship Earth.*[16] But spaceship Earth had increasingly turned into a blueprint of its circuitry and systems, equipped with gauges to measure the movements of matter and energy through them. This progressive naturalization of a biogeochemical structure of the cosmos is instrumental[17] to the current renaissance of interest in off-planet farming, supported by the so-called "new space age"—the fertile ground in which the WUR experiment grew.

After the Final Frontier

In the 1990s, the thawing Cold War stalled the thrust of the space race that had originally projected humans into outer space. But if the time of governmental projects of technoscientific nationalism has largely passed, the current renaissance in interest for space is usually characterized by the involvement of speculative financial investments and private venture capital. The resulting "new space age" depends on novel combinations of technological development, financial speculation, private interests, and mediatized publics. As a conference on this topic organized in 2017 by *The Economist* described it:

> Space is revolutionising the way people think about the Earth. New capabilities, rekindled dreams and an atmosphere of entrepreneurialism mean a new wave of terrestrial tech has forged a well-worn path now profitably travelled. "Big data" have transformed the planet into a gigantic set of data that can be both interrogated and extrapolated, transforming the way industries as diverse as farming and insurance operate. Space travel is moving from the world of government procurement and aerospace engineering giants to venture-capital-funded start-ups that rely on ever-cheaper services for ever more customers. As they prove to be profitable they will grow further, and fast.[18]

While the high stakes tables of this financial game still focus on the safer returns of technologies like remote Earth observation,[19] big data, and telecommunications, small companies, research projects, start-ups, and spin-offs that rely on this combination of private, public, and academic interests proliferate. The crowdfunding campaign for Wamelink's experiment at WUR is among them.

On the website of their campaign, *Worms for Mars*, the Wageningen University researchers inscribe their work along a path set by "NASA, Elon Musk and MarsOne." This path advocates the need for humanity to become multiplanetary as soon as possible. The rationale behind this call for humans to reach for the stars (or at least for other celestial bodies in our solar system) is a mesh of different considerations typical of the "new space age." Weaving together the long-term evolution of the species, the limits imposed on growth by the planet, the naturalization of human exploration and its colonizing imperative, the primacy of technosciences in shaping the future, and, importantly, the very notion of humanity as an unproblematic universal category—the experiment's imaginative horizon frames the colonization of other planets as the only way to escape the limits of Earth, and thus to ensure the continuity of humanity against planetary destruction. As the foreseen expansion of human settlements reaches the moon and Mars, the reasoning goes, a stable and safe provision of food must be secured for the colonists. Hence the WUR interest in off-Earth agriculture.

This vision of the future of humanity and of the relation between society and technosciences fits well with the ambitions of Wageningen University. Inspired by Stanford University and its pivotal role in bringing together higher education and private companies in what came to be known as the "Silicon Valley"—the site of an incredible concentration of venture-capital investment in information technology— WUR is the hub of the so-called "Food Valley." This Dutch region is the heart of the "knowledge-intensive agrifood ecosystem" that makes the small European country one of the largest agribusinesses in the world, second only to the United States. Embracing the promises of the rising outer-space business in the so-called Dutch "Space Coast,"[20] Wamelink's experiment pioneers the expansion of terrestrial technoscientific agriculture to off-Earth farming futures in the region. And to do so, it relies strongly on the biogeochemical cosmo-logic I traced here.

In considering another facet of the "new space age" that has received much attention lately—off-Earth mining—Kearnes and van Dooren bring to the fore the way this revamping of outer space made possible by this biogeochemical logic relies on the old trope of the frontier: "From space exploration, to terraforming and mining, the logic of the frontier is central here—variously configured as a new, final, or ultimate frontier" (2017: 182–83). The WUR experiment embraces the rhetoric of space as the final frontier; in fact, Wamelink's experimental crops grow next to a sign saying "to boldly grow where no plant has grown before," riffing off the famous opening narration of *Star Trek*. In their article, Kearnes and van Dooren stress how this frontier narrative and its naturalization of humanity inform the current demand for an ethics of regulation: if humanity is a naturally rapacious species, ethics must regulate this inevitable expansion to space so that it can provide the most benefits. But they refuse this characterization of humanity and its idea of ethics as regulatory. Instead, they call for "a thoroughly worldly ethics grounded in a cosmopolitan sensibility that seeks to mark out a notion of interstellar flourishing" (2017: 186). The ethics they suggest is more open to heeding the lessons of decolonial critiques of the inherently violent and imperialist dimensions of the unitary and amorphous humanity represented in frontier narratives—and, one should hope, of the biogeochemical circuitry on which this humanity relies. To phrase this critique along the lines of Jamaican writer and cultural theorist Sylvia Wynter, this figure of the human "is tied to epistemological histories that presently value a *genre* of the human that reifies Western bourgeois tenets; the human is therefore wrought with physiological and narrative matters that systemically excise the world's most marginalized" (McKittrick 2015: 9). This modern Western imaginary, which Wynter dubs "monohumanism," is all the more evident in the context of spacefaring, and in its tightest weave with the biogeochemical cosmo-logic of ecosystems. As Lydia Kallipoliti (2008) shows in considering the human that NASA placed at the center of its closed-systems architecture, to fit the cybernetic infrastructures of space the human who interfaces with the machine is made machinic, turned into its own (white, army-disciplined, healthy, male) physiological apparatus as accounted for by the biogeochemical cosmo-logic explored here. Only a few fit in this artificially, technoscientifically, and politically selected niche.[21] Even fewer stand to profit from it.

Soiling Logic

Once we understand how the biogeochemical cosmo-logic traced above in the emergence of modern technoscientific understandings of soil and planet and the postwar developments of their accounting practices feed into the monohumanist ethics of regulation that Kearnes and van Dooren encountered in off-Earth mining, it becomes clear why it is important to make space for other analytics. What kind of alternative cosmo-logic might open the path to the ethics of interstellar flourishing envisioned by the two authors? In answering a similar question, they write:

> Such an approach might begin from the question of "worlding," asking: What kinds of worlds are we helping to produce and with what consequences for whom? This is an approach concerned with the agency of, and impacts on, diverse peoples, places, organisms, and entities—always in the multiple, always specific. Such an approach would not assume that humans are the only subjects of ethical concern, holding open the question of which nonhumans—from Martian microbes to a lifeless asteroid—might make ethical demands on us.
>
> Kearnes and van Dooren 2017: 186

In the case of Wamelink's experiment, it is the particular kind of worlding that emerges in the encounter between Earth, dirt, and worm that takes center-stage. Here I refer to this particular form of worlding as *soiling*. I do so because this term allows me to simultaneously evoke the soil-forming processes that are at stake in the planetary encounters between worms and soil, and the interference that these processes can provide, by dirtying, or "soiling," the biogeochemical cosmo-logic at the heart of the experiment, and its clean narrative of a universal human off-planet future technoscientific agriculture.[22] The basic idea of the experiment is that since earthworms are crucial providers of soil services, being able to grow worms in martian soil simulants would mean being able to learn how to mobilize these processes in future off-planet agriculture. Yet, this idea depends on the functional and biogeochemical understanding of ecosystems and on their commensurability with economic accounting for ecosystem services.

To slow down this functionalist understanding of earthworms, it is useful to go back to the decolonial critique of the unitary version of humanity that emerged as the biogeochemical cosmo-logic reached outer space. Resisting the normalizing push to make all humanity fit into a Western, modern, and bourgeois (and biogeochemical?) version of the human, Wynter strives to put forward "an alternative, *yet not less secular*, version of humanness imagined outside liberal monohumanism," so that "her overall project can be identified as that of a *counterhumanism*" (McKittrick 2015: 11; here and in what follows, emphasis in the original). To open up to alternative versions of the human, crucially, "*humanness* is no longer a *noun. Being human is a praxis*" (2015: 23). Pushing this critique a step further, more-than-human scholarship seems to suggest that we learn also that *being more-than-human is a praxis*. This allows me to reconsider the role of the earthworm as a provider of "ecosystem services." From up close, even the worm's ecological function is more than just one thing. Not all earthworms behave in the same way. In fact, ecologists distinguish between three different categories of earthworms, based on their behavior and functional differences: anecic earthworms make permanent vertical burrows in the soil and drag surface litter into the soil; endogeic earthworms live in the soil and feed off organic matter in it; epigeic earthworms live on the surface of the soil in leaf litter. These three different categories have different impacts on soil dynamics. The worm species used in Wamelink's experiment, *Eisenia hortensis* (or *Dendrobaena veneta*, according to the old nomenclature they use in their study), is an epigeic worm. These worms are among the most common in Europe because of their widespread use in vermicomposting, making them easy to procure (in this case from one of the sponsors of the project, which sells the worms for composting and as live bait for fishing). But, while they are easy to procure and maintain, naturally epigeic worms do not burrow much as they live in leaf litter on the surface. In this sense, they make poor models for studies concerned with worms' impact on soil structure, while they could be more interesting in relation to their impact on the structure of microbial communities (Gómez-Brandón et al. 2012).

But there is more about this particular species that we can figure out by slowing down and attending to the details of its soilings. Commonly called European nightcrawler, this species is closely related to anthropogenic disturbance, as it lives pretty well in conditions that are facilitated by human presence. Together with other European and exotic species, these earthworms are well known for their role as biological invaders. Often moving unseen along the global trade of agricultural and horticultural products or intentionally imported for commercial applications like vermicomposting and fishing, they have exponentially expanded their geographical range. This is particularly well studied in the case of the temperate forests of North America. As in these environments native earthworms did not survive the last glaciation, these ecosystems evolved without the activity of earthworm assemblages. Until European colonization, that is. Since then, non-native earthworms began spreading in these habitats, profoundly transforming local ecologies. Given their relatively poor dispersal abilities, these ecological colonizations have been shown to be intimately connected to human activities and histories. In particular, epigeic species like *E. hortensis* seem to act as pioneer species in the invasion, thanks to their hardiness, making way for other underground assemblages to expand with them. This characteristic of the species used in Wamelink's experiment brings forward a transversal connection between the future colonization of space and past colonial enterprises—and their intended and unintended consequences. As such, they are reminders of the eventfulness[23] of nature. As Beauséjour and colleagues show in their study of historical human activities and current invasive earthworm distribution in a Québécois nature reserve, there is an evident and long-term connection between specific historical events (especially colonial construction of roads and settlements) and earthworm invasions (Beauséjour et al. 2015).

Far from a neutral, universal example of an imagined generic earthworm activity, *E. hortensis* is a historically specific species, and this specificity is relevant to the colonial character of Wamelink's agricultural dreams. This specific worm, a pioneer of agricultural modernization, comes, in turn, with a specific soil. This is a domesticated and modernized soil, intended for agricultural production. But, as Amundson and colleagues put it in a review article in *Science*, this soil is increasingly disappearing precisely because of its widespread and exponential use: "[T]he practice of farming greatly accelerated rates of erosion relative to soil production, and soil has been and continues to be lost at rates that are orders of magnitude greater than mechanisms that replenish soil" (Amundson et al. 2015: 647). As these authors also point out, the alarming rate of soil loss on Earth is intimately linked to the exponential growth of twentieth-century industrial agriculture with its narrative of technoscientific progress. Fueled by several "Green Revolutions," the increases in yields that industrial agriculture uses to justify itself came at the cost of increased financialization, corporatization, and technologicization of agricultural practices, accompanied by a tragic pauperization and dispossession of farmers in favor of transnational megacorporations, and an accelerated loss of ecological, cultural, and biological diversity and resilience.

Perhaps unsurprisingly, institutions like Wageningen University & Research had a key role in facilitating these processes of agricultural modernization and spreading their trademark practices of "self-devouring growth" (Livingston 2019). The soil in the experiment, then, is already the intensive industrial agribusiness soil, with its associated global rift in nutrients and wealth made possible by the cybernetic biogeochemical understanding of soil. The modern version of the soil as merely a substrate for biogeochemical flows cannot be easily separated from the concrete ways this understanding of the soil treats and affords real soils. Agribusiness's soil is not a generic, neutral one; instead, it is a specific and situated soil, one that is incrementally exhausted by the very practices it is enrolled into. The soiling logic I employed here, and its slowing down of this unitary push to fit a planetary biogeochemical circuitry, allows new stories and alternatives to emerge and brings new questions with them. For instance, if the kind of technoscientific agriculture behind the success of Wageningen's Food Valley has a significant role in the increase of soil loss on Earth, how can it provide a useful model when thinking of a context in which there's no soil to begin with, like on Mars? If humanity is really forced to become interplanetary because of the progressive devastation of terrestrial environments caused by the modern and colonial rush to industrial agriculture, can the same way of relating with soil be its guide to future martian colonization?

Conclusions

In this chapter, I traced the biogeochemical cosmo-logic that subtends the Wageningen experiment. Following its developments and its transformations that accompanied the postwar restructuring of technosciences and naturecultures, I showed how such a vision of a unitary cosmos relies on the political and epistemological imperialism of Western modernity. At the same time, I considered the very practices of the experiment more closely, attending to the concrete encounters it staged between soils, worms, and planets. This allowed me to show how an alternative cosmo-logic can be found already at work in practices. Soiling as an analytic, then, allowed me to question some of the assumptions grounding the experiment and muddying its clear narrative of a multiplanetary humanity. What do these questions and the dirty histories they bring to the surface do? Does the implicit monohumanism of the experiment compromise its whole mission? Are we better off without off-Earth farming? Shall we, following the Star Trek metaphor of Wamelink, retreat to Starfleet's Prime Directive and avoid any interference? Maybe. But, that too would fail to recognize the fundamental lesson that soiling teaches us. In assuming a "we" that can make such a prescriptive choice (a humanity, perhaps?), the risk is in overlooking the fact that the historical eventfulness characterizing our worlds is not one made up of such clean, neat, well-ordered, and liberal choices. What soiling as a cosmo-logic points at is that knowing the world also involves making one particular world and unmaking others. In this sense, soiling pushes us to consider that rather than aiming for ideal systems, we should adapt our knowledge practices and our forms of life to the other-than-ideal materialsemiotic messy becomings that really shape our worlds, not alone, not in a commensurable and ordered spreadsheet, but together in the dirt.

Notes

1 Aït-Touati (2011) explores the early history of this imaginative traffic through fiction and scientific literature, while Helmreich (2009) considers the current entanglements between terrestrial oceans and outer space.
2 For example, Praet and Salazar (2017), Battaglia et al. (2015), and Valentine et al. (2012).
3 I take this notion from Kearnes and van Dooren (2017), but I infuse it with the notion of logic as a materialsemiotic and intellectual infrastructure used by Mol (2008).
4 For a great exploration of this dynamic, see Markley (2005).
5 While an unusual funding instrument for research, crowdfunding is proving ideal for topics with an appeal to a broader audience, like this one. The role of crowdfunding for this experiment is especially interesting as it sheds light on the specific articulation of research and private interests promoted by WUR, as will become clear later [see https://crowdfunding.wur.nl/project/earthworms-for-mars?locale=en].
6 For more on Dokuchaev's work, see Evtuhov (2006, 2011), and Moon (2013).
7 These circumstances led Vernadskii's son George to find a position as a historian at Yale. For an interesting account of the fortunes of Vernadskii's work, including his contribution to Hutchinson's ideas, see Oldfield and Shaw (2013, 2016).
8 For more on the early history of US ecology, see Hagen (1992), Golley (1993), Worster (1994), and Cooper (2003).
9 It did this by guaranteeing a global primacy of US sciences through the economic and cultural hegemony funded by the Marshall Plan and American "soft" imperialism, among other things. This is why this section focuses particularly on US technoscientific changes. See Oreskes and Krige (2014) for a critical assessment of the Cold War's impact on technosciences.
10 For more on radiation ecology and its connection with systems ecology, see Kwa (1993).

11 See Kingsland (1995) for a closer look at the history of modeling in ecology.
12 Kwa (1987) explores in depth the relevance of the IBP for the success of ecosystem ecology.
13 The research with NASA environmental system management that Olson (2018) provides is invaluable to situate the importance of systems thinking in this genealogy.
14 Especially by enrolling algae in bioreactors like Algatron and Recyclostat. For a more in-depth approach to this history, see Munns and Nickelsen (2017), Aronowsky (2017), and Walker and Granjou (2017).
15 Especially significant are the contributions of this niche to vertical farming and controlled-environment agriculture, increasingly at the center of current dreams of automation in agriculture. The history of off-Earth farming research is usefully reviewed in Wheeler (2017).
16 Criticizing this move and exposing the connections it maintained with the military-industrial complex, Peder Anker characterizes this moment as "the ecological colonization of space" in his history of ecological design (2010). This phrase, I think, well describes the paradoxical hegemony of the biogeochemical logic I am tracing here.
17 Also thanks to its compatibility with neoliberal economics, which easily interfaces with this logic through the notion of ecosystem services and similar concepts from economic ecology, and thanks to the progressive datafication of nature.
18 From https://events.economist.com/events-conferences/americas/the-new-space-age-2017/
19 For example, with pharmaceutical and life sciences giant Bayer investing over $20m in Planetary Resources—an asteroid mining company—for remote Earth observation technologies to develop digital farming.
20 This term is also fashioned after the US Space Coast in Florida, reminding us of the closely woven hegemonic relations between American and Dutch sociotechnical imaginaries.
21 Luckily, thanks to the work of Lucianne Walkowicz, this critique reached NASA, which has been involved in an interesting effort to discuss and problematize the need to decolonize Mars [see https://www.decolonizemars.org/].
22 Furthermore, this term seems to fit well in a spectrum of ideas of transplanetary expansion moving away from colonizing and terraforming.
23 I use this term rather than historicity following Marisol de la Cadena, and her stress on the Western colonial legacy in lending historicity only to those events that are amenable to historiographic inscriptions that follow Western orderings of nature (Cadena 2015).

References

Aït-Touati, F. (2011), *Fictions of the Cosmos: Science and Literature in the Seventeenth Century*, Chicago, IL: University of Chicago Press.

Amundson, R., A. A. Berhe, J. W. Hopmans, C. Olson, A. E. Sztein, and D. L. Sparks (2015), "Soil and Human Security in the 21st Century," *Science*, 348 (6235): 1261071 [https://doi.org/10.1126/science.1261071].

Anker, P. (2010), *From Bauhaus to Ecohouse: A History of Ecological Design*, Baton Rouge, LA: LSU Press.

Aronowsky, L. V. (2017), "Of Astronauts and Algae: NASA and the Dream of Multispecies Spaceflight," *Environmental Humanities*, 9 (2): 359–77.

Battaglia, D., D. Valentine, and V. Olson (2015), "Relational Space: An Earthly Installation," *Cultural Anthropology*, 30 (2): 245–56.

Beauséjour, R., I. T. Handa, M. J. Lechowicz, B. Gilbert, and M. Vellend (2015), "Historical Anthropogenic Disturbances Influence Patterns of Non-Native Earthworm and Plant Invasions in a Temperate Primary Forest," *Biological Invasions*, 17 (4): 1267–81.

Cadena, M. de la (2015), *Earth Beings: Ecologies of Practice Across Andean Worlds*, Durham, NC: Duke University Press.

Certini, G. and F. C. Ugolini (2013), "An Updated, Expanded, Universal Definition of Soil," *Geoderma*, 192: 378–79.

Cooper, G. J. (2003), *The Science of the Struggle for Existence: On the Foundations of Ecology*, Cambridge: Cambridge University Press.

Creager, A. N. H. (2013), *Life Atomic: A History of Radioisotopes in Science and Medicine*, Chicago, IL: University of Chicago Press.

Darwin, C. (1881), *The Formation of Vegetable Mould, Through the Action of Worms, with Observations on Their Habits*, New York: D. Appleton.

Evtuhov, C. (2006), "The Roots of Dokuchaev's Scientific Contributions: Cadastral Soil Mapping and Agro-Environmental Issues," in B. P. Warkentin (ed.), *Footprints in the Soil: People and Ideas in Soil History*, 125–48, Amsterdam: Elsevier.

Evtuhov, C. (2011), *Portrait of a Russian Province: Economy, Society, and Civilization in Nineteenth-Century Nizhnii Novgorod*, Pittsburgh, PA: University of Pittsburgh Press.

Fuller, R. B. (1968), *Operating Manual for Spaceship Earth*, Carbondale, IL: Southern Illinois University Press.

Golley, F. B. (1993), *A History of the Ecosystem Concept in Ecology: More Than the Sum of the Parts*, New Haven, CT: Yale University Press.

Gómez-Brandón, M., M. Lores, and J. Domínguez (2012), "Species-Specific Effects of Epigeic Earthworms on Microbial Community Structure during First Stages of Decomposition of Organic Matter," *PloS One*, 7 (2): e31895 [https://doi.org/10.1371/journal.pone.0031895].

Hagen, J. B. (1992), *An Entangled Bank: The Origins of Ecosystem Ecology*, New Brunswick, NJ: Rutgers University Press.

Helmreich, S. (2009), *Alien Ocean: Anthropological Voyages in Microbial Seas*, Berkeley, CA: University of California Press.

Jones, C. G., J. H. Lawton, and M. Shachak (1994), "Organisms as Ecosystem Engineers," in F. B. Samson and F. L Knopf (eds.), *Ecosystem Management: Selected Readings*, 130–47, New York: Springer.

Kallipoliti, L. (2008), "Feedback Man," *Log*, 13/14: 115–18.

Kearnes, M. and T. van Dooren (2017), "Rethinking the Final Frontier: Cosmo-Logics and an Ethic of Interstellar Flourishing," *GeoHumanities*, 3 (1): 178–97.

Kingsland, S. E. (1995), *Modeling Nature: Episodes in the History of Population Ecology*, Chicago, IL: University of Chicago Press.

Kwa, C. (1987), "Representations of Nature Mediating Between Ecology and Science Policy: The Case of the International Biological Programme," *Social Studies of Science*, 17 (3): 413–42.

Kwa, C. (1993), "Radiation Ecology, Systems Ecology and the Management of the Environment," in M. Shortland (ed.), *Science and Nature: Essays in the History of the Environmental Sciences*, 213–49, Oxford: British Society for the History of Science.

Livingston, J. (2019), *Self-Devouring Growth: A Planetary Parable as Told from Southern Africa*, Durham, NC: Duke University Press.

Markley, R. (2005), *Dying Planet: Mars in Science and the Imagination*, Durham, NC: Duke University Press.

McKittrick, K. (2015), *Sylvia Wynter: On Being Human as Praxis*, Durham, NC: Duke University Press.

Meadows, D. H., D. L. Meadows, J. Randers, and W. W. Behrens, III (1972), *The Limits to Growth: A Report for the Club of Rome's Project on the Predicament of Mankind*, New York: Universe Books & Potomac Associates.

Mol, A. (2008), *The Logic of Care: Health and the Problem of Patient Choice*, London: Routledge.

Moon, D. (2013), *The Plough That Broke the Steppes: Agriculture and Environment on Russia's Grasslands, 1700–1914*, Oxford: Oxford University Press.

Munns, D. P. D. and K. Nickelsen (2017), "To Live Among the Stars: Artificial Environments in the Early Space Age," *History and Technology*, 33 (3): 272–99.

Odum, E. P. (1953), *Fundamentals of Ecology*, Philadelphia, PA: Saunders.

Oldfield, J. D. and D. J. B. Shaw (2013), "V. I. Vernadskii and the Development of Biogeochemical Understandings of the Biosphere, c. 1880s–1968," *British Journal for the History of Science*, 46 (2): 287–310.

Oldfield, J. and D. J. B. Shaw (2016), *The Development of Russian Environmental Thought: Scientific and Geographical Perspectives on the Natural Environment*, New York: Routledge.

Olson, V. (2018), *Into the Extreme: U.S. Environmental Systems and Politics Beyond Earth*, Minneapolis, MN: University of Minnesota Press.

Oreskes, N. and J. Krige, eds. (2014), *Science and Technology in the Global Cold War*, Cambridge, MA: MIT Press.

Praet, I. and J. F. Salazar (2017), "Familiarizing the Extraterrestrial/Making Our Planet Alien," Special Section, *Environmental Humanities*, 9 (2): 300–455.

Taylor, P. J. (1988), "Technocratic Optimism, H. T. Odum, and the Partial Transformation of Ecological Metaphor after World War II," *Journal of the History of Biology*, 21 (2): 213–44.

Valentine, D., V. A. Olson, and D. Battaglia (2012), "Extreme: Limits and Horizons in the Once and Future Cosmos," *Anthropological Quarterly*, 85 (4): 1007–26.

Vernadsky, V. I. (1926), *The Biosphere*, New York: Springer Science & Business Media.

Walker, J. and C. Granjou (2017), "MELiSSA the Minimal Biosphere: Human Life, Waste and Refuge in Deep Space," *Futures*, 92: 59–69.

Wheeler, R. M. (2017), "Agriculture for Space: People and Places Paving the Way," *Open Agriculture*, 2 (1): 14–32.

Worster, D. (1994), *Nature's Economy: A History of Ecological Ideas*, 2nd edition, Cambridge: Cambridge University Press.

8

Geosocial Polar Futures and the Material Geopolitics of Frozen Soils

Juan Francisco Salazar and Klaus Dodds

Introduction

In the last 150 years, the world has lost half of its topsoil due to erosion, intensive agriculture, and the industrialization and urbanization of the planet (Pimentel 2006). The scale of this impact becomes even more significant when considering that topsoil acts as an interface in the regulation of the flows and transfer of key elements between the atmosphere, biosphere, hydrosphere, and lithosphere. As David Pimentel concluded:

> Careful management of these vital resources [i.e., soils] deserve high priority to ensure the effective protection of our agricultural and natural ecosystems. If conservation is ignored, the 3.7 billion malnourished people in the world will grow and per capita food production will decline further.
>
> 2006: 132

As Maria Puig de la Bellacasa has made clear, historically, "the predominant drive underlying human–soil relations has been to pace their fertility with demands for food production and other needs, such as fiber or construction grounds" (2017: 169). In this chapter, we look at soils that are often considered marginal to conversations about topsoil and soil erosion, namely polar soils, as opposed to temperate and tropical soils or urban soils. Puig de la Bellacasa notes: "[A]t the turn of the twenty-first century, Earth soils regained consideration in public perception and culture due to global antiecological disturbances", and "[h]uman–soil relations are a captivating terrain to engage with the intricate entanglements of material necessities, affective intensities, and ethico-political troubles of caring obligations in the more than human worlds marked by technoscience" (2017: 169). These are precisely some of the questions that animate this chapter, which we use to develop a different approach from the perspective of geological politics and geosocial futures.

Rather than deem frozen soils as simply inert and infertile, we address a generative terrain where these soils service human and nonhuman communities, store carbon-rich resources, suspend past life in frozen animation, and, when thawed, reveal the contested politics of settler colonialism, resource capitalism, and anthropogenic change. Permafrost, a giant cold-storage compost heap stuffed full of frozen carbon, is ground that remains frozen for two or more consecutive years. It is the bedrock of Arctic terrestrial environments, containing rock, soil, sediments, bacteria, and varying volumes of ice that bind these materials together through a range of what Karen Barad has termed "intra-actions": a dynamism of elements and forces in which all the "stuff" of permafrost soil is constantly caught up in an "open process of mattering through which mattering itself acquires meaning and form through the realization of different agential possibilities" (2007: 141). Often found under a thin layer of topsoil, permafrost can range from less than one meter thick, like in the Antarctic, to 1,500 meters, as in many parts of Siberia or North America. It stores the carbon-based remains of plants and animals that froze before they could decompose. Permafrost can be frozen for tens or hundreds of thousands of years and is in a permanent process of geological becoming. However, as recent studies in the Canadian Arctic indicate, permafrost is now thawing at levels not previously expected until 2090, more than 70 years early because of climate change (Farquharson et al. 2019). Drawing on Tim Ingold's illustration of the temporality of materials (2012: 41), we argue that permafrost, like ice, not only exists in time but also is the "stuff of time" itself in the polar regions (Salazar 2018).

The Arctic and parts of the Antarctic Peninsula are warming at twice the rate of the rest of the planet. In both instances, they have become sources of evocative imagery and amplified sentiment concerning environmental change (Nilsson and Christensen 2019). They have also turned into a spatial setting for climate crisis discourses (Paglia 2016) and—in the case of the Arctic—an opportunity to expand economic exploitation and generate new controversies around militarization and securitization. The polar regions are no longer peripheral frontiers. Over the past century, polar landscapes have been subjected to extraordinary endeavors designed to probe their subterranean interiors and submarine environments (Dodds and Nuttall 2016: 64). At issue today are "scrambles" over resources, control over shipping routes, and increasing securitization (Dodds and Nuttall 2016: 14). Polar soils are not inert backdrops to these geopolitical and geo-economic dramas; they are active mediators in their expression. The extreme, as opposed to normal and seasonal thawing of permafrost, is overwhelming existing social-political practices and infrastructures. If the ground being frozen is no longer reliable, then travel becomes more dangerous and costly and infrastructure such as pipelines, roads, and housing is destabilized. Life in Arctic communities is infinitely more livable if things are kept perma-frozen (Dodds and Nuttall 2019). This is most significant, for instance, in the case of Shishmaref, Alaska, which has been home for millennia to a tightly knit Iñpuiat community and which observers have often called "ground zero for climate change in the Arctic" (Martin 2018). Drowning islands and the resistance of Indigenous communities is one facet of this predicament. In a recent study, Crate and colleagues (2017) show how Indigenous Sakha (Yakuts) in northeast Siberia have used thermokarst areas for animal husbandry for at least the last half millennium. This practice is encountering serious difficulties due to permafrost thawing. Thermokarst is a landscape characterized by topographic depressions because of thawing ground ice; these are today being transformed at an unprecedented rate due to climate change. Similarly, across the western Arctic (Canada and Alaska), the thawing of ice-rich permafrost is also significantly disturbing thermokarst landscapes, which is detrimentally affecting cultural resources, for instance, as recorded for the Gwich'in nation in the northern Yukon (Andrews et al. 2016). These are only two cases among dozens of profound instances of climate injustices against Indigenous peoples of the Arctic. As Kyle Powys Whyte (2017) would ask, is this a case of colonial déjà vu? Most certainly. Climate injustices associated with ice melt and permafrost soils thawing are the most recent episode of "a cyclical history of colonialism inflicting anthropogenic (human-caused) environmental change on Indigenous peoples" in the Arctic, who are facing climate risks "largely because of how colonialism, in conjunction with capitalist economics, shapes the geographic spaces they live in and their socio-economic conditions" (Whyte 2017: 88).

While topsoil in the polar regions was always too thin to cultivate under standard settler colonialism, colonialism has happened by other means. The Arctic is also tantalizingly rich in terms of what it is capable of incubating and revealing in terms of past life and future exploitation and microbial biodiversity. With melting and thawing, different worlds are being revealed—sunken, flooded, shifted, muddied, and displaced. Permafrost thaw is providing not only ample evidence of the past reborn (materials being exposed that were previously hidden) but also disruption with fears that native communities might "vanish." In the polar regions, it is clear that the planetary system is transitioning toward a different, and partly unpredictable, state, or what in paleoecology and ecological forecasting is sometimes referred to as "no-analogue climates" (Williams and Jackson 2007). The global climate emergency is being felt profoundly in the polar regions, and these changes indeed are also taking place below ground, fostering changes in "the climate of soil" (Granjou and Salazar 2019).

Polar soils are sites of and for promissory investment and speculative intent. To reappraise the ways in which we "think-with" soils in the polar regions, both materially and conceptually, we link our efforts to calls to think "beyond existing dependencies of social worlds upon particular geological strata and to imagine alternative 'geosocial' futures" (Clark and Yusoff 2017: 3). This has implications for thinking about a novel "geo-logic" of the polar regions (Salazar 2019). Drawing on the notion of "geosocialities," which Palsson and Swanson define as "the commingling of the geologic and the social and the sensibilities involved" (2016: 151), we also wish to picture the intricacies of geology in its relation to social life. In the case of the Arctic region, as Michael Bravo has shown, dominant discourses of Arctic geopolitics and geosocialities are often too blind to the realities of life in the Arctic as peoples and ecosystems are persistently trivialized or where an alternative arrangement of imaginings of a habitable Arctic interwoven with densely linked networks of Inuit routes, rich and deep in cultural meanings, is often rendered invisible (Bravo and Sörlin 2002; Bravo 2018).

Geosocial politics in the polar regions often unfold through a logic of abduction, an anticipatory politics of preemption, precaution, and preparedness (Anderson 2010) wherein a material event, such as permafrost thaw and melting sea ice, can quickly turn into an index or a proxy for a wider assemblage of geopolitical entanglements (Dittmer et al. 2011). This is much less the case in the Antarctic than it is in the Arctic, where the dynamic instability of ice sheets, for instance, or the thawing of permafrost, become a code through which the political instability of the Arctic region can be grasped. As Bravo attests through his long-term work in the Arctic, "the melting of sea ice and other frozen states such as permafrost adds another dimension to the accelerated warming of the atmosphere caused by greenhouse gases" (2017: 27). However, as Bravo adds, "what hasn't yet been adequately explained are the politics of frozen ecologies, and why they matter for the majority of citizens of the globe living in cities with no special interest in visiting the polar regions. Cryopolitics is the story of how the earth's frozen states have come to matter in the age of the Anthropocene" (ibid.).

We use the term "thermal geopolitics" as a framing device to examine how permafrost surfaces as a figure of both concern and hope in the northern polar region. Our discussion of frozen soils is attentive to what we call the everyday volumetrics of life and how it is being altered by thaw and melt. Sea ice and permafrost undergo seasonal thawing, which in many cases enables life forms to thrive and take advantage of summer light, open water, and additional moisture. Human and nonhuman communities, over millennia, have learned to work with what might be considered "normal" thermal regimes. Frozen soils are integral to "thermal geopolitics," because the state of permafrost has shaped the scope and potential of settler colonial states such as Canada to "land" the northern fringes of the North American Arctic. Abnormal thawing poses existential challenges to not only smaller Indigenous/native settlements but also settler colonial infrastructures. In the Arctic, thawing permafrost is generative of disaster imaginaries, a new and unwelcome world where the effects of contemporary global warming are felt first. Thereafter, we turn to Antarctica, which lacks the extensive landscapes of permafrost soils whose changing dynamics cause so much fascination

Figure 8.1 Permafrost in the National Petroleum Reserve-Alaska, 2017. Credit: David Houseknecht, USGS. Public domain.

and trouble in the northern hemisphere, but which is, however, abundant in microbes, as well as being actively reimagined as a frontier for biological prospecting. Polar soils prove to be anything but inert companions in our interrogation of a polar geopolitics, which is being animated by thawing and warming, or what we call might call, drawing on Puig de la Bellacasa (2019), a reanimating of polar soils through science, culture, and community.

Frozen Soils and Thermal Geopolitics

In many other parts of the world, soil enhancement and management are increasingly being enrolled in a range of social and political projects in response to concerns over climate change, environmental degradation, biodiversity loss, food security, and rural livelihoods (for an influential study, see Blaikie 1985). The capacity of humans to disrupt soil systems on an unprecedented scale has become apparent, at the same time as social life continues to be intensely underwritten by the biogeologic agency of the planet's soils. As Mark Whitehead (2014) reminds us in his geographical interrogation of the Anthropocene, the Dust Bowl storms of the 1930s provided a disturbing example of what is at stake when vast amounts of earth and topsoil are blown away by severe winds. Made worse by extreme drought compounded by inappropriate farming methods, the result was devastating to millions of American and Canadian families and communities. It remains one of the most serious environmental disasters in modern North American history.

When we turn to the colder parts of the world, the relationship between soils and human communities is less well appreciated. In the recent past, our temperate framings such as "dust bowl" would have made little sense in the Arctic region. Polar soils were considered "reliably frozen." The permafrost found in Alaska was different to the soils and ground that America novelist John Steinbeck narrated in *The Grapes of Wrath* (1939). Nowadays, however, dust storms are not uncommon in Arctic regions. When snow cover retreats earlier than it used to, glacial flour, river silt, and soil are suddenly a lot more exposed to late winter storms. Ice and snow cover used to hold things in place, in other words. Drier summers also allow for more material to be picked up by strong wind flows and then deposited elsewhere. These storms disrupt air and road transportation and, in the most severe cases, cost lives.

Unseasonal early snow cover retreat in combination with warmer and drier summers in the Arctic is inverting our geographical framings of polar soils and the subsurface. The implications are profound given the soils concerned. Scientists estimate that the world's permafrost holds 1,500 billion tons of carbon, almost double the amount of carbon that is currently in the atmosphere (Cho 2018). As permafrost thaws, the scope and diversity of change is mind-boggling. Rising temperatures cause frozen ground to thaw, and thus accelerate and facilitate decomposition of organic material. The conversion of soil organic carbon into methane and other greenhouse gases is not just restricted to the underground. Subsea permafrost located off the continental shelves of Russia and the North American Arctic is also adversely affected by rising temperatures.

The largest submarine permafrost stores are found in the 2 million km^2 of the East Siberian Arctic Shelf (ESAS). The ESAS was submerged around 12,000 years ago as the world entered the warming period known as the Holocene. The ESAS is so large that it has been calculated as holding 80% of the world's known subsea permafrost hydrate deposits. The ESAS is thought to be highly vulnerable to thawing and methane release because of ongoing warming trends.

The interaction of soils with humans is demanding ever greater attention because the evidence is mounting that anthropogenic change is leading not only to soil loss but also to a fundamental change of state; the Arctic ice is melting and warming in unprecedented ways. Forest fires in the summer are at an all-time high and permafrost thawing is destabilizing previously frozen ground. For thousands of years, the subterranean and submarine Arctic has captured a vast amount of carbon as plant life (roots and other organic matter which was not fully decomposed) was covered by ice and water. As the Arctic warms, subsurface permafrost (permanently frozen soil) is thawing and being broken down by microbial activity. As thawing continues, methane and carbon dioxide are being released. In short, Arctic soils are likely to be shifting from a net carbon reservoir to a net source. The thawing of the Arctic is one of the key stories of the present time. As we have described elsewhere (Salazar and O'Reilly, forthcoming), microbes awakening in the muddy permafrost thaw spew large amounts of methane as they chew and decompose organic matter. These processes are more than passive objects of human concern or regulation. The "thawing" of the Arctic is often being cited as productive of new geopolitical imaginaries, with wide-ranging implications for northern communities, Arctic states, and extraterritorial parties.

The release of carbon dioxide into the shallow waters of the continental shelf and thereafter the atmosphere exemplifies what Isabelle Stengers terms "Gaia's intrusion into collective historicity." The challenge for these "catastrophic times," as Stengers puts it, is to develop a more sustained engagement with the politics of varied matters (2015: 54, 117). As subsea permafrost thaws, it releases methane bursts. This has consequences beyond atmospheric change. The pressurized release of gas creates underground instability on the continental shelf. Scientists are able to use hydroacoustic technologies to monitor, measure, and represent methane release, which takes the shape of bubble clouds. As they breach the surface, these bubble clouds release further methane. Thawing subsea permafrost sets in motion a biophysical and geochemical pattern of change above and below the water surface.

A great number of human settlements in the Arctic are rooted in and structured by permafrost dynamics; thawing permafrost brings with it physical disruption and financial cost. Much of the Arctic's landmass is covered by permafrost, with vast and continuous areas found in Siberia and the North American Arctic. Permafrost is often termed "permanently frozen ground," but this description may not be the most accurate because permafrost is not necessarily "frozen," and, as recent studies have shown—and as Inuit have been experiencing first hand—it may not always be permanent. Several northern communities have incorporated research on changing permafrost conditions into their coastal adaptation planning. There are reports that thinning sea ice jeopardizes modes of transportation and that thawing permafrost destabilizes community infrastructure (Mustonen 2005; Sakakibara 2008). Thawing wreaks havoc when ice loses volume as it turns to slush and water. Thawing permafrost underneath or at the edge of a lake can cause it to drain like a leaky bathtub, with disruptive consequences for human and nonhuman communities. Landslides are common, and erosion exacerbates an already precarious situation.

Environmental writer Renée Cho (2018) vividly recounts how, in her time reporting in the Alaskan Arctic, thawing permafrost becomes a matter of concern for northern settler and Indigenous communities:

In Bethel, Alaska, walls are splitting, houses are collapsing, and the main road looks like a kiddy rollercoaster. In the coastal town of Kongiganak, sinking cemeteries prevent Alaskans from burying their dead in the ground. The village of Shishmaref, located on an island five miles from the western Alaska mainland, has eroded so much that it is contemplating total relocation. These communities are being plagued by permafrost that is thawing.

Permafrost invokes, embodies, and animates a particular relational ethics that, as Puig de la Bellacasa would argue, becomes "a lively *beingness*" that manifests "a world of 'companions' sharing the trouble" (2014: 33). The great "awakening" of the Arctic is one where frozen and inert elements are reanimated by warmth and moisture. Thawing permafrost releases methane fumes and restores life to bacteria and microbes preserved by low temperatures and lack of oxygen and sunlight. Thawing carcasses have enabled new bacterial and zoological possibilities to emerge, as reports of infections take hold of humans and animals. New pathogens are being discovered in ancient permafrost. New and old life forms commingle and co-produce one another. Arctic soils, long frozen, are incubators of microbial life, a reservoir of gases, and a crucible for past animal and plant life. Permafrost thaw is the textbook definition of positive feedback, where warming generates further thaw, microbial activity, and methane release.

All of this, we believe, needs to be understood as integral to a "thermal geopolitics." Permafrost shaped the scope and potential of settler colonial states like Canada to settle the northern fringes of the North American Arctic. Incapable of supporting agriculture and "land improvement," the boundary between sporadic and permanent permafrost necessitated a different form of colonial occupation. In Canada, Greenland, and Alaska, Indigenous peoples were displaced, dispossessed, and sent "south" to residential schools. Indigenous communities were also deployed in the occupational strategies of settler states. Notably, in Cold War Canada, an Indigenous community of 87 in northern Québec was relocated in 1953 to the Northwest Territories in a deliberate attempt to artificially populate remote spaces. This relocation, seen as an experiment, was designed to bolster Canadian sovereignty in the High North— prompting characterization of the community as "human flagpoles"—while providing new opportunities for communities affected by poor hunting in the north of Québec. The relocation proved disastrous. Indigenous peoples were in effect dumped on freezing permafrost and given insufficient support in terms of food and shelter. The end result was a heartbreaking tale of suffering and extraordinary courage in the face of elemental extremes and food shortages (McGrath 2006).

While Indigenous ontologies have long recognized land, ice, and water as living actors entangled with human lives and other communities, the 1953 High Arctic relocation was a telling example of a settler colonial conceit: that Indigenous peoples are well adapted and resilient and thus well able to cope with "Arctic" environments. No allowance was made for the fact that the human and physical geographies of the Arctic are diverse. The Canadian North was considered to be a "frozen desert." What mattered was that northern territories be populated and studied. Permafrost was a topic of considerable academic and political attention (Farish 2006). Attracting substantial government funding, universities across Canada focused their intellectual energies on cold-weather frontier engineering. Making sense of permafrost was integral for Canada's resource sector, government scientists, and armed forces.

What changed between the 1950s and the 2000s was a fundamental reframing of frozen soils in the North American Arctic. Permafrost used to be thought of as a problem that cold-weather engineers would study, advise upon, and find a solution for. The challenge for the communities of people in the military and the mining/petroleum industries working and living in the North was to anticipate and manage the active top layer of permafrost. Over time, however, more extensive experiences of permafrost thawing have unleashed a different imaginary: permafrost now evokes a vulnerable and disappearing archive of Arctic pasts rather than a problem space for cold-weather civil engineering. Thawing has become, in the contemporary Arctic, indicative of rapid and unwanted change, and complicit with new anxieties that the Arctic is distressed.

Scientists have not only recorded milder winters in the Arctic but also detected thick and slushy mud where frozen earth would have been expected. Higher snowfall in the polar winter has been credited with inadvertently trapping heat on the surface of the frozen ground. The stored heat then further contributes to the warming of the active layer and is capable of provoking new spatial forms such as sinkholes, craters, and ravines. Ground is hollowed out. Ice is stripped away. Air is altered by methane release. Fires in the Arctic summer season contribute further to the degradation of frozen ground. This lends credence to the claims by Peter Adey (2010) that we need to be attentive to "vertical reciprocity" of the subterranean, the surface, and the aerial, as volatile forces move and transform organic matter into mud and gas. Frozen territory becomes in part gaseous, as ice and soil are brought to the surface and exposed to the elements of wind and water.

Stuart Elden was among the first to argue that the volumetric can be mobilized as an expedient analytic within geopolitical (and also, in this case, geosocial) theorization, taking into consideration "the dimensionality implied by 'volume' and the calculability implied by 'metric'" (2013: 49). In the polar regions, the everyday volumetrics of life is being altered by thaw and melt, shifting the conjoined relations of what Peter Adey calls "vertical reciprocity" (2010: 2) that dwell between subterranean, subglacial, surficial, and aerial spaces (Bonilla 2017; Hemmings 2019; McNeill 2019). Geological strata emerge as "provocations for political issue formation" (Clark 2017). Interior and littoral landscapes change. Communities are disrupted as frozen ground no longer provides a reliable foundation for travel and inhabitation. Polar permafrost soils create a volumetrics of life that assembles through belowground, surface, and atmospheric conditions and forces.

On his presidential visit to Alaska in 2015 US President Barack Obama admitted that: Thawing permafrost destabilizes the earth on which 100,000 Alaskans live, threatening homes, damaging transportation and energy infrastructure, which could cost billions of dollars to fix … Consider, as well, that many of the fires burning today are actually burning through the permafrost in the Arctic. So, this permafrost stores massive amounts of carbon. When the permafrost is no longer permanent, when it thaws or burns, these gases are released into our atmosphere over time, and that could mean that the Arctic may become a new source of emissions that further accelerates global warming.

Obama 2015

The spatial reach and depth of life is complicated and disrupted. The state of frozen soil is intimately linked to matters of local, national, and international governance. Housing shortages are common in Arctic communities, and property, when it can be found, is expensive. In 2018, the Alaskan community of Newtok received federal funding to begin a relocation plan for its 350 residents. The town is becoming uninhabitable due to coastal erosion, landslides, and flooding. The US Army Corps of Engineers estimates that the final bill for the relocation will be around $130 million; so far $15 million has been allocated. Throughout Alaska, up to 30 villages have been identified as vulnerable due to excessive and accelerating thawing and melting (Mandel 2017). Relocation will be a resolutely geopolitical matter. Meanwhile, the Trump administration has been accused of delaying a federal response to climate change and the consequences of permafrost thaw, sea ice melting, and low-lying flooding. These changing states are only going to become more dramatic, more disruptive. The latest research from northern Canada and Alaska reveals that permafrost is extremely sensitive to climate change, and this is set to continue to degrade landscapes via retrogressive thaw slumps (Petley 2019).

As Isabel Stengers (2015) reminds us, there is no future where "nature" can be safely imagined as returning to a passive backdrop of human life. We are living in the ruins of the Holocene. And yet, the Arctic faces a situation where environmental imaginaries of a melting and thawing place don't produce the political outcomes that native communities might have hoped for. Instead, affected communities are expected to be resilient and adaptable, and wait for their time. During his visit to Alaska in February 2019, President Trump spoke about the state's strategic importance and the desire to license energy prospecting in the Arctic National Wildlife Refuge. He mentioned his grandfather's interest in gold prospecting. Permafrost thaw was not mentioned in his speech; nor was climate change (Trump 2019). The speech could be thought of as exemplifying what Laurent Berlant (2011) describes as impasse: a moment when ecological and political crisis does not produce expected outcomes.

Antarctic Soils: A New Frontier of Genetic Material

Antarctica lacks the extensive permafrost soils whose changing dynamics spark so much fascination and trouble in the northern hemisphere. The Antarctic's soils arguably posit a different set of futures where warming nourishes a framing of the continent's marine and terrestrial environments as an exploitable form of biodiversity. The polar regions, particularly the Antarctic, are being actively reimagined as a frontier for biological prospecting (Salazar 2017), with Antarctic biodiversity being identified as a great deal richer than previously thought, including in terms of diversity of soil biota (Chown et al. 2015). Biotechnology based on polar genetic resources ranges from enzymes (including in both life sciences research and industrial applications), anti-freeze proteins, and bioremediation to pharmaceuticals, nutraceuticals and dietary supplements, cosmetics, and other health and personal care uses (Leary 2008).

In Antarctica, climate change, in combination with human activities such as fishing, tourism, and scientific research expeditions, has been recognized as impactful. In terrestrial Antarctica, factors such as energy, shelter, and water have contributed to distinct patterns of soil and plant-life diversity. Comparative isolation and long periods of cold and darkness are pivotal to the biogeographies of Antarctica. Rising temperatures, accidental species introductions, and human mobility are changing Antarctica's biodiversity, and soil development is facilitated as ice-free areas expand. For much of Antarctica's history of human contact, the ice-free areas of the Antarctic Peninsula and McMurdo Valleys have attracted considerable interest from scientists eager either to understand their paleoclimates or, more lately, to work with NASA to develop and plan for Moon and Mars landings (Salazar 2017). Now other areas such as Signy Island are hotspots for research as scientists discover new species such as the flightless midge, which feeds on organic matter and has been responsible for affecting peat decomposition and soil structure (Bartlett et al. 2019).

The microbial communities in Antarctic soils have generated considerable interest because of their ability to survive in extreme environments such as polar deserts. Only about 0.4% of Antarctica's surface is permanently free of ice, and the soils concerned have very low levels of carbon and nutrients. These ice-free environments are more dynamic than previously thought. Drivers of change are found to include alien species introductions, the movement of microorganisms, meltwater runoff, rotting animal carcasses, and cumulative human impact including pollution (Cowan et al. 2014). Scientists have, over the last 30 years, invested ever more energy into analyzing and processing these soils and their compositional matter. While polar scientists warn about the absence of baseline knowledge of polar biota and non-native species management, others are racing ahead to capitalize on polar soils and biota (O'Neill 2017). The ice-free regions, of which about 90% are soil-forming, are located mainly on the coastline of the Antarctic continent, mostly on the Antarctic Peninsula and also in the McMurdo Dry Valleys within the Ross Sea region. Antarctic soils are characterized by extremely low soil temperatures, with an average mean annual temperature ranging between –15°C and –40°C, and low soil moisture (Manaaki Whenua Landcare Research, n.d.). Terrestrial ecosystems on the western side of the Antarctic Peninsula have patches of continuous vegetation that include not only mosses, lichens, microbiota, and algae but also two grasses (*Deschampsia antarctica* and *Colobanthus quitensis*), the latter the only vascular plant reported in Antarctica (Fretwell et al. 2011).

Antarctic soils are being conceptualized as genetic material to be studied, extracted, and commodified. In international law, where Antarctica is recognized as a global commons while at the same time governed by the 1959 Antarctic Treaty System, biological prospecting and extraction raises substantial issues regarding the freedom of knowledge exchange, benefit sharing, and intellectual property rights in a part of the world that has often been framed as exceptional for its levels of scientific and political cooperation. Antarctic biological prospecting is ongoing and attracting an ever greater diversity of scientific stakeholders. In February 2019, for example, Indian scientists working in a consortium of government, industry, and universities revealed that they were experimenting with Antarctic fungi in the hope that it might offer insights into the development of new chemotherapeutic methods for cancer treatment (*India Today Web Desk* 2019).

This biological imaginary of technoscientific optimism and potential was revealed in ethnographic interviews carried out between 2012 and 2014 in the Antarctic Peninsula. These interviews, carried out with a range of scientists while at sea meandering around the South Shetland Islands as well as in several research stations in the Antarctic Peninsula, were regarded as "agential conversations" (Müller and Kenney 2014). For Müller and Kenney, reframing research interviews as "agential conversations" that interfere with the contexts they seek to understand is key to creating "situated moments of reflection, connection, and disruption" (2014: 539), which in this particular case serve as a basis for discussing the problematic conditions of bioprospecting in the Southern Ocean and on Antarctic soils.

The prospect of discovering new organisms offers biotechnology the great promise of finding new geochemical and genetic properties that might be developed for scientific and commercial activities. This offers a profound contrast with the imaginaries of doom and disaster that frame public engagement with climate change science in the Arctic. As Helmreich's (2009) anthropological work on "microbial seas" attests, microbes can be thought as "embodied bits of vitality" that define a new resource frontier in marine microbiology and ecology, where genomics and bioinformatics afford new multiscalar associations "linking genomes to biomes." Unlike commercial mining, which threatened to undermine the Antarctic Treaty System in the 1980s, biological prospecting does not generate anywhere near the same level of political and public passion. The Antarctic is routinely considered the "last wilderness on Earth" and a "continent for peace and science." These framings and narratives are, one would think, incompatible with resource extraction. The Antarctic Treaty System, especially the Protocol on Environmental Protection, bans any form of mineral prospecting and mining and values Antarctica for its wilderness qualities, which need to be protected. Political value is attributed to the containment of mineral extraction while recognizing that other forms of activity such as fishing have to be carefully managed.

The framing of Antarctica as an emerging pharmacopeia is narrating and legitimizing new forms of extraction that do not appear to conflict with the framing of a "continent for peace and science." Ratified in 1991, the Environmental Protocol to the Antarctic Treaty has been, Alan Hemmings suggests, "largely driven by the success of Antarctic science, which has been given an entrenched and privileged role in the international Antarctic governance regime provided by the Antarctic Treaty System over the past half century" (2010: 6). As reported by the Antarctic Treaty Consultative Meetings held every year in Antarctic Treaty states, more than 200 research organizations and companies from at least 27 states are undertaking research for commercial purposes in the Antarctic. The greatest concentration of genetic resources in Antarctica comes from the research by pharmaceutical and medical technology industries (20%), followed by molecular biology and biotechnology (18%), industrial applications (12%), chemical processing (11%), cosmetics and personal care (6%), aquaculture and agriculture (6%), culture collection or databasing (3%), and environmental remediation (1%) (Joyner 2012).

As the hunt for new medicines and biotechnological applications turns to the Antarctic and the deep seabed, Antarctica is being reframed as a space of opportunity, as a biotech cornucopia of discoverable genetic riches. Drawing on Veronica Davidov's (2013) analysis of the commonly deployed imaginary of the Amazon as a pharmacopeia, we argue that a similar metaphor could be used in the Antarctic, notwithstanding that the rich biodiversity of the Amazon is not directly comparable to that of the Antarctic. As Davidov reminds us, it was not so long ago that the Amazon was being framed as "the lungs of the earth," a vital organism for a "healthy" planet. As "pharmacopeia," however, the Amazon is reimagined as an inviting biological resource that can be safely prospected and sustainably exploited. Moreover, the politics of bioprospecting in the Amazon is facilitated by its co-option of Indigenous traditional knowledge of plants and other bioresources.

Bioprospecting also raises particular and distinctive geopolitical issues in Antarctica by virtue of its peculiar historical and legal arrangements (Jabour-Green and Nicol 2003; Hemmings 2010; Jabour 2010; Joyner 2012; Rogan-Finnemore 2017). The Antarctic Treaty System does not directly regulate bioprospecting activities in the Antarctic. To the extent that rules for bioprospecting now exist, they stem from the host government under which the researching company or group of scientists is carrying out the bioprospecting. Nonetheless, certain provisions of the Antarctic Treaty, the Protocol for Environmental Protection, and the Commission on the Conservation of Antarctic and Marine Living Resources (CCAMLR) have relevance for bioprospecting, and these may provide the genesis for a future regulatory regime. As many voices claim, the extraction and use of any resources from the Antarctic Treaty area is highly controversial because such extraction "has the potential to impact the Antarctic environment, and the use of Antarctic resources always awakens the dormant argument on Antarctic sovereignty and sovereign rights" (Meduna 2015). Without some institutional separation of science as actor from science as independent advisor, bioprospecting may "risk moral hazard for science in the Antarctic Treaty System" (Hemmings 2010).

A number of unresolved bioprospecting issues could pose serious challenges for the Antarctic Treaty Consultative Parties as a group, particularly, though not exclusively, between claimant and non-claimant states. One fundamental issue is the lack of a consensus definition of biological prospecting as a research activity. The geopolitics and ethics of earthly bioprospecting certainly speak to current modes of thinking about terraforming and planetary ecosynthesis. During visits to sub-Antarctic islands and follow-up visits to the biologists and ecologists working on sampling trips, and in laboratory work on King George Island, descriptions of how extremophilic microbes present raw material for innovative science loomed large (Salazar 2017). This is similar to Stefan Helmreich's observations on the work of marine biologists, where the ocean microbes were seen, on the one hand, as "potential ancestors of all life, helpful monitors of climate control, raw material for new life-saving drugs, and, on the other, beings always erasing the trace of their own origins, entities indifferent and adaptable to human ecological disaster, vehicles of seaborne disease" (2009: xi).

In contrast to this depoliticized vision of bioprospecting, the Antarctic and Southern Ocean Coalition has warned:

> One of the biggest controversies is whether companies and governments should be able to profit from Antarctic species. Antarctica is set aside under the Environment Protocol to the Antarctic Treaty as a protected area dedicated to open science and environmental protection. Allowing a free-for-all on biological prospecting is inconsistent with those values and would allow some countries and companies with an unfair advantage to profit off of Antarctica's fragile ecosystem.
>
> ASOC 2019

Conclusion

As we invert Cymene Howe's focus on "vitalities, materials, and movements that are skyward, spacey, and atmospheric" (2015: 203), we ask how a new generation of researchers in the human sciences can write on what she terms "climate inhabitants living within weather-weathered political economies" (2015: 207) and what it means to analytically inhabit life below earth's surface in ways that provoke seeking out forms of porous mutuality (Howe 2015; Granjou and Salazar 2019). Polar soils provide entrées into very different sociopolitical worlds. We might ask in this context: What do polar soils promise? What do polar soils do? And what do polar soils reveal? In the Arctic, the thawing of permafrost has informed and escalated an imaginary of ecological breakdown and potential disaster. For some Arctic coastal communities, thawing permafrost in combination with melting and retreating sea ice has contributed to repeated vulnerabilities from coastal storms, landslides, and flooding. As Sheila Watt-Cloutier, in *The Right to Be Cold* (2016: 3), noted:

> We are all accustomed to the dire metaphors used to evoke the havoc of climate change, but in many parts of the Arctic the metaphors have already become a very literal reality. For a number of reasons, the planet warms several times faster at the poles. While climate experts warn that an increase of two degrees in the global average temperature is the threshold of disaster, in the Arctic we have already seen nearly *double* that. As the permafrost thaws, roads and airport runways buckle. Homes and buildings along the coast sink into the ground and fall into the sea.

The "buckling of infrastructure" reveals evidence of a social and material terrain that is riddled with uneven geographies of inequalities and vulnerabilities. Infrastructure is integral to northern communities and often extraordinarily important because communities are small, scattered, and often dependent on frozen ground and ice for mobility. Roads are often absent or sparse, and air transport is expensive and irregular.

An unstable Arctic is an expensive Arctic, and a thawing subterranean Arctic generates a landscape akin to Swiss cheese—full of holes and cracks, and prone to subsidence. Melting and thawing is disruptive, and its effects are felt disproportionately by Indigenous and northern communities who have borne the brunt of power plays, security projects, and community relocation for much of the Cold War and since. When soils and ground thaw and flood, it more often than not reveals the precariousness of northern communities, the limits of distributional justice, and the aspirations of political elites in the southern part of national territories. Thawing and melting have been regarded by many as providing opportunities for further resource extraction and cargo transportation.

Indigenous peoples have dwelled on and inhabited northern frozen soils for millennia. These spaces today continue to be contested, fossil-resource rich, and thawing, which makes their political economies very different to the geologic politics of Antarctic soils. In this chapter, we further trouble the imaginary of soils as "inert." Frozen soils are lively assemblages that both depend on and develop with this inertness and participate in its animation. This very inertness turns out to be agentic—by "keeping things in," the permafrost makes life livable.

As geosocial formations, polar soils offer up rich possibilities for thinking about the intersection of social and political life and the geological and ecological processes and spaces that make up the proverbial "ends of the earth." Within ancient Arctic permafrost and the low-carbon soils of ice-free Antarctica, we find evidence for multiple imaginaries and geosocial formations. Thinking with and through polar soils and frozen ground enables us to ask new questions about warming, the organic, and the mutual interconnectedness of ice, water, and air (Clark and Yusoff 2017). The polar subterranean and submarine is revealing itself to be highly stratified, home to multiple species and thermal energy regimes. There is now a growing recognition that the remotest parts of the earth such as the deep oceans and poles are anything but inert and incapable of hosting life.

Acknowledgments

Klaus Dodds acknowledges the Leverhulme Trust for the award of a Major Research Fellowship (2017–2020).

References

Adey, P. (2010), *Aerial Life: Spaces, Mobilities, Affects*, Oxford: Blackwell.
Anderson, B. (2010), "Preemption, Precaution, Preparedness: Anticipatory Action and Future Geographies," *Progress in Human Geography*, 34 (6): 777–98.
Andrews, T. D., S. V. Kokelj, G. MacKay, J. Buysse, I. Kritsch, A. Andre et al. (2016), "Permafrost Thaw and Aboriginal Cultural Landscapes in the Gwich'in Region, Canada," *APT Bulletin: The Journal of Preservation Technology*, 47 (1): 15–22.
Atlantic and Southern Ocean Coalition (ASOC) (2019), "Biological Prospecting" [https://www.asoc.org/advocacy/antarctic-environmental-protection/biological-prospecting].

Barad, K. (2007), *Meeting the Universe Halfway: Quantum Physics and the Entanglement of Matter and Meaning*, Durham, NC: Duke University Press.

Bartlett, J. C., P. Convey, and S. A. L. Hayward (2019), "Life Cycle and Phenology of an Antarctic Invader: The Flightless Chironomid Midge, *Eretmoptera murphyi*," *Polar Biology*, 42 (1): 115–30.

Berlant, L. (2011), *Cruel Optimism*, Durham, NC: Duke University Press.

Blaikie, P. (1985), *The Political Economy of Soil Erosion in Developing Countries*, London: Longman.

Bonilla, L. (2017), "Voluminous," Theorizing the Contemporary: Speaking Volumes series, *Society for Cultural Anthropology*, October 24 [https://staging.culanth.org/fieldsights/voluminous].

Bravo, M. (2017), "A Cryopolitics to Reclaim our Frozen Material States," in J. Radin and E. Kowal (eds.), *Cryopolitics: Frozen Life in a Melting World*, 27–57, Cambridge, MA: MIT Press.

Bravo, M. (2018), *North Pole: Nature and Culture*, London: Reaktion.

Bravo, M. and S. Sörlin, eds. (2002), *Narrating the Arctic: A Cultural History of Nordic Scientific Practices*, Canton, MA: Science History Publications.

Cho, R. (2018), "Why Thawing Permafrost Matters," State of the Planet, Earth Institute, Columbia University, January 11 [https://blogs.ei.columbia.edu/2018/01/11/thawing-permafrost-matters/].

Chown, S. L., A. Clarke, C. I. Fraser, S. C. Cary, K. L. Moon, and M. A. McGeoch (2015), "The Changing Form of Antarctic Biodiversity," *Nature*, 522 (7557): 431–38.

Clark, N. (2017), "Politics of Strata," *Theory, Culture & Society*, 34 (2/3): 211–31.

Clark, N. and K. Yusoff (2017), "Geosocial Formations and the Anthropocene," *Theory, Culture & Society*, 34 (2/3): 3–23.

Cowan, D. A., T. P. Makhalanyane, P. G. Dennis, and D. W. Hopkins (2014), "Microbial Ecology and Biogeochemistry of Continental Antarctic Soils," *Frontiers in Microbiology*, 5: 154 [https://doi.org/10.3389/fmicb.2014.00154].

Crate, S., M. Ulrich, J. O. Habeck, A. R. Desyatkin, R. V. Desyatkin, A. N. Fedorov et al. (2017), "Permafrost Livelihoods: A Transdisciplinary Review and Analysis of Thermokarst-Based Systems of Indigenous Land Use," *Anthropocene*, 18: 89–104.

Davidov, V. (2013), "Amazonia as Pharmacopia," *Critique of Anthropology*, 33 (3): 243–62.

Dittmer, J., S. Moisio, A. Ingram, and K. Dodds (2011), "Have You Heard the One about the Disappearing Ice? Recasting Arctic Geopolitics," *Political Geography*, 30 (4): 202–14.

Dodds, K. and M. Nuttall (2016), *The Scramble for the Poles: The Geopolitics of the Arctic and Antarctic*, Cambridge: Polity Press.

Dodds, K. and M. Nuttall (2019), *The Arctic: What Everyone Needs to Know*, New York: Oxford University Press.

Elden, S. (2013), "Secure the Volume: Vertical Geopolitics and the Depths of Power," *Political Geography*, 34 (1): 35–51.

Farish, M. (2006), "Frontier Engineering: From the Globe to the Body in the Cold War Arctic," *Canadian Geographer*, 50 (2): 177–96.

Farquharson, L. M., V. E. Romanovsky, W. L. Cable, D. A. Walker, S. V. Kokelj, and D. Nicolsky (2019), "Climate Change Drives Widespread and Rapid Thermokarst Development in Very Cold Permafrost in the Canadian High Arctic," *Geophysical Research Letters*, 46 (12): 6681–89.

Fretwell, P. T., P. Convey, A. H. Fleming, H. J. Peat, and K. A. Hughes (2011), "Detecting and Mapping Vegetation Distribution on the Antarctic Peninsula from Remote Sensing Data," *Polar Biology*, 34 (2): 273–81.

Granjou, C. and J. F. Salazar (2019), "The Stuff of Soil: Belowground Agency in the Making of Future Climates," *Nature and Culture*, 14 (1): 39–60.

Helmreich, S. (2009), *Alien Ocean: Anthropological Voyages in Microbial Seas*, Berkeley, CA: University of California Press.

Hemmings, A. D. (2010), "Does Bioprospecting Risk Moral Hazard for Science in the Antarctic Treaty System?," *Ethics in Science and Environmental Politics*, 10 (1): 5–12.

Hemmings, A. D. (2019), "Subglacial Nationalisms," in E. Leane and J. McGee (eds.), *Anthropocene Antarctica: Perspectives from the Humanities, Law and Social Sciences*, 33–56, Abingdon: Routledge.

Howe, C. (2015), "Life Above Earth: An Introduction," *Cultural Anthropology*, 30 (2): 203–9.

India Today Web Desk (2019), "IIT Hyderabad Researchers Find Antarctic Fungi that Could Make Childhood Cancer Treatment Cheaper, with Fewer Side Effects," *India Today Web Desk*, February 19 [https://www.indiatoday.in/education-today/news/story/iit-hyderabad-researchers-find-antarctic-fungi-that-could-make-childhood-cancer-treatment-cheaper-with-fewer-side-effects-1459708-2019-02-19].

Ingold, T. (2012), "Toward an Ecology of Materials," *Annual Review of Anthropology*, 41: 427–42.

Jabour, J. (2010), "Biological Prospecting: The Ethics of Exclusive Reward from Antarctic Activity," *Ethics in Science and Environmental Politics*, 10 (1): 19–29.

Jabour-Green, J. and D. Nicol (2003), "Bioprospecting in Areas Outside National Jurisdiction: Antarctica and the Southern Ocean," *Melbourne Journal of International Law*, 4 (1): 76–111.

Joyner, C. C. (2012), "Bioprospecting as a Challenge to the Antarctic Treaty," in A. D. Hemmings, D. R. Rothwell, and K. N. Scott (eds.), *Antarctic Security in the Twenty-First Century: Legal and Policy Perspectives*, 197–214, London: Routledge.

Leary, D. (2008), "Bi-polar Disorder? Is Bioprospecting an Emerging Issue for the Arctic as well as for Antarctica?," *Review of European, Comparative and International Environmental Law*, 17 (1): 41–55.

Manaaki Whenua Landcare Research (n.d.), "Antarctic Soils" [https://www.landcareresearch.co.nz/science/soils-and-landscapes/antarctic-soils].

Mandel, K. (2017), "America's Climate Refugees Have Been Abandoned by Trump," *Mother Jones*, October 17 [https://www.motherjones.com/environment/2017/10/climate-refugees-trump-hud/].

Martin, A. (2018), "An Alaskan Village Is Falling into the Sea. Washington Is Looking the Other Way," *PRI*, October 22 [https://www.pri.org/stories/2018-10-22/alaskan-village-falling-sea-washington-looking-other-way].

McGrath, M. (2006), *The Long Exile: A Tale of Inuit Betrayal and Survival in the High Arctic*, London: Vintage.

McNeill, D. (2019), "The Volumetric City," *Progress in Human Geography* [https://doi.org/10.1177/0309132519863486].

Meduna, V. (2015), "The Search for Extremophiles: Antarctic Biological Prospecting," in D. Liggett, B. Storey, Y. Cook, and V. Meduna (eds.), *Exploring the Last Continent: An Introduction to Antarctica*, 463–76, Dordrecht: Springer.

Müller, R. and M. Kenney (2014), "Agential Conversations: Interviewing Postdoctoral Life Scientists and the Politics of Mundane Research Practices," *Science as Culture*, 23 (4): 537–59.

Mustonen, T., ed. (2005), *Stories of the Raven—Snowchange 2005 Conference Report, Anchorage, Alaska, USA*, Snowchange Cooperative, Alaska Native Science Commission, Inuit Circumpolar Conference Alaska.

Nilsson, A. E. and M. Christensen (2019), *Arctic Geopolitics, Media and Power*, London: Routledge.

Obama, B. (2015), "Remarks by the President at the GLACIER Conference—Anchorage, AK," speech delivered at Dena'ina Civic and Convention Center, Anchorage, Alaska, August 31 [https://obamawhitehouse.archives.gov/the-press-office/2015/09/01/remarks-president-glacier-conference-anchorage-ak].

O'Neill, T. A. (2017), "Protection of Antarctic Soil Environments: A Review of the Current Issues and Future Challenges for the Environmental Protocol," *Environmental Science and Policy*, 76: 153–64.

Paglia, E. (2016), "The Northward Course of the Anthropocene: Transformation, Temporality and Telecoupling in a Time of Environmental Crisis," PhD thesis, KTH Royal Institute of Technology, Stockholm.

Palsson, G. and H. A. Swanson (2016), "Down to Earth: Geosocialities and Geopolitics," *Environmental Humanities*, 8 (2): 149–71.

Petley, D. (2019), "Thawing Permafrost Is Triggering Thousands of Landslides Across the Arctic," *The Conversation*, April 3 [https://theconversation.com/thawing-permafrost-is-triggering-thousands-of-landslides-across-the-arctic-114702].

Pimentel, D. (2006), "Soil Erosion: A Food and Environmental Threat," *Environment, Development and Sustainability*, 8 (1): 119–37.

Puig de la Bellacasa, M. (2014), "Encountering Bioinfrastructure: Ecological Struggles and the Sciences of Soil," *Social Epistemology*, 28 (1): 26–40.

Puig de la Bellacasa, M. (2017), *Matters of Care: Speculative Ethics in More than Human Worlds*, Minneapolis, MN: University of Minnesota Press.

Puig de la Bellacasa, M. (2019), "Re-animating Soils: Transforming Human–Soil Affections through Science, Culture and Community," *Sociological Review*, 67 (2): 391–407.

Rogan-Finnemore, M. (2017), "What Bioprospecting Means for Antarctica and the Southern Ocean," in G. Leane and B. von Tigerstrom (eds.), *International Law Issues in the South Pacific*, 211–40, Abingdon: Routledge.

Sakakibara, C. (2008), "'Our Home Is Drowning': Iñupiat Storytelling and Climate Change in Point Hope, Alaska," *Geographical Review*, 98 (4): 456–75.

Salazar, J. F. (2017), "Microbial Geographies at the Extremes of Life," *Environmental Humanities*, 9 (2): 398–417.

Salazar, J. F. (2018), "Ice Cores as Temporal Probes," *Journal of Contemporary Archaeology*, 5 (1): 32–43.

Salazar, J. F. (2019), "The Anthropocene Melt: Antarctica's Geologic Politics," in E. Leane and J. McGee (eds.), *Anthropocene Antarctica: Perspectives from the Humanities, Law and Social Sciences*, 73–84, Abingdon: Routledge.

Salazar, J. F. and J. O'Reilly (forthcoming), "Materials after Ice Thaw: Methane, Microbes, Mud," in R. Ruiz, P. Schönach, and Rob Shields (eds.), *After Ice: Cold Humanities for a Warming Planet*, Durham, NC: Duke University Press.

Stengers, I. (2015), *In Catastrophic Times: Resisting the Coming Barbarism*, London: Open Humanities Press.

Trump, D. (2019), "Remarks by President Trump to U.S. Service Members, Anchorage, Alaska," Joint Base Elmendorf-Richardson, Anchorage, Alaska, February 28 [https://www.whitehouse.gov/briefings-statements/remarks-president-trump-u-s-service-members-anchorage-alaska].

Watt-Cloutier, S. (2016), *The Right to Be Cold*, Harmondsworth: Penguin.

Whitehead, M. (2014), *Environmental Transformations: A Geography of the Anthropocene*, London: Routledge.

Whyte, K. P. (2017), "Is it Colonial Déjà Vu? Indigenous Peoples and Climate Injustice," in J. Adamson and M. Davis (eds.), *Humanities for the Environment: Integrating Knowledge, Forging New Constellations of Practice*, 88–105, New York: Routledge.

Williams, J. and S. Jackson (2007), "Novel Climates, No-Analog Communities, and Ecological Surprises," *Frontiers in Ecology and the Environment*, 5 (9): 475–82.

9

A Mend to the Metabolic Rift? The Promises (and Potential Pitfalls) of Biosolids Application on American Soils

Nicholas C. Kawa

Introduction

We live in a time of ecological crisis, or what is known in Marxian theory as the *metabolic rift*—the disruption of the Earth's socioecological systems brought on by industrial capitalism (Foster 1999; see also Moore 2011). Recently, McKenzie Wark has proclaimed that we are in fact experiencing "a series of metabolic rifts, where one molecule after another is extracted by labor and technique to make things for humans, but the waste products don't return so that the cycle can renew itself" (2015: xiv).

Marx himself originally located this rift in the English soil. As the environmental sociologist John Bellamy Foster (1999) explains, Marx had studied the works of the chemist Justus von Liebig, who had identified declines in soil fertility driven by the removal of soil nutrients under capitalist agriculture and a neglect for their systematic restoration. In *Capital Volume 1*, Marx declared: "All progress in capitalist agriculture is a progress in the art, not only of robbing the worker, but of robbing the soil" (1979: 506). Later, in *Capital Volume 3*, he specifically lamented how human excrement, which was once a resource for agricultural fertilization, had become a source of pollution and waste:

> Excretions of consumption are of the greatest importance for agriculture. So far as their utilisation is concerned, there is an enormous waste of them in the capitalist economy. In London, for instance, they find no better use for the excretion of four and a half million human beings than pollute the Thames with it at heavy expense.
>
> Marx 1999: 69

Which is to say, Marx really pinpointed the metabolic rift in the modern treatment of human excrement.[1]

This chapter examines attempts in the United States to mend the metabolic rift and turn human excreta into a viable agricultural fertilizer once again. Currently, the US Environmental Protection Agency (EPA) estimates that more than 8 million dry tons of biosolids (i.e., treated sanitation sludge) are produced in the country annually, but only about half of that material is applied to land, and US Department of Agriculture (USDA)-certified organic farms are prohibited from using it (EPA 2019). While some researchers, sanitation engineers, and farmers view the use of biosolids as a beneficial model for fertilization on a planet of finite resources (Basta 1995; Cofie et al. 2005; Cordell et al. 2011), others have raised concerns about its possible consequences for public health, and some communities have even accused farmers of conspiring with the sanitation industry to spread "toxic sludge" on agricultural lands (Snyder 2005; LeBlanc et al. 2009). And, for the majority of Americans, the realities of sewage treatment and disposal remain largely hidden in plain sight. As Gay Hawkins argues, the hydraulic sanitation system is a "public secret," aided by modernist infrastructure that blinds people from knowing "where shit ends up" (2002: 40).

This chapter relies on participant observation and semi-structured interviews ($n = 26$) conducted in 2017 and 2018 with wastewater treatment specialists, soil scientists, and grain farmers in three sites in the United States—Ohio, Illinois, and Washington State. Through this ethnographic research, I explore the contemporary regulation, production, and application of biosolids. Specifically, I highlight different experts' insights into the productive benefits of biosolids, including the remediation of degraded industrial sites, the return of nutrients to agricultural lands, and the incorporation of much-needed organic matter into soils vulnerable to erosion. However, I also bring attention to the emergent concerns facing contemporary sanitation systems, from unregulated industrial chemicals in the waste stream to public fears regarding the application of biosolids on rural lands. In doing so, I question the extent to which the growing movement to adopt biosolids in industrial agricultural production reflects either a trend of "salvage accumulation" (Tsing 2015)—the amassment of wealth in the ruins of late industrialism—or a new, albeit uncertain, frontier for ecological sustainability in the Anthropocene. To conclude, I offer reflections on the challenges of sustainable agricultural management under late industrialism (Fortun 2014). Ultimately, I contend that while the use of biosolids is proving effective in various sites in the United States, the increasing complexity of late industrial excreta (see Blanchette 2019) should draw our attention to the problematic practices and pollutants further upstream from biosolids processing rather than fixate solely on the endpoint of their application.

Background: From Agricultural Resource to Human Waste (and Back Again)

Prior to the development of the modern hydraulic sanitation system, people across the world commonly relied on human excrement as a source of agricultural fertilization, sometimes known euphemistically as "night soil" (Kawa 2016). An extensive history of this practice can be found in the Americas (see, for example, Becerril and Jiménez 2007; Birk et al. 2011), Africa (Van Der Geest 2002; Cofie et al. 2005), Europe (Gandy 2004), and Asia (Hanley 1987; McNeill and Winiwarter 2004; Xue 2005). The earliest document describing the application of night soil as a fertilizer appears in *Qi Min Yao Shu*, the first Chinese agricultural instruction book, written between 553 and 554 AD

(Jia and Huang 1977). During the Qing dynasty (1736–95 AD), night soil grew into such a prized agricultural resource that farmers not only sought out night soil for fertilization of their fields, but many also became involved in its sale and trade, traveling long distances to procure high-quality night soil (i.e., high in nitrogen and other nutrients) from wealthy, urban areas that had protein-rich diets (Xue 2005). Night soil depots or trading houses (*fenchang*) were even established to handle the collection, transport, treatment, and sale of night soil, with many farmers eventually abandoning their agricultural work in the late nineteenth and early twentieth century to become night soil traders instead. Until the 1970s, urban toilet cleaners still paid for the night soil they collected from residents' houses in southern Chinese provinces like Jiangnan (Xue 2005). By the mid to late twentieth century, however, the rise in adoption of chemical fertilizer along with growing concerns regarding night soil's role in the spread of diseases (see Kim et al. 2014) led to a drastic reduction in its use in Asia (Ferguson 2014). The large-scale abandonment of night soil in China mirrored a similar trend witnessed in Europe and North America nearly a century earlier.

Before the development of the modern hydraulic sanitation system, most European cities like London relied on night soil collectors to remove excrement from cesspits and privies. As in Asia, night soil was collected and then spread on agricultural fields in the rural countryside. With the growth in popularity of the flush toilet in the mid-nineteenth century, however, private toilets directed increasing volumes of water into urban cesspits, which considerably diluted night soil and diminished its value for agricultural application (Gandy 2004: 366). To complicate matters, the expansion of cities pushed night soil collectors greater distances to reach their markets in rural areas—not to mention that the cost of emptying a cesspit was double the daily wage of an average skilled laborer, which presented an additional obstacle to timely removal (Johnson 2006: 10). Together, these factors created the conditions for bacteriological disaster—between 1831 and 1866, Britain was ravaged by four distinct cholera epidemics due to the contamination of drinking wells.

At the time, there was much debate in Europe over the flushing of human feces into newly constructed sewer systems that were originally designed to handle urban storm water and that alone. Despite such debate, the idea of channeling human excrement into city sewers became the most practical option, especially since running water was not believed to be at serious risk of contamination (Benidickson 2011: 4). The model of the private flush toilet encouraged this "culture of flushing," sending urban wastes into underground tunnels and off into rivers and the open oceans. And so, the modern hydraulic sanitation system was born.

The spread of disease from feces leaking into drinking water is what spurred the adoption of the modern sanitation system, but it never fully addressed the problem of keeping human excrement out of water. Instead, it largely attempted to resolve it by flushing it further downstream, where it would become someone else's problem. For this reason, by the end of the nineteenth century and beginning of the twentieth, sewage treatment became the focus of intensive scientific inquiry (Schneider 2011). Some European cities, including Paris and Berlin, relied on "sewage farms"—open fields where urban excreta were applied—but the extensive tracts of land needed to sustain such operations led to alternative methods (Schneider 2011: 13). In the early twentieth century, a critical breakthrough occurred with the invention of the "activated sludge method." Under this new process, sewage was placed in aeration tanks with large populations of bacteria. As Daniel Schneider explains:

> After treating the sewage for just a few hours, the bacteria-rich sludge was allowed to settle out, cleansing the sewage of solids and leaving a clear effluent. Like a sourdough starter, some of the settled sludge was added back into the aeration tank to treat new sewage. The engineering press quickly heralded the activated sludge process, and cities around the world began to experiment with it.
>
> 2012: 172

But the problem still remained of what do with all the remaining residues.

American cities like Milwaukee and Chicago were quick to recognize the potential value of treated sludge as an agricultural amendment, and began to employ it as such. Many other metropolitan areas resorted to landfilling, incineration, or dumping into waterways. However, when the United States Congress passed the Clean Water Act in 1972 and then later the Ocean Dumping Ban Act in 1988, the disposal of sewage sludge into oceans and waterways was prohibited, and the use of sanitation sludge became more highly regulated (EPA 2019). As agronomists and soil scientists had argued before, the alternative solution appeared to be in the soil.

Biosolids: Their Regulation and Possibilities for Use on a "Damaged Planet"

The word "biosolids" was developed in the early 1990s by the Water Environment Federation as an attempt to rebrand sewage sludge and promote "beneficial use" of it, particularly as a soil amendment. The term was adopted by the US EPA in 1992, and it has stuck ever since. And there is a good reason for that: just say the word "biosolids" and let it hang in the air for a second or two. You can't even smell it, can you?

Part 503 of the United States Clean Water Act outlined the federal guidelines for the oversight and monitoring of agricultural use of sludge, including testing for nine heavy metals. Following those regulations, there are two distinguishable grades of biosolids: Class A and Class B (EPA 2019). In Class A biosolids, pathogens must be reduced to undetectable levels and strict standards are applied with regards to heavy metals and offensive odors. This class of biosolids can be applied to land without restrictions and is frequently sold as a fertilizer or compost to ordinary homeowners and gardeners. Many different US cities have marketed their own brands of Class A biosolids, including Milorganite from Milwaukee, TAGRO from Tacoma, Dillo Dirt from Austin, and Com-Til from Columbus.

In contrast, Class B biosolids undergo treatment and must meet the same regulations with regard to heavy metals, but they are allowed to contain marginal levels of detectable pathogens and odors. For this reason, they also require EPA permits for their use on agricultural lands. Still, many large-scale agricultural operations use Class B biosolids, particularly for the production of commodity crops like wheat, corn, and soy. Perhaps unsurprisingly, the use of Class B biosolids has generated the most public resistance.

While interviewing Tony,[2] an environmental chemist who has worked with biosolids across the United States for decades, I asked what he thought of the ongoing debates regarding the safety of using biosolids in agriculture. He admitted that at their onset, early biosolids might have had some "nasty stuff" in them. However, the EPA developed what he described as a "carrot-and-stick approach" by the early 1990s. "They said if you produce Class A biosolids, then the regulatory burden will be taken off your shoulders. If you don't, then we will regulate the hell out of you." And, according to Tony, it pretty much worked. Having studied metals in soils since the 1980s, all the biosolids are—in his words—"clean" today.

But what is more interesting, he added, is that while people are worried about all the things that end up in biosolids, they are often present at reduced amounts when compared to what people typically ingest or expose themselves to. Take triclosan, for example. Tony described it is a "pesticide," although I later found it to be identified as "an antimicrobial agent" (Bhargava and Leonard 1996). Regardless of its classification, it is a common ingredient in hand soap as well as toothpaste. Products like Colgate Total rely on triclosan to reduce plaque build-up on teeth, but it has been shown to pose possible health risks—including disruption of sex and thyroid hormones (Zorrilla et al. 2009). Triclosan is also suspected to contribute to broader bacterial resistance and the rise of so-called "superbugs." Tony laughed as he described attending meetings in which wastewater treatment plant managers berated executives from the multinational consumer goods corporation Procter & Gamble, demanding they take antibacterial agents out of soaps and other products because they messed with the ability of microbes in wastewater aeration tanks to "do their job." Tony conceded that triclosan is usually "shredded up" pretty quickly by microbes in wastewater treatment facilities, but it invites one to wonder: what other chemicals might be found in the sanitation system that are not so easily eaten up?

Before meeting with Tony, I had naïvely thought of biosolids as treated human excreta that served as agricultural fertilizer. But that is not really the case. When human excrement is channeled into a wastewater treatment plant, it is devoured by microbes. The resulting byproducts are largely constituted by the remains of those microbial bodies—in fact, Tony told me that the biomass in sludge actually *increases* during the wastewater treatment process. And, even before raw sewage enters into treatment, it is already so much more than just human excrement.[3] For a minute, think about all the things that people might put down their drains or toilets besides water and excrement: toilet paper, tissues, tampons, toothpaste, dental floss, baby wipes, shampoo, shaving creams, soap suds, matches, ashes, pet snakes, solvents, slimes, fats, grease, goldfish, paints, condoms, bleach . . . the list goes on and on. This does not even account for all the refuse dumped by businesses and manufacturers. Although we know and understand this, it is only on rare occasions that we reflect upon all the unwanted things that are channeled into the sanitation system, much less how they might complicate attempts at "closing the loop" in agricultural systems, or address the widening metabolic rift.

In recent years, Tony has been developing research at the southernmost edges of the city of Chicago, where he and others are hoping to bio-remediate old slag heaps at abandoned industrial sites using biosolid blends. Planting native grass species into what he describes as a "biosolids dream treatment," he and his colleagues are seeking to build a different model of ecological restoration for a less-than-pristine world. Already, in several different areas of the eastern United States, old strip mines are being rehabilitated with deep row hybrid poplar plantations that are fertilized with biosolids (Felix et al. 2008). Trenches are dug into the denuded lands and large seams of biosolids are deposited before bare-root poplars are planted above. Over time, the root systems of the trees break through the rocky land, while drawing from the nutrient-rich biosolids. In six to nine years, the poplars can be harvested and made into mulch. Prior to their harvest, they can help rebuild the soil and reduce run-off from the site. While biosolids might not be perfect or "pure," Tony and others reason that they offer significant opportunities for reclaiming otherwise severely degraded lands.[4]

The edited volume *Arts of Living on a Damaged Planet* (Tsing et al. 2017) highlights the tensions inherent to such ventures as the ones undertaken by Tony and his colleagues in this time of ecological crisis. In the introduction to that volume, Elaine Gan and colleagues (2017) argue that today we are living in the midst of haunted landscapes that carry vestiges of past ways of life, including the ruins of an earlier industrial era and species now extinct. But, the authors note that present landscapes are simultaneously haunted by imagined futures and "dreamworlds of progress" (Gan et al. 2017: G2). By rehabilitating slag heaps and strip mines—wasted landscapes borne out of the modern industrial push for progress—it is difficult to discern whether the application of biosolids today represents an opportunity to make up for past mistakes, or instead serves to reinvigorate the same technoscientific optimism that will ultimately yield the same (toxic) results. Framed somewhat differently, one might ask: is the adoption of biosolids in ecological rehabilitation part of a new model for thinking about environmental sustainability on a damaged planet, or is it nothing more than an attempt to squeeze profit out of its accumulated ruins?

To understand the challenges of mending the metabolic rift today—and the role of biosolids in urban ecologies and contemporary agricultural production—I decided before venturing any further to look into the site of biosolids production in the city where I live.

Biosolids Production and the Problems of Purity

"It's not shit anymore," Rachel said plainly. We were driving through the facility where the City of Columbus produced its compost known as Com-Til, derived from treated sanitation sludge and wood mulch. It was the dead of winter and steam was rising off the piles as the thermophilic microbes did their work

I asked Rachel if the taboo surrounding human waste made Com-Til a difficult product to market. "Fifteen years ago, it was a harder sell. People have a foothold now," she told me. Part of this she attributed to interest in kombucha and probiotics. "There's a cultural swell," she said, "that's focusing more attention on the importance of healthy microbial populations both in our bodies and in the soils."

Figure 9.1 A pile of Com-Til—composted woodchips and biosolids from the City of Columbus, Ohio—releases steam as thermophilic microbes "do their work." Photo by Nicholas C. Kawa.

With the "intestine of the city," she told me, "we can create a story." The story that Rachel wanted people to understand is how microbiota circulate from bathrooms into the wastewater system to rendered sludge, then to Com-Til and then back to the soil, hopefully to make food. "Composting waste and using it for agriculture," Rachel continued on, "everyone is contributing to the cycle. YOU are helping close the carbon cycle, YOU are helping close the phosphorus cycle, YOU are helping close the potassium cycle." In this way, people can begin to see their role in this broader ecology, she insisted.

In 2017, the City of Columbus achieved 100% beneficial use of its sanitation sludge. Now, it directs biosolids into the compost program but also does liquid land application of Class B biosolids, working with large commodity-crop farmers. It also supports hybrid poplar production in eastern Ohio, and some of the sludge even goes to biodigestors for energy production. But Rachel added that there were still limits—both legal and cultural—to the acceptance and application of biosolids. "What kind of hurts my heart is that you can't sell this as an organic amendment." She shared that she had bought lots of organic food in the past, but she also saw how the vision of organic farming could become restrictive, especially in its obsession with—in her words—"its own purity."

"Does this have triclosan in it? Yes, probably it does. But," she argued, "organic farmers really have to hustle to get their needs met when it comes to building healthy organic matter in the soil." And Class A biosolids could be a way to do that, she indicated. But the concern over purity remained.

"Is it [Com-Til] pure? No. Is it pretty damn good? Yes," she insisted. "What's pure anyways? It's like a how-many-angels-on-the-head-of-a-pin question. If you take it from the perspective of 'what's our best option?', it's a pretty damn good option," Rachel concluded.

In her book *Against Purity*, Alexis Shotwell observes: "To be against purity is ... not to be for pollution, harm, sickness, or premature death. It is to be against the rhetorical or conceptual attempt to delineate and delimit the world into something separable, disentangled, and homogenous" (2016: 15). Similarly, Rachel insinuated that the ideals of purity in organic agricultural production had their own dangers, or at the very least, they could stand in the way of pragmatic forms of sustainable resource management, including the use of biosolids as a soil amendment. More than just a source of fertilization, Rachel pointed out that biosolids could help return much-needed organic matter to soils that had suffered from erosion and even contribute to soil health by bolstering soil microbial populations. Her comments, along with those of contemporary social theorists like Shotwell, seemed to demand recognition that we live in a world that is deeply compromised, and yet that should not stop us from trying to make it more livable, despite the inevitable flaws in any of our designs. This also suggested that attempts to mend the metabolic rift should be stripped free of any romanticized notions about returning to a time of living in "equilibrium with nature." Clearly, the conditions of late industrialism are far different from those of only a few hundred years ago, and as such, they require negotiation with a whole series of different questions, concerns, and modern messes that are not so easily cleaned up or straightened out (Fortun 2014). Yes, triclosan and PFOAs and PCBs run through the waste stream, as do Viagra, Xanax, Prozac, Vicodin, and many other pharmaceuticals and personal care products that individuals consume and excrete. But with a growing ecological crisis before us, Rachel and many others working with biosolids reason that we simply cannot afford to hide from our waste anymore.

Back to the Land: Biosolids Application and Attempts to "Close the Loop"

To see what the use of biosolids could do on a large agricultural scale, Rachel had recommended that I visit the state of Washington where efforts to promote biosolids were—in her words—"years ahead" of the American Midwest. In August of 2017, when I happened to be traveling through Seattle, the King County Biosolids Program graciously offered to take me on a day-long tour of their operation in Mansfield (more than three hours away by car from Seattle), where they had been working with dryland wheat farmers for decades.

Amy from the program picked me up just before 6:00 am at a coffee shop on the outskirts of downtown Seattle. On our way out of town, I asked her about the emergent issues in biosolids that she had been tracking. She listed off bans in the northeastern United States and new concerns about PFOAs (perfluorooctanoic acids) in sludge.

There had also been attempts to ban biosolids in Kern County (southern California), but they ultimately failed. And, she said, there was a lot of controversy over biosolids in neighboring Canada.

In response, I asked Amy about what they had been doing to attempt to change public perception or bring attention to the beneficial use of biosolids. "We try to use more social media, but often get trolled online, and our partners do too, so it's kind of a disincentive to promote the work," she shared. But they also do other things. Currently, King County has an urban farm at a treatment site that relies strictly on biosolids for fertilization. The program also hosts a dinner during Seattle's Local Food Week with food produced with biosolids. But, in general, Amy observed that "hardcore gardeners are a lot more accepting" of biosolids than the populace at large.

After picking up three additional team members—James, Alan, and Susan—the team gave me a background on the history of the King County Biosolids Program. James informed that in the late 1980s, King County had wanted to diversify beyond the use of biosolids in forestry and hoped to find a location to do agricultural application. They held a public meeting in Grant County (eastern Washington State), and there one individual spoke up. He thought it wouldn't be right for him, but it might be useful to his brother. Not long after, the brother and two other men decided to give biosolids a shot—later, becoming known as "the Big Three" in the local farming community. They started with a 5,000-acre test plot of wheat, and that year it outperformed conventional fertilizer in total yield. Today, they and others work with biosolids on 100,000 acres of land, and more than 100 landowners are involved in all.

But despite their success, there is still resistance. In neighboring Lincoln County, some farmers at higher elevation—who produce mostly dryland grain crops—were interested in adopting biosolids, but organic fruit and vegetable farmers situated at lower elevations were "freaking out," James said. Nearby in Kittitas County, one citizen opposition group with the acronym CRAP even formed to protest biosolids use.

"You get resistance from the same four 'antis' [private citizens against biosolids] who always say that if you use biosolids the world is gonna end," Susan chimed in. One locally vocal critic was even caught trespassing at their operation in Mansfield, although they joked that they were happy to let him take some biosolids home with him. "He claims that Snoqualmie Pass Forest application is affecting Puget Sound forty miles out and that it's killing the rabbits!" Susan continued. "It's a 'toxic brew,' the antis all say!"

Despite the occasional outburst of the naysayers, 82% of biosolids are land applied in the state of Washington. In fact, biosolids are required to be directed to beneficial use in the state. Only in scenarios where land application is not possible does landfilling or incineration occur. Susan said that following the Clean Water Act, the state came to the realization that "what was toxic to a river was beneficial to land." But communicating this key point to the public was largely lost, she told me. In front of us, a truck carrying biosolids from Seattle suggestively advertised its product with the catchphrase "Turn your dirt around."

When we reached Mansfield, we joined up with Dan, who managed their operations there. He reiterated that there were over 100 landowners and farmers involved. Dan explained to me that dryland wheat is produced every other year (one year in production and one year left fallow). Best management practices dictate that the application of biosolids occurs only once every four years. The second crop in the rotation is often able to capture residual nitrogen from biosolids in the soil, he explained.

Switching gears, Dan acknowledged that there were still some landowners and farmers in the area who didn't want to get involved. "Some don't want it—they see the gremlins," he commented wryly. But there were also cases in which landowners convinced farmers renting their land to adopt it. To put it plainly, he said: "[If you] hate biosolids, [then you] don't want the money." In other words, Dan contended that farmers who avoided biosolids had missed an opportunity to increase the profitability of their operations.

Originally, King County paid farmers in the area fifteen dollars per acre to till biosolids into the soil. Since then, the initiative has grown, and farmers now pay for the fertilizer. Dan summarized: "It's all about the money for the farmers . . . especially for the younger, poorer farmers. The older guys [still] have some cookie jar money."

But it is also about more than just the economics. "Are there noticeable improvements to the tilth?" I asked. "Oh yeah," Dan responded, "especially the no-till guys. Lots of organics [soil organic matter], which is what they want." Over the last few decades, more and more American farmers have adopted no-till management as a soil conservation practice, which requires farmers to abstain from tilling the land to minimize soil disturbance and erosion. Dan said about half of those with whom they worked had gone to no-till, particularly as government subsidies were made available. Alan, the soil scientist on their team, shared that other research had shown that biosolids application could help increase carbon sequestration, particularly when applied in conjunction with continuous no-till management (Spargo et al. 2008). And Dan said that the application of biosolids appeared to boost soil microbial health, which helped to break down the stubble left from the previous cropping cycle when farmers practiced no-till.

Dan showed me a photo hanging on his office wall that was taken at a nearby farm. A strikingly clear line could be seen between the land that received biosolids application and land that did not. Dan explained that the field where biosolids were applied had no remaining wheat stubble from the previous cropping cycle, likely due to higher microbial activity in the soil, while the adjacent field still had rows of old wheat stalks waiting to decompose. "See, clear line between 'poop' and 'no poop,'" he joked. "I'm a salesman—you know a lie. But the plants don't lie to you."

Of course, biosolids surface application can present problems too. One of the primary concerns among farmers was soil compaction. With large spreaders used to haul and disperse dried biosolids across the land, the heavy machinery can compact the soils. This can compromise the soil structure by reducing pore space and limiting the overall soil volume. Compacted soils also require plants' roots to work harder to penetrate compacted layers. But Dan argued that the concerns over compaction were overblown and the economics of biosolids outweighed any downsides in the end. "What's the difference between a 747 [jet airplane] and a farmer?" Dan asked, flashing a grin. "The 747 quits whining when it gets to Hawai'i."

Near the end of our tour, Dan took us to a field where Class B biosolids were being applied. The land was dry and large dust storms had begun to kick up. "God only waters

Figure 9.2 A photograph that demonstrates the difference that biosolids application can make. Photo by Nicholas C. Kawa.

here every once in a while," he observed. Nearby, several different piles of biosolids were mounded up, each marked with a different sign that indicated a point of origin. For example, the city of Alderwood, a wealthy community in the Seattle metropolitan area, produced a high-quality Class A product, but because the city was not interested in marketing it independently, it was used in Mansfield along with the other Class B material. Most other cities, however, did not produce the same high-quality material. Dan informed that they worked with over thirty cities in Washington State, which each generated biosolids with distinct nutrient contents and qualities. For that reason, they were required to make calculations to determine the appropriate rate of application for each batch of biosolids. Four tons of biosolids from some cities could be equivalent to three tons of material from others in terms of total nitrogen. It quickly became apparent that not all biosolids were created equally.

On our last stop, flies swarmed around a particularly ripe pile of biosolids and then followed us back into Dan's suburban. As we swatted the flies, Dan acknowledged that between them and the dust, application was not always pretty. But, at least for him and many of the farmers in Mansfield, it seemed to be working well enough. And there was something to be said for that.

Figure 9.3 A large mound of Class B biosolids are hauled across a future dryland wheat field near Mansfield, Washington. Photo by Nicholas C. Kawa.

After leaving Washington, I wondered what Dan and the farmers of Mansfield might have to say about their work in relation to the metabolic rift. Did they see themselves as fighting back against the trends of soil degradation—including the mining of soil nutrients as well as the loss of topsoil—that began during industrialization? Or did they simply understand themselves as savvy businessmen capitalizing on an opportunity in an increasingly competitive agricultural market? Or perhaps they stood somewhere in between? My hosts from the King County Biosolids Program argued that the use of biosolids in the state of Washington is a win-win for farmers and their soils. By this they meant that farmers are able to take advantage of a soil amendment that not only offers macro- and micronutrients at an affordable cost but also contributes vital organic matter to soils otherwise prone to weathering and erosion. After visiting with Dan and others in Mansfield, it was hard not to see things from this vantage point. But part of me still had questions. And, yes, maybe even some doubts too.

Conclusions

Anthropological investigations into contemporary soil management—and the use of biosolids in particular—might not offer a clear vision for the future of sustainable agriculture in the United States, or elsewhere. However, such investigations can help to scrutinize the systems and resources that enable agricultural production under the conditions of late industrialism. The case of biosolids, for example, helps draw attention to the compromises that late industrialism demands between idealized models of sustainable agricultural management and more practical strategies that are accessible but plagued by uncertainties, including the long-term impacts of industrial compounds (from triclosan to PFOAs) on the microbiota that sustain agricultural lands.

Through my interviews and visits with wastewater treatment professionals, soil scientists, and others involved with biosolids production and application in Washington State and the American Midwest, I have come to see the expanding use of biosolids as encouraging productive futures for human "waste" by returning valuable nutrients and organic matter back to agricultural lands that have suffered from soil erosion, nutrient depletion, and losses in microbial health. However, it is also apparent that this soil amendment can open the door for a vast array of other substances and wastes—from chemical compounds in personal care products to residual pharmaceutical agents—to be redirected and concentrated in agricultural landscapes. At the end of 2018, the EPA released a report that reignited concerns surrounding the safety of biosolids (EPA 2018). The report highlighted 352 unregulated chemical compounds in the waste stream that can persist in biosolids and might ultimately pose some risks for environmental and public health. Because there are so many unknowns regarding the waste stream, there are just as many (if not more) concerning the treatment and application of biosolids. For now, the questions will remain.

Regardless of the ultimate fate of biosolids in American agriculture, more sustained and systematic examinations of the waste stream can have other important consequences for addressing the metabolic rift. If the potential value of human excrement as an agricultural resource is severely compromised by triclosan or PFOAs or other unregulated chemical compounds, then this may serve to amplify the problems posed by these toxicants that are already ubiquitous in the lives of consumers. In such a way, the anthropological study of soil and how we sustain it under late industrialism can force a broader rethinking of industrial ecosystems and their management. If the current system does not allow for the viable production of agricultural fertilizer from bodily excreta (human or otherwise), then we should ask what conditions need to be in place to develop systems that can.

As Marx argued nearly 150 years ago, industrial capitalism turned human excrement from an agricultural resource into a source of waste. Ironically, biosolids may prove to be profitable under the conditions of late industrialism, but how they can be employed to reverse trends of the metabolic rift as outlined by Marxian scholars is a far greater challenge. Despite many unanswered questions lingering, there is a growing recognition that our bodily substances are necessary elements of our socioecological systems, and that we simply cannot hide from our waste anymore. Perhaps in learning to live with our wastes, we might come to more critically assess the broader industrial ecologies in which they circulate.

Notes

1   As noted in the Introduction, John Bellamy Foster (1999) was the first to explicitly
articulate this notion of the metabolic rift. Since then, Jason W. Moore (2011) and
many others have expanded this line of Marxian ecological thinking. However,
Schneider and McMichael (2010) have critiqued the idea that the metabolic rift is
solely rooted in the disruption of nutrient cycling from human bodies to agricultural
lands. They note that some forms of capitalist agriculture could be deemed
ecologically sustainable—such as eighteenth-century English high farming that relied
on crop rotation with sheep manuring—even while they were socially exploitative.
Conversely, there are many examples of precapitalist societies that practiced
unsustainable forms of land use that mined nutrients from the soil. The point that
Schneider and McMichael ultimately make is that agricultural practice itself demands
consideration in any examination of the metabolic rift. In this chapter, I specifically
focus on the use of human excreta as a source of fertilization in contemporary
capitalist agriculture in the United States, but I also take into consideration the
agricultural practices that enable its use.
2   The names of all individuals interviewed have been replaced with pseudonyms.
3   It is arguable whether human excreta is even largely "human," since it is mostly
composed of diverse microbial bodies that inhabit the human gut. Walker and Granjou
(2017) make this point explicit in their study of the European Space Agency program
known as MELiSSA, which is working through the tricky problem of managing human
"waste" in space along with all of the microbial bodies that thrive in the human gut.
4   Soil scientific research has shown that biosolids application can improve soil structure
and soil porosity while also increasing soil organic carbon on degraded lands
(García-Orenes et al. 2005; Tian et al. 2009). In New Mexico, a study by Aguilar and
Loftin (1992) demonstrated that biosolids were more effective at restoring degraded
rangelands suffering from soil erosion and nutrient depletion due to overgrazing than
rangeland management through natural regeneration (i.e., by removing cattle).
Biosolids have also been effective in land reclamation, particularly for reestablishing
vegetation on lands degraded by extensive mining activity (Brown et al. 2003).

References

Aguilar, R. and S. R. Loftin (1992), "Sewage Sludge Application in Semiarid Grasslands:
Effects on Runoff and Surface Water Quality," in C. T. Ortega Klett (ed.), *Proceedings:
36th Annual New Mexico Water Conference; Agencies and Science Working for the
Future*, Report No. 265, 101–11, Las Cruces, NM: New Mexico Water Resources
Research Institute.

Basta, N. T., ed. (1995), "Land Application of Biosolids: A Review of Research Concerning
Benefits, Environmental Impacts, and Regulations of Applying Treated Sewage Sludge,"
No. B-808, Oklahoma Agricultural Experiment Station and Center for Agriculture and
the Environment, Division of Agricultural Sciences and Natural Resources, Oklahoma
State University [http://factsheets.okstate.edu/wp-content/uploads/2017/05/B-808.pdf].

Becerril, J. E. and B. Jiménez (2007), "Potable Water and Sanitation in Tenochtitlan: Aztec
Culture," *Water Science and Technology: Water Supply*, 7 (1): 147–54.

Benidickson, J. (2011), *The Culture of Flushing: A Social and Legal History of Sewage*,
Vancouver, BC: UBC Press.

Bhargava, H. N. and P. A. Leonard (1996), "Triclosan: Applications and Safety," *American Journal of Infection Control*, 24 (3): 209–18.

Birk, J. J., W. G. Teixeira, E. G. Neves, and B. Glaser (2011), "Faeces Deposition on Amazonian Anthrosols as Assessed from 5β-Stanols," *Journal of Archaeological Science*, 38 (6): 1209–20.

Blanchette, A. (2019), "Living Waste and the Labor of Toxic Health on American Factory Farms," *Medical Anthropology Quarterly*, 33 (1): 80–100.

Brown, S. L., C. L. Henry, R. Chaney, H. Compton, and P. S. DeVolder (2003), "Using Municipal Biosolids in Combination with Other Residuals to Restore Metal-Contaminated Mining Areas," *Plant and Soil*, 249 (1): 203–15.

Cofie, O., G. Kranjac-Berisavljevic, and P. Drechsel (2005), "The Use of Human Waste for Peri-urban Agriculture in Northern Ghana," *Renewable Agriculture and Food Systems*, 20 (2): 73–80.

Cordell, D., A. Rosemarin, J. J. Schröder, and A. L. Smit (2011), "Towards Global Phosphorus Security: A Systems Framework for Phosphorus Recovery and Reuse Options," *Chemosphere*, 84 (6): 747–58.

Environmental Protection Agency (EPA) (2018), "EPA Unable to Assess the Impact of Hundreds of Unregulated Pollutants in Land-Applied Biosolids on Human Health and the Environment," Report 19-P-0002, Washington, DC: EPA Office of Inspector General [https://www.epa.gov/sites/production/files/2018-11/documents/_epaoig_20181115-19-p-0002.pdf].

Environmental Protection Agency (EPA) (2019), "Frequent Questions about Biosolids" [https://www.epa.gov/biosolids/frequent-questions-about-biosolids].

Felix, E., D. R. Tilley, G. Felton, and E. Flamino (2008), "Biomass Production of Hybrid Poplar (*Populus* sp.) Grown on Deep-Trenched Municipal Biosolids," *Ecological Engineering*, 33 (1): 8–14.

Ferguson, D. T. (2014), "Nightsoil and the 'Great Divergence': Human Waste, the Urban Economy, and Economic Productivity, 1500–1900," *Journal of Global History*, 9 (3): 379–402.

Fortun, K. (2014), "From Latour to Late Industrialism," *HAU: Journal of Ethnographic Theory*, 4 (1): 309–29.

Foster, J. B. (1999), "Marx's Theory of Metabolic Rift: Classical Foundations for Environmental Sociology," *American Journal of Sociology*, 105 (2): 366–405.

Gan, E., N. Bubandt, A. L. Tsing, and H. A. Swanson (2017), "Introduction: Haunted Landscapes of the Anthropocene," in A.L. Tsing, H.A. Swanson, E. Gan, and N. Bubandt (eds.), *Arts of Living on a Damaged Planet: Ghosts and Monsters of the Anthropocene*, G1–G14, Minneapolis, MN: University of Minnesota Press.

Gandy, M. (2004), "Rethinking Urban Metabolism: Water, Space and the Modern City," *City*, 8 (3): 363–79.

García-Orenes, F., C. Guerrero, J. Mataix-Solera, J. Navarro-Pedreño, I. Gómez, and J. Mataix-Beneyto (2005), "Factors Controlling the Aggregate Stability and Bulk Density in Two Different Degraded Soils Amended with Biosolids," *Soil and Tillage Research*, 82 (1): 65–76.

Hanley, S. B. (1987), "Urban Sanitation in Preindustrial Japan," *Journal of Interdisciplinary History*, 18 (1): 1–26.

Hawkins, G. (2002), "Down the Drain: Shit and the Politics of Disturbance," *UTS Review*, 7 (2): 32–42.

Jia, S. and P. Huang (1977), *Qi Min Yao Shu*, Zhongguo Zixue Mingzhu Jicheng Bianyin Jijinhui.

Johnson, S. (2006), *The Ghost Map: The Story of London's Most Terrifying Epidemic—and How It Changed Science, Cities, and the Modern World*, London: Penguin.

Kawa, N. C. (2016), "What Happens When We Flush?," *Anthropology Now*, 8 (2): 34–43.

Kim, M. J., H. C. Ki, S. Kim, J.-Y. Chai, M. Seo, C. S. Oh et al. (2014), "Parasitic Infection Patterns Correlated with Urban–Rural Recycling of Night Soil in Korea and Other East Asian Countries: The Archaeological and Historical Evidence," *Korean Studies*, 38: 51–74.

LeBlanc, R. J., P. Matthews, and R. P. Richard (2009), *Global Atlas of Excreta, Wastewater Sludge, and Biosolids Management: Moving Forward the Sustainable and Welcome Uses of a Global Resource*, HS/1030/08E, Nairobi: UN-Habitat.

Marx, K. (1979), *Capital*, Vol. 1, New York: International Publishers.

Marx, K. (1999), *Capital*, Vol. 3, New York: International Publishers.

McNeill, J. R. and V. Winiwarter (2004), "Breaking the Sod: Humankind, History, and Soil," *Science*, 304 (5677): 1627–29.

Moore, J. W. (2011), "Transcending the Metabolic Rift: A Theory of Crises in the Capitalist World-Ecology," *Journal of Peasant Studies*, 38 (1): 1–46.

Schneider, D. (2011), *Hybrid Nature: Sewage Treatment and the Contradictions of the Industrial Ecosystem*, Cambridge, MA: MIT Press.

Schneider, D. (2012), "Purification or Profit: Milwaukee and the Contradictions of Sludge," in S. Foote and E. Mazzolini (eds.), *Histories of the Dustheap: Waste, Material Cultures, Social Justice*, 171–97, Cambridge, MA: MIT Press.

Schneider, M. and P. McMichael (2010), "Deepening, and Repairing, the Metabolic Rift," *Journal of Peasant Studies*, 37 (3): 461–84.

Shotwell, A. (2016), *Against Purity: Living Ethically in Compromised Times*, Minneapolis, MN: University of Minnesota Press.

Snyder, C. (2005), "The Dirty Work of Promoting 'Recycling' of America's Sewage Sludge," *International Journal of Occupational and Environmental Health*, 11 (4): 415–27.

Spargo, J. T., M. M. Alley, R. F. Follett, and J. V. Wallace (2008), "Soil Carbon Sequestration with Continuous No-Till Management of Grain Cropping Systems in the Virginia Coastal Plain," *Soil and Tillage Research*, 100 (1/2): 133–40.

Tian, G., T. C. Granato, A. E. Cox, R. I. Pietz, C. R. Carlson, and Z. Abedin (2009), "Soil Carbon Sequestration Resulting from Long-Term Application of Biosolids for Land Reclamation," *Journal of Environmental Quality*, 38 (1): 61–74.

Tsing, A. L. (2015), *The Mushroom at the End of the World: On the Possibility of Life in Capitalist Ruins*, Princeton, NJ: Princeton University Press.

Tsing, A. L., H. A. Swanson, E. Gan, and N. Bubandt (2017), *Arts of Living on a Damaged Planet: Ghosts and Monsters of the Anthropocene*, Minneapolis, MN: University of Minnesota Press.

Van Der Geest, S. (2002), "The Night-Soil Collector: Bucket Latrines in Ghana," *Postcolonial Studies*, 5 (2): 197–206.

Walker, J. and C. Granjou (2017), "MELiSSA the Minimal Biosphere: Human Life, Waste and Refuge in Deep Space," *Futures*, 92: 59–69.

Wark, M. (2015), *Molecular Red: Theory for the Anthropocene*, New York: Verso Books.

Xue, Y. (2005), "'Treasure Nightsoil as if It were Gold': Economic and Ecological Links between Urban and Rural Areas in Late Imperial Jiangnan," *Late Imperial China*, 26 (1): 41–71.

Zorrilla, L. M., E. K. Gibson, S. C. Jeffay, K. M. Crofton, W. R. Setzer, R. L. Cooper et al. (2009), "The Effects of Triclosan on Puberty and Thyroid Hormones in Male Wistar Rats," *Toxicological Sciences*, 107 (1): 56–64.

10

Reclaiming Freak Soils: From Conquering to Journeying with Urban Soils

Germain Meulemans

Introduction: Ecological Narratives of Conquest

November 2014. We are in the middle of St-Blaise district in eastern Paris, a low-income neighborhood, and one of the most densely populated in Europe. A shy summer's heat soothes the square of La Réunion. It is early in the afternoon, and the sounds of the weekly market dissipate as the stallholders fold up their stands one after the other. As they tidy up, they bring stacks of fruits, vegetables, and plants to a big pile of broken trays and cardboard boxes. It's a mound of leftovers, all the groceries that were too damaged, too rotten, or too ugly to be sold. From the heap emanates the characteristic smell of early fermentation processes as bacteria kick-start into action under the auspices of the afternoon sunbeams. The acetone smell of overripe mangoes soon merges with that of fermenting tomato juices and rotten onions. Several of the district's inhabitants have gathered on the market place to glean their weekly groceries from among the recoverable items. They are soon joined by wasps, and a timid rat sometimes furtively enters the scene to catch its share. Léo jokes as he hands me a box of spinach: "You smell that? It's the smell of very young compost." Unlike our fellow gatherers, we are here to get not only food but also "organic matter" to build soil for a garden Léo has started—or should I say "cleared"?— on a nearby section of the Petite Ceinture, an abandoned railway that is home to homeless people and migrants, and as many plant and animal species as are found in the woodlands that circle the city. I have come here to learn soil-building techniques with the gardeners. Today, we gather rotten vegetables. Tomorrow, it will be fallen leaves or the wooden planks of discarded pieces of furniture. All these will be brought back to the ceinture's garden to continue transforming its hard ground into soil.

* * *

My encounter with Léo and the *ceinture*'s garden took place at a specific turning point in my doctoral research. In November 2013, I had begun fieldwork in Paris at an abandoned industrial site in eastern France to research "urban soil science." The urban soil sciences are an emerging technoscientific trope that aims at guiding the ways in which soils should be protected, managed, and even "made" in cities (Lehmann and Stahr 2007; Morel et al. 2015). For thirteen months, I interviewed most of the soil scientists and technicians involved in researching these urban soils in France, and had followed them in their daily research work in laboratories and experimental zones as they dug the soil in search of "aggregates" and "collaborated" with earthworms to grow fertile soil in controlled conditions (Meulemans 2020).

Unlike previous generations of soil scientists, these researchers' goal was not to describe and classify these soils but to grow artificial soils that could mimic and improve the functioning of natural soils, and implement these made soils within and around cities to carry out "functions" that natural soils could no longer carry out. These included water filtration and retention, heat mitigation, and hosting vigorous urban biodiversity. Scientists working on the development of these synthetic soils were often soil ecologists rather than more traditional pedologists, and they were convinced that soils were a living entity. In the last twenty-five years, soil has increasingly come to be seen as a lively compound. It has now become common to write about "the living soil"—an expression used as a motto by defenders of an ecological approach to soil (Gobat et al. 2004). In 2015, the Food and Agriculture Organization's International Year of Soils initiative showcased the idea that once soil is understood by the wider public as a living compound rather than an inert substrate, more ethical and careful relations with it would ensue (FAO 2015).

Like most contemporary ecologists that engage in the study or restoration of anthropogenic environments, urban soil scientists are wary of misplacing nature as an unchanging "out there." They refuse the tenacious idea of there being a "balance of nature." Instead, to them, ecosystems are inherently changing and processual realities that always intertwine with human becomings. Because human projects and ecosystem processes entangle, the latter cannot be enframed, as with the old modernist tropes of "controlling nature" through territorial intervention, but can only be "followed" (Pickering and Guzik 2008). Furthermore, since human interventions can neither appeal to a great outside of nature nor ignore the possibility of unintended consequences, they can only consist in open-ended "real-world experiments" (Gross and Hoffmann-Riem 2005) that invent new combinations between engineering and care. As Bruno Latour has summarized in a memorable few words: "It is as though we had to imagine Prometheus stealing fire from heaven in a cautious way!" (2008: 4).

As I witnessed the ways in which the urban soil sciences were swiftly addressing the challenge of caring for anthropogenic soils, it quickly appeared to me that their claim to further human "management" of soils and their "services" often boiled down to an extension of green technologies and markets to soils. Ecologists' practices of soil construction were indifferent to social or political matters, and often fell quite in line with a capitalistic understanding of the world, with young researchers getting their soil mixtures patented at the end of their PhDs, and the waste and construction industries designated as its principal allies, in the idea of improving the "territorial metabolism" (Barles 2015) of cities.

Through the trope of "making better soils than nature" also came the age-old hylomorphism that places human will or agency as the modeler of inert nature or ecologies in need of taking up a better form. Scientists often spoke of "reconquering" wastelands and biodiversity, and occasionally described themselves as heirs to Middle-Age land-clearer monks, and their conquest of new agricultural land over the environing wasteland. These narratives connect to well-known stories of frontier pioneers, industrialization, and progress that have been used across the ages to justify the shattering of local ecologies and cultures in the name of improving the productive capacity of landscapes in so many places. They were yet another story that staged humans as lords of creation.

To me, this revealed how narratives of care can subtend appropriative or colonizing practices in ways that are not always easy to detect at first. Susan Leigh Star's (1990) warning to always ask oneself the crucial question *Cui bono?* comes in handy here. Who does this benefit? And who does this harm? As Tom van Dooren (2016) notes in the context of conservation, "care" for endangered species can sometimes justify a lot of violence to other species or people, or render such violence invisible. Could scientists' claims of caring for the soil come into tension with other, more local care practices regarding urban soils? Can we think of building and reclaiming soils in ways that do not necessarily foreground human dominance and mastery?

In this chapter, I address these questions by attending to the practices of Léo and Henri, a pair of activist gardeners who reclaim urban wasteland by (re)building soil in these places. I concentrate on a railway brownfield site which they have turned into a school for themselves and others, a place to learn about and experiment with the kind of life and spirit that thrives in the city's cracks—the very life that discourses of ecological conquest fail to acknowledge. In this, I follow Bettina Stoetzer's proposal to attend to ruderal worlds (and their soils) in order to redirect ethnographic attention toward "often unnoticed, cosmopolitan yet precarious ways of remaking the urban fabric" (2018: 297), and thereby help us think about how we might inhabit an urbanized world.

In the first two sections that follow, I suggest that these practices can be inspiring for a critical and ecologically informed ethnography of relationships between soils and people in cities. Indeed, these gardeners have become experts in following urban materials and lives as they coalesce into the soil, indicating an ecological understanding of soil processes that does not disconnect the material and human histories that make and unmake the city. Because of this, they guide us through marginalized lives and landscapes that tell alternative stories than those of progress and green policing.

Then, in the following two sections, I examine the ways in which the gardeners help soil grow on the railway brownfield where Henri used to live. My aim is to show that these techniques not only are imaginative and highly sensitive to the fragile entanglements that make life possible, they also radically depart from a managerial conquering impetus by placing the emphasis on the shared creativity of people, other organisms and materials. Indeed, these urban gardeners do not view themselves as managers of soil assemblages. Rather, they *participate* in forms of creativity that encompass more than just human invention, and that bring forth new reciprocal functionalities between people, organisms, and materials. The practices they explore make worlds where soil's entangled lines may thrive, and help us understand soils as fellow beings to learn from rather than as spaces for occupation or extraction. I conclude by providing some reflections on how these gardeners' work can help us inform ecological thinking and cultural theory.

A Bootleg Garden on Old Train Tracks

Because of the ambiguities of ecologists' "careful experimentations," I decided, in October 2014, to return to Paris to interview actors in the waste management sector who were pushing to develop "made soils" as a new commodity in the sector of construction materials. This is when I met Léo Nguyen Van Thé, by chance, sitting next to each other at a conference on the recycling of urban waste. Léo describes himself alternatively as "a gardener and dry-stone wall builder" and as "someone in between a gardener and a forager." He immediately told me about a derelict train station where he was building a garden. As Natasha Myers notes, "gardens are crucial sites for examining the more-than-human dimensions of social, political and economic life, offering profound insights into forms of governance, political economy and ecology, industry, labor, and more" (2019: 126). As we spoke, however, I understood that the place he was talking about was just concrete and gravel and that he was actually building soil there. The more I learned about Léo's soil-building project for his garden, the more I became intrigued by this place that both related to and departed from the ecologists' reclaiming projects. For six months, I regularly returned to Paris and met Léo, and our friendship continued to develop after the end of my PhD. I regularly went with him to local markets or public gardens to gather organic waste and grow soil in ways rather different from the ones I had encountered with the soil ecologists.

Léo was trained in the city school of gardening as a garden worker, after which he worked for several years for the city council and private landscaping businesses. During this period, he mowed lawns, watered flower beds, and was exposed to pesticides on several occasions. In parallel with this, he explored the city and started to gather the weeds he was paid to get rid of and plant them elsewhere. He started to participate in spontaneous neighborhood projects inspired by the Food Not Lawns[1] movement, in which inhabitants turned the well-tended lawns of their social housing estates into permaculture gardens. The authorities, however, did not approve of these unsolicited reclaiming practices and wanted the lawns to remain lawns. The gardens were soon dismantled, and the gardeners were fined. Léo remembers this time as one during which he became growingly angry at mainstream gardening practices and the way they framed urban nature simply as a pleasant backdrop, without any possibility of touching or relating to it more meaningfully. He became involved in local guerilla gardening groups and left his job in 2012 to participate in the opening of several community gardening projects. As he moved away from the traditions for well-tended gardens he had been trained in, he opened or helped open both legal and illegal gardens in several places within the city, and started to work with "freak soils"—his name for the local polluted brownfield soils —and the ruderal[2] plants that thrive in these areas.

Léo met Henri Taïb in 2012. Henri is an artist. Between the late 1990s and 2017, he lived in a decommissioned *ceinture* train station and transformed it into a place open for artistic and cultural experiments. The train station was once part of the *Petite Ceinture*—literally the "little belt"—a 32-kilometer long circular railway connection around Paris that was progressively abandoned in the second half of the twentieth century, until its complete decommissioning in 1993. The *ceinture* has often been described as the archetype of a "terrain vague" (Lizet 2010), a place "in between," that is "hiding in plain view" (Foster 2014), cutting through every outer arrondissement of Paris. The *ceinture* is an "interstitial landscape" (Jorgensen and Tylecote 2007) in which novel cultural practices can thrive without needing official assent (Hatzfeld et al. 1998). Because it currently falls outside of projects of urban planning and control, it has become a laboratory for other ways of inhabiting the city.

One can easily feel disoriented after crawling through one of the rabbit holes that provides access to the *ceinture*. It is hard to know whose kingdom we have just entered. Certainly it is an animal and plant territory more than a modern-human one. Bursting with smells of compost, urine, and wet spray paint, pulsating with plant and insect life, the *ceinture* seems to abide by a wholly different temporality than the large metropolis around it. It is home to foxes, bats, feral cats, birds, and wild orchids, and its "degree of biodiversity" is as important as that of the city's two major woodlands, the Bois de Boulogne and Vincennes (APUR 2011). Many people come here for shelter—homeless people and migrants find temporary or more permanent refuge under its bridges—but also because the place is bursting with experimentations and other modes of living together (or alongside) other humans and animals. A disorienting place, but also one where I definitely could feel a force.

In line with the colonizing narratives I alluded to in the introduction, the *ceinture* is often framed as an "internal frontier" by planners and the *mairie* (city council). The *mairie* regularly speaks of "reconquering" the *ceinture*, while dismissing it at the same time as vacant and dangerous. "Reconquering" here means managing the *ceinture* in the name of democratic access for all citizens to this biodiverse space. It is also a way to dismiss already present forms of life by favoring what the city council calls "peaceful use: conviviality, strolling and gardening" (Mairie de Paris 2018).[3] Henri's life has been directly affected by this reconquering impetus. For years, the national railway company (SNCF), which owns the station and the tracks, had allowed Henri to live there in exchange for a low rent, as part of its open policy regarding artistic and cultural projects. In 2009, however, the SNCF decided to redirect its wastelands to more lucrative uses everywhere it could, delegating the management of these estates to a private society. The rent rose to twice the amount Henri had had to pay until then, and he soon could no longer cope. When I did fieldwork with him, he still lived in the old station, but he was regarded as a squatter and faced threats of eviction.[4]

Henri started gardening by the train tracks just behind his home in the early 2000s. He started the garden on his own, with the help of his teenage son, and was soon joined by Léo. He often says that his involvement there came from "his concern for the place." He showed me pictures of the place when he first arrived, in the 1990s, highlighting the mineral universe he dwelt in. There was no soil in sight, only mineral surfaces, well maintained over decades by glyphosate treatments, still extensively used by the SNCF for track maintenance. These were typical "surfaces of empire": concrete, hard-surfaced city ground, supposedly dead, abiotic, and meant to afford only walking and upright posture (Ingold 2004). Asphalt, which covers most of the ground in Paris outside of buildings, is representative of a specific urbanistic approach to the senses. Because it remains solid, doesn't slip, and doesn't have a smell, asphalt is thought to civilize the world. It lends itself to be made into a surface that is just a surface: smooth, hard, and stable. It participates in the ambition of silencing all forms of life other than human—to establish soil as a countryside feature, far away from the sight of urbanites, who, no longer distracted by muddy streets and smelly decomposition processes, can concentrate on "higher" matters like politics, business, and trade (see Ripoll 2016). Soil sealing and the effective demise of soils it hastens are a key aspect of the modern alienation from nature, of the split between daily life and the environmental relationships one depends on to live (Tsing 2015).

Even though Léo and Henri do grow food in the garden, their reasons for growing plants mostly stem from a sheer interest in what the place affords, and a passion for its transformations, soils, and botany. This feeds into a very particular interest in the city's biological cycles, the hands-on development of an uncanny botany. As a complement to their other militant commitments, they created the Special School of Free Spaces (ESEL), a gathering of activists and neighbors who wanted to learn together about growing soil in wastelands. A lot of the work done with ESEL entails constructing soil on, and from, the crumbling concrete platform, to transform it into something like an interface of exchange, rather than the hard surface it once was. As they once explained to me: "We want to produce ideas, like you would when writing your thesis. But we want to do it by growing soils. We want to explore the art of soiling." Léo and Henri do not just enjoy the aesthetics of these ruderal ecologies. They have become apprentices of the city's queer ecologies.

Léo and Henri are far from being the only ones who want more soil and more gardens in the city. However, to them, making soil is what really sets their project apart from the many gardens that have opened in the last twenty years in Paris, which often rely on the bringing in of topsoil. Topsoil is the name used for the superior, fertile horizon of forest or agricultural soils. It is considered a construction material and is sold on the construction market. When a new garden is opened in Paris with the help of the municipality, the latter offers the soil as a courtesy—meaning it brings a few big bags of topsoil to the site to make sure vegetables aren't grown in polluted soil (Daniel 2015). This clean soil, however, is actually agricultural soil scraped off fields that have been preyed upon by property developers in the periphery of the city. There can be no such delivery of soil without the destruction of soil elsewhere. Commodified soil depends on the same business as that of urban sprawl and soil sealing. To Henri and Léo, making their own soil is, therefore, a way of contesting the recourse to commodified soil. It is a political gardening act. As Léo explains, "It annoys me that we move soil around like that, that we compact it, that we are not at ease with what we have already ... If there is no soil, it does not matter—we will build it gradually." Soil construction is a vital practice to them, a weapon of choice against the transformation of the city into an abiotic, sealed, and mineral environment. In this place at least, no council worker will spread pesticides for a while. They can create a space for the city plants they like, where they can strive to form novel ecosystems.

Figure 10.1 Henri and the *Petite Ceinture* garden in winter 2013, not long after he started gardening on the old train platform. Photo by Léonard Nguyen Van Thé.

Noticing Soils: The Intruders' Point of View

We often tend to think of soil as something that sits in a place, or that even embodies a place such that it confers it its unique character, its identity. However, this idea of soil, as a well-defined, measurable skin of the earth, only recently emerged in the modern West, and is not shared by many peoples. The anthropologist Kristina Lyons (2014) explains that for the Colombian farmers she met on fieldwork, "soil" is not a fixed entity that can be located somewhere on the farm. It is primarily an entanglement of relations that bring together the forest, farmers' hard work, their hopes for the future, and the governmental politics that hinder these hopes. Likewise, Léo and Henri's mode of pedological observation starts not by scrutinizing a specific spot but by walking around the city and observing how life develops in its cracks. Indeed, to guerrilla gardeners, soil doesn't appear as something that sits in a place. It isn't a terroir but rather a temporary knot of open-ended lines of life and materials. Their explorations of the art of soiling start not in the garden itself, but whenever they walk around in the city. Unlike the static gaze of landscape admirers, looking while walking prevents romantic contemplation. As Vergunst and colleagues note, "Vision during movement is not a singular gaze, but involves glances, distractions, and a specific and lively being-aware rather than the generalised awareness of consciousness" (2012: 7). Cultivating their passion starts with observing the city not just as a backdrop for urban (human) life (as critiqued in Stoetzer 2018: 299) but as a chaotic, ruderal, and spontaneous garden space. This change in perspective relies on their effort to see the city from the eyes of its intruders: the soil and flora that spontaneously appear between pavements, on roofs, or in gutters. This is very different from the kind of vision pedologists develop when looking at specific grounded entities such as soil profiles, but rather resembles the "precise modes of inattention" (Picard et al. 2016) that experimental artists such as Lois Weinberger deploy in following the vegetable exuberance in the fissures of urban modernity—modes in which the observer does not know in advance where to look in order to find ruderal communities.

Developing an art of noticing soils in cities means learning to pay attention in a world where what one is looking for has been carefully hidden away by asphalt and concrete. To Anna Tsing, the arts of noticing that we need in order to address the current ecological situation are directed toward "the divergent, layered, and conjoined projects that make up worlds" (2015: 22). They allow us to become aware of ways of life that have been removed from dominant narratives of progress, to retrace the effects that this ideology has on them, and to provide situated answers to situations of alienation. The hard surfacing of soils is an ideology of progress that makes us believe that we do not need muddy companions. But careful observation reveals that life continues everywhere in spite of it.

Hence, Léo and Henri's city is not one of forms and structures, but of compost. When they walk in the city, they look both up and down: to the roofs and to the ground. Soil for them can be in a gutter or a layer of decayed leaves on a roof, and high up on buildings. They spot every little plant and speculate on how it got there. They once brought me to a ruined building just to observe concrete decay, to contemplate how in cities the wind is one of the strongest soil-creating forces, as it carries dust, leaves, trash, and sand to corners and interstices where it gets trapped. Trash and dust are soon taken over by a host of organisms that start digesting them and transforming them into something else—something some are happy to call soil. Even in newer and well-maintained buildings and streets, once a crack appears in concrete, the dust that starts accumulating in it will benefit from the humidity and the heat the concrete stores during the day to develop into a young soil. In becoming an expert urban gardener, one develops an eye for this life that develops in city interstices. The city, then, takes on a whole new dimension. Far from the cold concrete façade that many see, it becomes one in which life is everywhere, weaving in and out of the mineral surfaces of the city. As Léo explains:

When you suddenly see trees of heaven, medlar trees and apricot trees that start growing altogether in the same spot in town, you can guess that there is some sort of soil and microclimate that enables this. Then when elsewhere, you see only dry liana plants, you know there is probably little soil depth, but you will still find mosses or other living things. There is always something going on.

To follow these materials and their transformations is to enter a world in formation—one in which the city is a socio-material composite, taking in processes of decomposition and recomposition that we might dare call pedogenetic. When they walk through the city, not only do Henri and Léo look at such micro-climates and the spontaneous flora they foster, they also intervene. When they can reach them, they prune trees or displace stones to protect plants and gather heat; they add compost; they collect seeds and re-sow them. Sometimes, they also dig up these plants to replant them by the old station.

Growing Soils: "Soiling Mounds" and "Dry-stone Soils"

In creating mound-gardens, urban gardeners emulate the processes of growth, degradation, and recomposition that they notice in their urban surroundings. For Léo and Henri, to construct soil is to resonate with the strange ecology of the place. Gardening and constructing soils, taken together, are means to reclaim the city through its strata, not just its surface and to further an understanding of plants and soils by constantly experimenting with them. They are both practices of knowing and of making the world. At the intersection of epistemology and ontology, they are "ontological politics" (Mol 1999) that shape reality as gardeners engage in soil knowing and making.

Soiling Mounds

Their basic reclamation technique consists in building what they call a *soiling mound* (in French: *une butte de sol en devenir*). Constructing such a mound starts with gathering rotten vegetables, discarded wood, leaves, or cardboard found on the streets. A mound's basic design is simple: it consists in laying a base of cardboard, then alternating layers of "green" matter such as fresh leaves to provide nitrogen, and layers of "brown" matter such as straw or dried leaves to provide carbon. The mound is then planted and left to develop. As seeds from the now fully degraded vegetables sprout and grow, they contribute to the degradation of the layers, which in turn become a fertile substrate for these plants. Once arranged in layers, the rotting materials ferment and interact with one another to form a new entity bursting with life: the juices of some smoothening others while the cardboard placed underneath retains nutrients. When the wet mix starts settling down, plants, bacteria, and fungi take up and continue the process, until all the rotting materials are digested down to a thick layer of fertile compost. The climate also comes into play. Water penetrates through the pores of decaying materials and further smoothens them. With time, however, it also washes nutrients away. If left unattended, the mound eventually loses its fertile properties and sags down. At the time I worked with them, the fertile layer was still shallow and the mounds were quickly washed away or consumed entirely by the plants. The process of

Figure 10.2 Léonard Nguyen Van Thé sets the first layers of a new mound on the abandoned platform. Shredded greens from the market mixed with straw or dried leaves will be placed on top of the cardboard layer. Photo by Germain Meulemans.

mound building thus had to be repeated every season, using the earth remaining from previous living mounds to infuse new ones with their microorganisms.

Constructing soil from and on the impermeable ground thus implies repeated work on the boundaries, limits, and surfaces of the garden. The boundary of the garden isn't marked by a fence but follows the surface onto which they can build and maintain a thick enough soil. To work on the limits of the garden is to work on the whole surface and the thickness of it, to make it more or less permeable and organic. In turn, the surfaces and boundaries that materialize through the growth of plants need care to maintain their existence. It takes constant rebuilding for this soil to hold. Far from being an isolated background in the landscape, it is what Galarraga and Szerszynski (2012) call a "metastable artifact" that can only hold because of the web of relations that traverse it. Its natural tendency is not to persist, and the plants can only exist "through the controlled exchange of material and energy with their environment" (Galarraga and Szerszynski 2012: 223). As a gathering that is greater than the sum of its parts, the *ceinture* soil is constituted by the intricate fold of material fluxes that circulate across and within it or are derived from it, and the constant re-doing of the soil by the gardeners and the environing forces are all at once what counts as gardening. Again, the *ceinture* soil isn't a specific localizable entity, but a going-on, or "a place where several goings-on become entwined" (Ingold 2010: 96). It is a condensate of its surroundings that leaks outside of its space, as multiple trajectories are enfolded into it to give it its particular existence.

Dry-stone Soil

Among the various soil-building techniques used by Léo and Henri to build soil, the one that best exemplifies the intermingling of materials, recomposition processes, skills, and sociality is the making of what they call *dry-stone soils* (in French: *un sol en mur de pierres sèches*). These combine a lasagna bed and a dry-stone wall—a kind of wall made from stones assembled without cement, typical of rural regions in southern France and Europe, where it was long used to cultivate and stabilize mountain slopes. In the mountains, dry-stone walls are erected to build soil, retain it so it does not get washed away by the rain and wind, and drain it while also retaining a certain level of warmth and humidity. Dry-stone wall building does not separate horticulture from earthwork construction, architecture, and the force of plants, soil, and climate. In the mountains, not only do walls hold the soil that holds a grapevine or apple tree, the root system of the tree also allows the wall and the soil to hold together, and the heat stored by the stone wall, in turn, creates the conditions for the roots to thrive. Stones hold the soil, which holds the tree, which holds the stones. Léo and Henri learned from their observation of city recomposition cycles that the city is a lot like a mountain: "Just like in cities, a lot of mountain soil comes in carried by the wind and water. So peasants

Figure 10.3 Léonard Nguyen Van Thé builds a dry-stone wall around a tree of heaven (*Ailanthus altissima*) on a brownfield site in Aubervilliers. The pit will later be filled with vegetable waste and dry leaves to make a bateau—a walled lasagna. Photo by Jens Denissen.

have to subtly capture this before it continues its course." In the mountains, these walls are built from stones removed from the fields when plowing. They are built by "paying maximal attention to frictions between stones, which provide the stability of the whole, as if geological layers were there, re-woven by the hands of the peasant-builder" (Vidalou 2017: 37). In Léo's case, the "stones" are technogenic—they are bits of crumbled concrete, bricks, and asphalt—but the building process is the same.

Dry-stone wall constructions are in fact an apt metaphor for thinking about anthropogenic pedogenesis, in which soil, plants, and human activity co-constitute each other in the making process. Indeed, on mountain slopes, the shape that a wall takes is organic; the tree and the weather are as responsible for it as is the human builder. It emerges not from planning but in the repetition of the building and rebuilding process, in the constant struggle with the forces of rain, wind, and gravity. As the philosopher and dry-stone mason Jean-Baptiste Vidalou explains, the dry-stone walls that pepper rural landscapes in southern France and Europe have nothing in common with what we call infrastructure, because they do not flatten the territory or participate in dreams of control. They have not been "designed following a pre-established plan, but woven from day to day on and from the mountain of which they constitute a texture of subsistence" (Vidalou 2017: 37). This is perhaps why each dry-stone wall and terrace is contextual and different, as each "emerges from the local needs of a house, a hamlet or a village" (ibid.). They originate in toying around with the forces and materials at hand, in striving to stay one step ahead of the weathering process. As Léo explained to me, "It's like homeopathy: peasants could not 'treat' the whole mountain and make it a field, so they work around every tree. It's much-localized earthwork construction."

In building a dry-stone wall, the forces of sun, rock, and recomposition are brought together. The wall emulates the conditions of cracks in concrete buildings in which wild urban plants normally grow—and it does it by reusing materials. Unlike narratives framing landscapes as deserts to be conquered, dry-stone soil-making leads one to become attentive to the conditions of a place, the materials it affords, and their potentialities. Making dry-stone walls is material poetry. It is to make worlds for soil's entangled lines of life to thrive, to stop seeing the soil as a den of natural resources and start seeing it as a fellow being to learn from, to make kin with (Haraway 2016).

In the urban form of dry-stone wall-making that Henri and Léo developed, the concrete seal of the station platform and the excavated clay bricks are no longer what they were. They now hold and drain soil, and their interstices are soon inhabited by colonies of insects and fungi. Not only do plants, soil, and stones rely on one another in this arrangement: we can think of them as growing together, as undergoing a process of "concrescence" (Whitehead 1929).

The Reanimation of Soils, Skills, and Community

Thinking about how soils not only grow but concresce, or grow-with, helps us think of soil as something that transcends boundaries between the material and the social, and to further question the prevalence of human agency in processes of making soils. In the gardens that Natasha Myers studies, "it is not just the plants that are 'cultivated' or 'cultured' in gardens; the plants also remake the people who tend, harvest, and enjoy them" (2019: 126). We can connect this observation to the processual understanding of soil-making that I underline here by turning to Tim Ingold's studies of markers' and growers' engagement with materials in art, archaeology, and architecture. Ingold relates the Western dichotomy between making and growing to that between artifacts and organisms. We tend to think that artifacts are made according to an external organizing pattern while organisms grow according to internal organizing patterns (often identified with genetic information). The point for Ingold is to reverse the analysis of the making process from one based on the putting of raw matter into a form to one in which materials take their form in an unfolding field of forces, which includes both the properties of materials and the action of the maker. Thus, for him, artisans do not transform the system, but their activity is "part and parcel of the system's transformation of itself" (Ingold 2000: 345). In this view, organisms too grow into shape, in a process that he describes as autopoiesis: "the self-transformation over time of the system of relations within which an organism or artefact comes into being" (ibid.). To emphasize that the gardener's activity is part of a system's larger transformation of itself implies that the life of the garden and that of the gardener are tied in a common becoming of which they both are the emergent results.

These loops of growth also imply human sociabilities and the many human neighbors of the *ceinture* garden. The *ceinture*, indeed, is far from being the vacant space that the city council sometimes speaks about. The *ceinture* garden neighbors one of the largest social housing estates in Paris, and for many teenagers who live there, the *ceinture* is a place to meet and relax. When Henri began gardening there, his compost box was regularly used by graffiti-makers as a stepstool to reach up higher. His lasagna beds were also regularly trampled by careless walkers or dismantled for fire fuel. However, instead of building a fence around his composting box he decided to stop using it and try other composting techniques. He often explains that for him, graffiti-makers were only a problem until he remembered to think of them as part of the ecology of the site. Hence, trampling came to participate in shaping the mounds. The garden grows with trampling rather than despite it. Léo and Henri constantly rebuild their walls to follow the paths of walkers or to guide them when possible. The pathways that have to be observed are those of plants and the weather, but also of other humans, with whom it is important to "live alongside" (Latimer 2013). Gardeners learn to cultivate a "polite distance" (Candea 2010) with the many forms of sociability taking place on the *ceinture*, while remaining aware of the "the frictions, the rubbings, the hesitations that make [them] feel [they] are not alone in the world" (Stengers 2018: 81).

The story of the *ceinture* garden shows how the reclaiming of ruins can be something else than another story of inventing better techniques for building soil. Instead, it conjures up a sense of invention that places the emphasis on the shared creativity of people and materials. It isn't really that Henri and Léo invent new techniques. They rather *participate* in the invention of new reciprocal functionalities between organisms and materials. The kind of creativity at play encompasses more than just human invention. Hence, Léo and Henri build soils as participants in processes of growth, in joining forces with the active materials and activities at hand, by embarking on an adventure with them.

Conclusion: Growing with Soil as Becoming Capable

In the Western world, city planning is currently undergoing an ecological turn. At the same time, it remains largely captured by the hegemonic forces of the state and capitalistic investment, which subtends an understanding of urban interstices and their soil as places to be conquered and policed. In this chapter, I have followed soil-making practices that thrive in the cracks and fissures of the hierarchically planned city, participate in the emergence of concerned groups of people, and render palpable other possible ways of cultivating urban soils.

The chapter started with the movement of gardeners in the city and how they learn to focus their attention on plants and soils. It continued with the correspondence between the gardener's exploratory movements in the city and its materials. In this, skilled movements and materials converge in the building of a mound-garden. Learning to notice soil processes through walking in the city and growing mound-gardens go hand in hand. The making of a garden is based on processes in which the materials of the garden are active and have to be joined in their movements of growth. This refutes the idea of there being a superimposition of form and rather suggests forms of co-action. In soil-making, humans do not control these processes but strive to work with them, to collaborate with material flows, to vectorize (Gatt 2013) them through constant attention to a material arrangement. In this, Henri and Léo's skills, their relationship, and their knowledge grow together with a loose community of *ceinture* squatters and fellow gardeners.

Now, how can such engagement with a place's lines of life inspire ethnographers and cultural theorists? How might thinking about local practices of soil-building open our imaginations to other forms of living with the damaged soils of cities or postindustrial landscapes? For the great archaeologist and theorist of techniques André Leroi-Gourhan (1965), technology—the science of techniques—must start from the description of making processes—what he called the "operational sequences." To him, careful descriptions of sequences of gestures and tools would make it possible to "dethingify" objects. They would show all the invisible moves and detours necessary for the existence of the setup, and provide a better basis for understanding than that afforded by a more formal analysis of the finished objects. Just seeing the finished boat-shaped dry-stone wall could lead us to think of its beautiful design, or to praise the intelligence of how it espouses the walking movement of passers-by. But its real beauty—as Léo attests every time he talks about it—lies in the stories and journeys through which soil comes to be in this place. Léo and Henri's following of materials and processes in cities, and their vectorizing in making soil for the *ceinture* garden, is exemplary of what Maria Puig de la Bellacasa calls ecological thinking: a way of thinking that is "attentive to the capacity of relation-creation, to how different beings affect each other, to what they do to each other, the internal 'poiesis' of a particular configuration" (2016: 52). Léo and Henri's soils do not acquire "social meaning" after they are made. Rather, socialities, skills, and soils grow together in the permanent process of their making and remaking. They too undergo concrescence. The specificity of their way of making soil also lies in the unexpected associations that develop between the city's activities, the soil, and the plants.

This is also how their practices can open up new political spaces through the cultivation of care and sustained attention to the meaningful networks that bring about soil on the *ceinture*. In contrast to engineers' mode of reclaiming, inspired in the large-scale transformation of landscapes for human use, Léo and Henri's reclaiming practices link to a healing impetus that goes far beyond the soil. To them, reclaiming does not link to a narrative of conquest or control over ruderal land, but resonates with the idea of becoming capable, of learning to be sensitive to what makes and unmakes living conditions for the city's more-than-human life.

Notes

1 Food Not Lawns is an international movement founded in Oregon in 1999 that aims to turn urban lawns into collective food-producing gardens (see Flores 2006).
2 Ruderal is a botanical term that comes from the Latin word for rubble (*rudus*). It refers to organisms that spontaneously grow in disturbed environments usually considered to be hostile to life (see Stoetzer 2018).
3 The chief of the "mission homeless" at the city council explains clearly in an interview (https://youtu.be/sLcKaB2aigE?t=21m40s) that the way in which the abandoned buildings of the *ceinture* can become dwellings for the homeless is a source of disorder, an endless problem that will only be overcome once the space becomes used by "the Parisians"—the other Parisians, the official ones. Opening the *ceinture* is, therefore, part of a strategy of occupation to prevent such "illicit" use.
4 Later, in 2017, Henri was eventually evicted for unpaid rent, and the place was soon occupied by new squatters. The garden is still in place, and Léo and Henri continue to build soil on the platform, even though access has been made more difficult.

References

APUR (2011), "Situation et perspectives de la place de la nature à Paris," report, Paris: Atelier parisien d'urbanisme.

Barles, S. (2015), "The Main Characteristics of Urban Socio-ecological Trajectories: Paris (France) from the 18th to the 20th Century," *Ecological Economics*, 118: 177–85.

Candea, M. (2010), "'I Fell in Love with Carlos the Meerkat': Engagement and Detachment in Human–Animal Relations," *American Ethnologist*, 37 (2): 241–58.

Daniel, A.-C. (2015), "Les 'terres végétales' en Île de France : Éléments de compréhension sur un marché peu connu," report, Paris: JASSUR.

Flores, H. (2006), *Food Not Lawns: How to Turn Your Yard into a Garden and Your Neighborhood into a Community*, White River Junction, VT: Chelsea Green Publishing.

Food and Agriculture Organization (FAO) (2015), "What Do Soil Microorganisms Do?," brochure, Rome: Food and Agriculture Organization of the United Nations.

Foster, J. (2014), "Hiding in Plain View: Vacancy and Prospect in Paris' Petite Ceinture," *Cities*, 40 (Part B): 124–32.

Galarraga, M. and B. Szerszynski (2012), "Making Climates: Solar Radiation Management and the Ethics of Fabrication," in C. J. Preston (ed.), *Engineering the Climate: The Ethics of Solar Radiation Management*, 221–35, Lanham, MD: Lexington Books.

Gatt, C. (2013), "Vectors, Direction of Attention and Unprotected Backs: Re-specifying Relations in Anthropology," *Anthropological Theory*, 13 (4): 347–69.

Gobat, J.-M., M. Aragno, and W. Matthey (2004), *The Living Soil: Fundamentals of Soil Science and Soil Biology*, Enfield, NH: Science Publishers.

Gross, M. and H. Hoffmann-Riem (2005), "Ecological Restoration as a Real-World Experiment: Designing Robust Implementation Strategies in an Urban Environment," *Public Understanding of Science*, 14 (3): 269–84.

Haraway, D. J. (2016), *Staying with the Trouble: Making Kin in the Chthulucene*, Durham, NC: Duke University Press.

Hatzfeld, H., M. Hatzfeld, and N. Ringart (1998), *Quand la marge est créatrice: Les interstices urbains initiateurs d'emploi*, La Tour d'Aygues: Éditions de l'Aube.

Ingold, T. (2000), *The Perception of the Environment: Essays on Livelihood, Dwelling and Skill*, London: Routledge.

Ingold, T. (2004), "Culture on the Ground: The World Perceived Through the Feet," *Journal of Material Culture*, 9 (3): 315–40.

Ingold, T. (2010), "The Textility of Making," *Cambridge Journal of Economics*, 34 (1): 91–102.

Jorgensen, A. and M. Tylecote (2007), "Ambivalent Landscapes—Wilderness in the Urban Interstices," *Landscape Research*, 32 (4): 443–62.

Latimer, J. (2013), "Being Alongside: Rethinking Relations Amongst Different Kinds," *Theory, Culture & Society*, 30 (7/8): 77–104.

Latour, B. (2008), "A Cautious Prometheus? A Few Steps Toward a Philosophy of Design," in F. Hackne, J. Glynne, and V. Minto (eds.), *Proceedings of the 2008 Annual International Conference of the Design History Society*, 2–10, Irvine, CA: Universal Publishers.

Lehmann, A. and K. Stahr (2007), "Nature and Significance of Anthropogenic Urban Soils," *Journal of Soils and Sediments*, 7 (4): 247–60.

Leroi-Gourhan, A. (1965), *Le geste et la parole II: La mémoire et les rythmes*, Paris: Albin Michel.

Lizet, B. (2010), "Du terrain vague à la friche paysagée: Le square Juliette-Dodu, Paris, X^e," *Ethnologie Française*, 40 (4): 597–608.

Lyons, K. M. (2014), "Soil Science, Development, and the 'Elusive Nature' of Colombia's Amazonian Plains," *Journal of Latin American and Caribbean Anthropology*, 19 (2): 212–36.

Mairie de Paris (2018), "Premiers travaux à l'été 2018 pour l'ouverture de la Petite Ceinture" [https://www.mairie12.paris.fr/actualites/les-projets-2018-pour-le-12e-573; accessed January 15, 2019].

Meulemans, G. (2020), "Wormy Collaborations in Practices of Soil Construction," *Theory, Culture & Society*, 37 (1): 93–112.

Mol, A. (1999), "Ontological Politics: A Word and Some Questions," *Sociological Review*, 47 (suppl. 1): 74–89.

Morel, J.-L., C. Chenu, and K. Lorenz (2015), "Ecosystem Services Provided by Soils of Urban, Industrial, Traffic, Mining, and Military Areas (SUITMAs)," *Journal of Soils and Sediments*, 15 (8): 1659–66.

Myers, N. (2019), "From Edenic Apocalypse to Gardens Against Eden: Plants and People in and After the Anthropocene," in K. Hetherington (ed.), *Infrastructure, Environment, and Life in the Anthropocene*, 115–48, Durham, NC: Duke University Press.

Picard, C., E. Gan, and B. Stoetzer (2016), "The Multispecies World of Technology," *Anthropocene Curriculum: The Technosphere Issue* [https://www.anthropocene-curriculum.org/pages/root/campus-2016/feral-technologies/the-multispecies-world-of-technology/; accessed July 2, 2019].

Pickering, A. and K. Guzik, eds. (2008), *The Mangle in Practice: Science, Society, and Becoming*, Durham, NC: Duke University Press.

Puig de la Bellacasa, M. (2016), "Ecological Thinking, Material Spirituality, and the Poetics of Infrastructure," in G. C. Bowker, S. Timmermans, A. E. Clarke, and E. Balka (eds.), *Boundary Objects and Beyond: Working with Leigh Star*, 47–68, Cambridge MA: MIT Press.

Ripoll, D. (2016), "Du caillou roulé au ciment coulé: Métamorphoses du revêtement de sol à Genève (19e-20e siècles)," in P. Mantziaras and P. Viganò (eds.), *Le sol des villes— Ressource et projet*, 101–12, Geneva: MētisPresses.

Star, S. L. (1990), "Power, Technology and the Phenomenology of Conventions: On Being Allergic to Onions," *Sociological Review*, 38 (1): 26–56.

Stengers, I. (2018), *Another Science Is Possible: A Manifesto for Slow Science*, Cambridge: Polity Press.

Stoetzer, B. (2018), "Ruderal Ecologies: Rethinking Nature, Migration, and the Urban Landscape in Berlin," *Cultural Anthropology*, 33 (2): 295–323.

Tsing, A. L. (2015), *The Mushroom at the End of the World: On the Possibility of Life in Capitalist Ruins*, Princeton, NJ: Princeton University Press.

Van Dooren, T. (2016), *Flight Ways: Life and Loss at the Edge of Extinction*, New York: Columbia University Press.

Vergunst, J., A. Whitehouse, N. Ellison, and Árnason, A. (2012), "Introduction," in A. Árnason, N. Ellison, J. Vergunst, and A. Whitehouse (eds.), *Landscapes Beyond Land: Routes, Aesthetics, Narratives*, 1–14, Oxford: Berghahn Books.

Vidalou, J.-B. (2017), *Être forêts: Habiter des territoires en lutte*, Paris: La Découverte.

Whitehead, A. N. (1929), *Process and Reality: An Essay in Cosmology; Gifford Lectures Delivered in the University of Edinburgh During the Session 1927–28*, Cambridge: Cambridge University Press.

11

Soil Refusal: Thinking Earthly Matters as Radical Alterity

Manuel Tironi

Introduction

Olivia had been telling me about planting a magnolia tree for a while. She is an enthusiastic and skillful gardener and spends long hours among her plants. Every time I visit her, I return home with seeds, baby plants, lemons, and even small trees. She talks passionately about the cactuses, roses, and lavender bushes she nurses in her garden. The toxicity of La Greda, her hometown, hasn't discouraged her. La Greda is a small hamlet in the Puchuncaví Valley in central Chile, and adjacent to the infamous Centro Industrial Ventanas (CIV), one of the most polluted industrial compounds in Latin America. CIV hosts 27 petrochemical industries, including one copper-smelting complex and four coal-burning energy stations. Stories of ecological collapse abound in the area—and are dramatically evident after spending some time in La Greda. Actually, Olivia and her plants live just across from the now abandoned La Greda elementary school, closed down in 2012 after several children and teachers fainted owing to high levels of sulfur trioxide. Visible from almost all sides of her home, the abandoned building is a ghostly reminder of the chemical violence to which Olivia and her plants are constantly subjected.

For the last decade, I have been paying attention to soil–plant–human relations, in Puchuncaví and elsewhere. I'm interested in how people like Olivia establish deep ethico-practical commitments with plants and soils in a context of chronic industrial violence, and in the way these human–soil–plant embroilments allow for a politics of intimate resistance (Tironi 2018). I have also paid attention to how earth scientists relate to inapprehensible geological matter, including topsoil, and to what extent these engagements recompose *bio-geo* arrangements (Tironi 2019). Spending time with neighbors from Puchuncaví and with geophysicists as they relate, sound, remediate, and work upon soily things has allowed me to get a sense of the kind of alliances articulated among different kin for vital endurance and knowledge production.

One week after Olivia got the magnolia tree, I visited her so that we could plant it together. It was perfect timing, she told me, ideal for planting because of the full moon. When I arrived, she had already decided where the magnolia tree would be sited: a corner of her front garden, where she already has ornamental flowers and cactuses, beautifully distributed among the panoply of stuff that inhabits her garden—including both her flowers and the toxicants, chiefly particulate matter—carbon, arsenic, lead—that tarnishes the leaves and acidifies the soil, dusty reminders that Olivia and her vegetable companions spend their days in a sacrifice zone. And then there is the constellation of abandoned things. To plant the magnolia tree we had to maneuver through various kinds of rubble and trash. Truck tires, the skeleton of an old washing machine, and construction materials interfered in our task.

Neither this panoply of discarded junk nor the toxic layer sedimented on top of the soil hindered our gardening mission. We were fully committed to the task, and I was happy to join Olivia in her careful and laborious work of creating a space for human–vegetable companionship. But as I dug the hole for the magnolia tree, I cut my finger on a broken glass bottle buried in the hardened soil. It wasn't a bad cut, but it bled enough to dot the soil with a red stain. My thumb throbbed painfully, and suddenly a sense of resistance grew between my body and Olivia's garden. Previous feelings of communion transmuted into a sensation of distance. An aloofness. An indifference. As if the blood, the toxic chemicals, the dry soil, and the abandoned objects were indexing an inhospitableness that my analytics hadn't rendered palpable before.

The somatic rejection I experienced in Olivia's garden was hardly new. In my fieldwork in Puchuncaví and collaborations with geoscientists, I've come to see and feel moments in which soils, plants, rocks, and other vegetable and mineral things did not respond to my call for friendship (Tironi et al. 2018; Tironi 2019). My analytics, however, often lagged one step behind, not fully grasping what was at stake. My accounts of the gardening practices I witnessed in La Greda, for example, had been attuned to a sensibility toward gardens as a *becoming together* between soils, plants, and humans. An analytics saturated with images of mutual flourishing where soils allowed themselves to affect and be affected in an ecology of connections and interdependences. My bloody thumb painfully confirmed a different form of relationality. Actually it made me consider whether plants and soils had an outside *outside* relationality—a form of existence that could not be exhausted in the pragmatics and ethics of entanglements, conviviality, and symbiosis. As I stood with my wound and the magnolia tree waiting to be planted amidst the ruins of industrial development, I wondered how to account for this and other pushbacks and what I might learn from them to find cues for renewed political practices in a time of enhanced ecological sensitivity.

In this chapter, I pay attention to those moments in which soils, in close proximity to plants, chemicals, and animals (human and otherwise), emerge as radical alterity—as a sovereign Other not fully amenable to relationality. I coin the phrase "soil refusal" to indicate situations of human–soil encounters in which the form and content of the encounter itself are alien to what "encounter" is supposed to be and do. Soil refusal does not imply rejection of the "encounter" as the critical concept for thinking multispecies worlds; neither is it an attempt at disposing from "relation" as a phenomenological cue for engaging with more-than-human realities. Rather, soil refusal points at situations that force us to open up what "encounter" and "relation" mean when thinking about soil–human interactions—and *geo*-human exchanges more amply. Borrowing from

Mario Blaser and Marisol de la Cadena (2009), what interests me is to think about the *unthinkable* in and of soil–human encounters—which is not the possibility of the encounter itself, but the terms upon which this encounter has been conceptualized.

My aim in this chapter is to draw the contours for a conceptual framework able to render visible the manifold moments of entanglement, symbiosis, and interdependence in soil–human relations, while accounting for the potency of soils and their *inhuman* capacity for non-concurrence as a possible form of these relations. So while ethnographically grounded, the notion of soil refusal emerges from a conceptual disaffection with the way soil–human relations are thought and theorized in certain quarters of science and technology studies (STS), geography, and anthropology. It grows also from a broader discomfort with how calls for engaging with the geological, including soils, in the perspective of planetary catastrophe conceal entrenched anthropocentric logics and analytics. By exploring the limitations of the relational approach to soils, in this chapter I challenge soil scholars to think human–geological encounters by being attentive to the categories of existence demanded by soils, instead of projecting the parameters of the One into the dynamics of the Other.

In the next section, I summarize the literature on soils, particularly the work that has focused on soil as relationality. I then turn to two ethnographic instantiations of soil refusal. They are drawn from different settings and are led by different protagonists, but they both index the soil alterity I'm looking for. What I attempt with these two vignettes is rather simple: to show chemical processes and lived experienced in which soil does not accept the biontological invitation for communion, and hence where the encounter between soil and humans needs to be redrawn. I then engage with discussions coming from feminist geophilosophies to explore how they can help us knit a conceptual alternative for thinking soil–human encounters.

Relational Soils

Soil has become a charismatic entity. While relatively marginal within the natural sciences (Puig de la Bellacasa 2015), it has grown in relevance in many discussions in STS, anthropology, and geography, particularly at the intersection between the "material turn" and feminist approaches to the politics of knowledge production.

Critical at this juncture is the power of soil to invoke, represent, and energize relational ethics and theories in social engagement with more-than-human worlds. Countering a positivist–objectivist position according to which material realities exist beyond and despite practices and relations (see Mol 1999; Law 2004), interactions with the soils of scientists (Latour 1999), amateurs (Puig de la Bellacasa 2014), and farmers (Shiva [1999] 2016; Lyons 2014) render visible the multifarious practices that bring soil and soil ecologies into being. Soils are relational materialities that are entangled in complex webs of thought and action.

This ontological dynamism is not restricted to the constitution of soil. Soils are also the medium and the site of generative provocations and entanglements. They issue forth flows of life that flourish, intersect, and die in open webs of co-dependency and symbiosis. Soils, as put by Puig de la Bellacasa, are "a lively *beingness*" that manifest "a world of 'companions' sharing the trouble" (2014: 33).

Soil is hence also a point of departure for conceptualizing *elementally* relational ontologies and ethics in a time of extended crisis. Its exuberance points to the ecological sensitivities needed to live and die well on a damaged planet. Particularly, soil's generative capacities and potencies confront us with the task of recognizing that "we require each other in unexpected collaborations and combinations, in hot compost piles. We become-with each other or not at all" (Haraway 2016: 4).

Thinking with Donna Haraway is helpful for drawing the relational condition of soils. In her speculative fabulations, Haraway takes the figure of compost and composting—as "theory in the mud, as muddle" (2016: 31)—to think about humanness and worldliness more broadly as a messy tentacular "become-with each other" in processes in which we "compose and decompose each other, in every scale and register of time and stuff in sympoietic tangling" (Haraway 2016: 97). Compost is a metaphor for reimagining and empowering the meaning and practice of togetherness (Abrahamsson and Bertoni 2014), conviviality (Hinchliffe and Whatmore 2006), cordiality (Tironi 2014), or friendliness (Bingham 2006)—that is, for celebrating the political apertures made possible by those beings and collaborations that "make attachments and detachments" in multiple, open, and situated ways, weaving "paths and consequences but not determinisms" (Haraway 2016: 31). Importantly, the togetherness invoked in composting involves a "cooking" process (Lynes and Symes 2016), both in the sense of a hands-on and worldly practice and in that of a transformational mesh that provokes life into being. Like life itself, compost is prepared with sticky and ordinary stuff and requires our bodily, affective, and sentient engagement with an alchemy that cannot be fully controlled. Compost is the result of various beings—soil, vermin, fungi, bacteria, oxygen, plants, and humans—collaborating in a continuous process that has no teleological framing. Compost and composting, and by extension soils and soil ecologies, are ways of attending to the material yet always relational condition of life.

Relationality helps me understand the lively and messy imbrications between soils, plants, and humans that I have witnessed doing fieldwork with geologists or spending time with farmers. But the focus on abundance and extension—on the profusion of life rather than on its scarcity (Yusoff 2012)—blurs the pragmatics of many situations in which relations cannot be taken for granted: situations in which relations were not absent, but forced me to rethink the ontological politics of "the relation" between soils and humans. In the next section, I offer two ethnographic vignettes that may help illustrate the form of these situations.

Barren Life

We meet Miguel and Rafael in a sunny morning in March 2015. They are longtime activists and the founders of the Consejo Ecológico de Puchuncaví (Puchuncaví Ecological Council), the first environmental organization in the area. I'm accompanied by a colleague visiting from Catalonia, and I try to keep hidden my chemical caveats. Although I've been doing fieldwork in Puchuncaví for several years, my body still feels a kind of sensorial hesitancy. I always feel *enveloped* in Puchuncaví, atmospherically conditioned—however minimally—by suspended toxicants and energies. I've grown to experience Puchuncaví as a mood (Tironi et al. 2018).

Miguel and Rafael want to show us what they call "environmental passives," the technical name for those sources of pollution that were not properly dealt with and continue to cause harm. They have identified 21 illegal dumping sites for chemical residues used by the copper smelting plant and at least two carbon-burning electric plants over the last five decades.

After driving around Campiche, the site of an infamous conflict over the approval for a fourth fossil-burning energy plant, we park in a hilly patch of land surrounded by wire fences, yellowish bushes, and plenty of bare, grayish land. After slipping over the wire fence, we begin climbing a small hill. The soil below our feet feels extremely dry and dusty. Our boots slip and each step kicks up a trail of suspended material. We climb surrounded by a phantasmagoric cloud. Fifteen meters away there are *malvavisca* (*Sphaeralcea obtusiloba*) and romerillo (*Baccharis linearis*) bushes delimiting the exposed and acidified land we walk through, among the few plants capable of living in highly polluted soils in Central Chile (Ginocchio et al. 2004). I feel a bit dizzy.

We are walking over a large "industrial barren" (Kozlov and Zvereva 2007). The term was coined to call attention to ecologies in which, due to extreme pollution, soil services and reproduction capacities are severely curtailed. Life is not (can never be) completely absent within and across these barren soils, but in industrial barrens soil deterioration reaches "its nearly final point" (Kozlov and Zvereva 2007: 232). Industrial barrens can be defined as extreme habitats characterized by land that is open and bleak due to the deposition of airborne pollutants, sparsely vegetated (coverage of 10% or less), severely eroded, and with acidic (pH < 4.0) and metal-contaminated soils. Industrial barrens often develop near non-ferrous smelters and refineries, primarily those of factories producing copper, nickel, zinc, or lead. Several areas around the CIV in Puchuncaví, including the one I visited with Miguel and Rafael, are categorized as industrial barrens (Ginocchio 2000). The term helps me to situate the chemical and ecological refusal of soils. Life finds its way. Pure excess: left on its own, nature folds and unfolds exuberantly as a "potency, insurgency, and unstoppable force" (Myers 2018). Soils are not outside this ongoingness. They also expand, connect, embroil, multiply, decompose, and issue forth. Although sometimes they don't. Sometimes soils disconnect. Sometimes they reject or become rejectable. Sometimes, for example in Campiche, they are not hospitable to the ever-expanding motion of nature, or at least to that form of "nature" that we assume is always engaged in an endless movement toward expansion and entanglement.

When we reach the hilltop we get the full view and experience of an industrial barren. Not inert. Not dead—actually "dead" would be too easy an adjective. As I scrutinize the soil under my feet I keep thinking that nothingness—the complete absence of life—would be much more soothing than what I have below—and above and in front of—me. The soil is still soil, as I can identify some organic elements, at least in aspect. Some dry but at least slightly brownish soil lies a few centimeters below the surface. There is some nitrogen left here, I say to myself. But the very top layer is a thick clay-looking coat. Arsenic, I think automatically, propelled more by the anxieties of my body in interaction with this landscape than by my biochemical expertise. But I'm not too far off. Industrial barrens show systematically high levels of toxic pollution. In all cases reviewed by Kozlov and Zvereva (2007), the concentration of at least one pollutant in the uppermost soil layer exceeded 1,000 micrograms per gram (that is, 1 gram of pollutant per kilogram of soil). In Campiche, it might not be arsenic, but maybe lead, sulfur dioxides, and definitely copper. Research in Puchuncaví has shown that copper increases significantly at sites near the CIV, such as the place we visited with Miguel and Rafael, compared to sites as far as 5.5 km from the CIV. Sulfur concentration follows the same pattern, which is four times higher nearer to the CIV (Ginocchio et al. 2004). Inversely, organic matter decreases by half and nitrogen concentration by 1.7 times from the furthest surveyed point to the one closest to the CIV.

Since most of the heavy metals accumulated in soils are non-soluble, their complete leaching from upper soil horizons takes centuries—for example, 100–200 years for copper. These long-term conditions have a negative effect on fundamental processes for soil enrichment. An example is biodiversity, which in industrial barrens is one-third of that observed in undisturbed habitats (Kozlov and Zvereva 2007). Having lost their protective vegetation cover, industrial barrens suffer from extensive erosion, and most are devoid of topsoil, sometimes even showing acute loss of subsoil (McCall et al. 1995). This is associated with a reduction in microbiota, which in industrial barrens has been shown to lose its resilience to disturbances and its ability to perform normal processes of nutrient cycling, assimilating organic residues, and maintaining soil

Figure 11.1 Barren soil in Campiche, central Chile. Photo by Manuel Tironi.

structure. The thick clay-looking layer under our feet renders these biochemical (un) processes brutally real.

But the soil is not completely unfriendly to vegetable life. In addition to romerillo and *malvavisca* bushes, we can see here and there *dondiego de la noche* (*Oenothera chilensis*) and *chinitas* (*Noticastrum sericeum*), herbaceous plants that have proved resilient to industrial violence in Puchuncaví (Ginocchio et al. 2004). Further away, like a bad omen, we can see some eucalyptuses, those water-insatiable trees that have become the symbol of extractivism, water scarcity, and climate change in Chile. The presence of these plants and trees doesn't attenuate my feeling of being unwelcomed by the soil under our feet. The problem in industrial barrens, warn Kozlov and Zvereva (2007), is not the elimination of vegetable life but the impossibility of conducting a fundamental ecological function, that of *restoration*. In fact, the scant vegetation that manages to survive in intensely contaminated sites is often able to produce viable seeds, and sometimes even in larger amounts than at unpolluted sites. However, due to heavy concentrations of toxicants in the uppermost soil layers that stunt radicle growth, natural regeneration is absent or nearly absent in industrial barrens. Even when seeds manage to germinate, their root growth is so inhibited that seedlings quickly dry up and die off completely (Winterhalder et al. 2001; Kozlov 2005). In Puchuncaví, plant abundance decreases by 59.5% toward the CIV, and seed species richness is 1.5 times greater 5.5 km away from where we are with Miguel and Rafael. And maybe this what is at the root of my discomfort: not the fact that "life" is absent (it is not), but that "life" in an industrial barren, against our bioimagination of exuberance and continuity, is finite and astringent. The feeling that any relation with this soil would work against my will to connect and engage—hard, frictional, and not devoid of pain. A place for extremophiles.

At some point in our visit, Miguel connects this site with the larger history of toxicity in Puchuncaví—a history of soils that became hostile to vegetable and microbial life. He remembers the time when, in the 1970s, the cattle began to die, their insides green as a result of copper sulfates. "And then agriculture began to die—in this part [Los Maitenes and Campiche] it died," he continued. "Nowadays it is practically a desert, a desert with a few trees, with a few plants and nothing else." He scrapes the dusty soil with his foot, as if looking for something buried in this industrial barren. "Nothing grows here," he adds with a tone of sorrow and realism in equal amounts.

(Un)Diggable

One year later and it is also a sunny morning. I'm in Cáhuil, 200 km south of Santiago. I'm doing fieldwork with a team of geophysicists led by Elías. He is characterizing the Pichilemu-Vichuquén seismic fault (P-V fault) from Cáhuil near the Pacific coast all the way to the Teno Valley in the Andes using a technique called magnetotellurics (MT). This technique involves a complex apparatus that requires the deployment of a 100 × 100 meter, north–south/east–west-oriented matrix of bobbins, dipoles, and magnetometers. MT draws upon the Earth's electromagnetic fields, which constantly interact with solar winds on the one hand and thunderstorms worldwide on the other.

When this external energy reaches the Earth's surface, part of it is reflected back while the rest penetrates the earth, where it encounters rocks and minerals with different physical properties, from highly resistive crystalline igneous rocks to highly conductive saline-filled sedimentary rocks. The interaction of this energy with variegated geological structures produces electric currents (known as telluric currents), which in turn produce a secondary magnetic field. MT measures, at ground-level sites, time variations between the magnetic field and the electric field, with the ratio of the electric and magnetic variations providing a measure of electrical resistivity. In turn, electrical resistivity is associated with factors such as rock composition, porosity, and permeability, as well as rock fluid composition and temperature. Since low-frequency signals can penetrate deep into the subsurface, MT is able to measure the electromagnetic features of geological structures at depths of hundreds of kilometers. The functioning of the apparatus is, it became evident working with Elías and his team, rather uncertain. To begin with, MT requires a plot of land large enough to accommodate the apparatus. After installation it has to be a secured in place to avoid being stolen. And since some drilling is needed to deploy the bobbins and electrodes, hard, rocky soils are problematic.

Elías had located by GPS all the points along the P-V fault where magnetotelluric measurements were required for his project. After an hour driving around looking for the third spot of the day, which was proving extremely elusive, we entered what seemed like a forestry allotment. "F**k it, here is fine," said Elías. As he had told us, when undertaking geophysical fieldwork it is not unusual to find vigilantes or nervous landowners carrying rifles to make sure their land is protected. We were not scared, but an intense energy was palpable. Once we trespassed into the field, I felt a shot of adrenaline circulating through my body—and through the bodies of my colleagues, whose heightened energy I could see and sense.

We drive two pickup trucks. One is filled with digging materials, including an industrial auger. I wondered why such heavy equipment was needed. Once we began the installation of the MT apparatus I understood. The dried and acidified soil was so hard to drill that even the auger proved completely ineffective. *Pinus radiata*, the industry-introduced species that ubiquitously covers this region, had done its erosive work. The site had been filled with *Pinus* not long before, as the remaining stumps and the unfriendliness of the soil made evident. The soil was not rendering itself available for scrutiny. Dry, hard, rocky. Our efforts to engage with the lithosphere was encountering nothing but resistance in its uppermost layer.

Elías was starting to lose his temper. He commanded us to use shovels to dig the holes for the bobbins and electrodes. The shovels were also useless against the hardened soil. We begin digging with our bare hands. The land was just rocks, abandoned lumber, and thorny bushes. I felt intense pain in my fingertips as I tried to make a dent in a yellowish soil that was utterly unresponsive. A remoteness stood between us and the earth we were supposed to be interacting with. I felt frustrated. But I could also sense something similar to excitement, as if the impenetrable soil we were confronted with invited us to a game of strength, a peculiar joust between our shovels and the Earth's crust. In the field, says Frodeman, "the scientist must adjust herself to nature's patterns, cultivating a disposition of alert repose and anticipating the moment when the world

Figure 11.2 Doing magnetotellurics in Cáhuil, central Chile. Photo by Manuel Tironi.

reveals itself" (2003: 68). I second this observation, but digging the soil in Cáhuil with my lacerated hands I also felt that the human–lithic choreography of geophysics was as much based on adjustment, anticipation, and revelation as it was on fragmentation, negativity, and withdrawal.

The summer sun was punishing, and we had at least one more station ahead of us. We were exhausted. The undergraduate members of the team joked about the infernal working conditions imposed by Elías. "Come on, guys! Really?" he responded half-jokingly, half-seriously, "Do you *really* want to be geophysicists? Toughen up!" Elías's scolding was partly aimed at the masculine bravado that surrounds geosciences, but also at invoking what anthropologist Tim Ingold (2000) calls "enskilment," or the necessary entanglement between perception, body, and environment in the process of acquiring a skill. Forty minutes later the holes were dug. We were all covered in dirt and sweat, hungry and worn out, but also fully physically committed to the task. We had managed to place and bury all the dipoles and electrodes, and with our hands still painful, or maybe *because* our hands were feeling the perilousness of rocky animosity, we were energized. A rush, an enchantment, an impulse, perhaps a variation on what Jeffrey Jerome Cohen (2015: 25) calls *geophilia*, or the "material magnetism" to the petric. Inhospitality, instead of weakening our excitement, was intensifying our engagement with the soil, as if our bodies had found a way to stay with the trouble (Haraway 2016).

Alongside Soils

The two vignettes presented above are nothing more than that: two moments, two situations, two anecdotes even. And they are different. Different settings, actors, and dramatic arcs. But they intersect at one critical point, at least in the perspective of my engagement with soil and soil ecologies. They both point to a situation in which soil becomes *unavailable*: unavailable to extension, to connections, to engagement.

Not completely, of course. The point is not whether the soils of Puchuncaví and Cáhuil I have presented here are without life. They are not. As suggested by Helmreich (2016: xii), life "is in a volatile state, pragmatically and theoretically," and thus its abundance or absence is an issue of scale and the efficacy of the materials upon which it is made visible. In Puchuncaví and Cáhuil, soil–human relations were not lacking either: on the contrary, my encounter with these soils was full of affection and apprehensions. All ecological relations have their own complexities and frictions, their own mode of defining the demarcation between excess and scarcity. Relations, in brief, were not absent.

But they were different, and this is what interests me: to what extent the soils of Puchuncaví and Cáhuil—and elsewhere for that matter—instead of being readily amenable to ecological relations sometimes make them difficult, frictional, or painful. How to think about soil–human relationality when soil does not render itself relatable?

Debates around the geological articulated in and around feminist geophilosophies seem apt points of departure for exploring this question. As stated earlier in this chapter, ontological theories, particularly those of a material-semiotic bent, have made it possible to draw connections between geology (including soils) and larger ethical projects for ecological perseverance. This is sustained, on the one hand, through the possibility of granting agential sovereignty to otherwise inert matters and things, and, on the other, by integrating them into the compositional processes making up diverse worlds. By interrupting stubborn demarcations between the animate and its opposite, "[l]ife is liberated from its confinement in living beings to become a general property of relationality," as observed by Kai Bosworth (forthcoming).

However, geological matter sits uncomfortably within the compositional and animist narrative. Geological things, abysmally withdrawn from human sensoria, temporality, and imagination, render problematic the normative grammar of relation, assemblage, and entanglement (Clark 2010). The brute and dark matter of earthly interiors, "the fractured and the inorganic" (Bosworth, forthcoming) that sustains our existence on Earth, is completely indifferent from human endeavors—from microbacterial dynamics to the molten rocks of deep geology, indeed all the way to cosmic processes, the geological is not always readily available for connections (Harman 2010). Actually, violence is a fundamental mode of being in biotic and non-biotic worlds, and a constitutive part of our relation to the diversity and dynamism of life on Earth (Yusoff 2012). The issue at stake in this line of thinking is not the denial of the multifarious spaces in which heterogeneous elements gather, relate, and act in complex webs of interdependence. It is rather to pause the proclivity of certain vitalist or new materialist discourses to overlook the excess, recalcitrance, and radical autonomy of earthly matter.

Moreover, the propensity to look for relations, vitality, and entanglements in human–geology encounters is mediated and fueled by a transubstantiation in which the human structure of being becomes the analytics for *reality*. "Western ontologies are covert biontologies," asserts Elizabeth Povinelli (2016: 5), in the sense that they have imposed "the qualities of one of its categories (Life, Leben) onto the key dynamics of its concept of existence (Being, Dasein)" (2016: 18). "Relation" might be a critical mode of inter- and intra-action and being-in-adjacency for existents inhabiting a reality in which "life" is predicated upon the life/death binary, but may be inconsequential for those partaking in the realm of Nonlife, existents that have never been alive and thus can never lose their lived condition—existents for whom the absence of life does not mean "death": things and processes that "cannot merely be included in the ways we have understood the qualities of being and life but will need . . . to displace the division of Life and Nonlife as such" (2016: 15).

These threads inspire a mode of attention to soils that I find helpful for thinking about what I observed in Puchuncaví and Cáhuil. Soils can, at least in part, be included in the geological insofar as they point us toward mineral and chemical processes and elements that cannot be easily framed under the arc of the *bios*. Soils are in this sense *inhuman*, elements intimately necessary for human earthly existence but radically and even violently other to humanness (Cohen 2015). Thinking soil as an inhuman matter allows for an analytics in which soil existence, borrowing from Yusoff, "is necessary for life, but its force is not *for* life, insomuch as its teleology is not that of the organism" (2015: 206).

The challenge is how to think of soils as elements that are *both* obliged into relationality *and* exceed it. Here I am at one with Kathryn Yusoff. In her reflection on the ethico-political programs enacted in discourse and action around biodiversity loss, Yusoff invokes the notion of the *insensible* as a way "into an expanded realm of relationality that queries the exclusions that govern the sphere of intelligibility, and might help us think *between natures* to promote a noncontemporaneous ethics of apprehension of the biotic world" (2013: 208). Crucial for Yusoff is the political openings made possible when biodiversity loss is apprehended from a "radical nonrelationality," that is, "modes of recognition beyond 'our' abilities to make nonhuman worlds intelligible" (2013: 209).

Following the lead of Yusoff's proposition: what are the consequences of engaging with soils without imposing a human-centered phenomenological program of visibility, recognition, and existence? Maybe, as radical non-relationality, soils demand alternative ways for conceptualizing how two or more things connect or are relevant to each other. Maybe radical otherness requires modes for *staying alongside* rather than *becoming with*. Joanna Latimer defines *alongsideness* "as a form of intermittent and partial connection [which] eschews the obfuscation of difference entrenched in contemporary emphasis on connectivity" (2013: 77). Being alongside is thus a mode of relationality among different kinds that stresses "the possibility of dwelling with non-humans as preserving division and alterity as much as connectivity and unity" (2013: 98). In Campiche's industrial barren, the polluted soil proposed relations hard to follow without harm; interdependence and collaboration were implausible without physical damage, but the inhospitable condition of the soil was in extension (Latimer 2013) with our presence – not intermingling, not becoming together, but being alongside each other. As we lay on the eroded ground of Cáhuil, cheeks against the dirt to remove rocks and cover holes with our bare hands while thorns and horseflies punctured our skin, we were being alongside earthly matters. A sort of ecological intimacy between our bodies and the acidified soil had flourished. Intimacy, to be sure, that did not rely on a vital connection or sharing, or on a hybridizing wholeness, but on a *proximity* between divergent existents that encountered and even exchanged propensities, yet always equivocally and asymmetrically.

Maybe what was at play in Puchuncaví and Cáhuil was not a "relation" proper but something closer to what Emmanuel Levinas (1969) calls *enjoyment*, or the amalgamation of feelings, sensitivities, and pleasures that emerge from the bodily openness to the sheer world: a sheer world that can be refractive, and hence an openness that is always risky and not without pain. Being-with is not always a story that culminates in symbiosis. It is, however, this partial and even violent encounter with divergent and inhuman things, and not its exhaustion through entanglement, that might be defining "relationality." What I've learned in Puchuncaví and Cáhuil is that relating to soils that resist and withdraw requires not just *becoming* with them— adapting to, sensing with, and being transformed by their forces and specifications— but also assuming a background of relentless abjection and indifference: the fact that in spite of our attempts at engaging with soily things, they can, and will, always exert an inhospitable resistance. Soils are part of that indifferent Gaia that Myra Hird (2010) has brought to our attention: a living Earth sustained by processes, whether microbial or geological, that are profoundly indifferent to human life.[1]

Conclusion: Soil Refusal

By way of conclusion, I want to return to soil refusal as a framework for engaging with soils as sovereign existents. While the term emerged in close connection with polluted and degraded soils, it indexes a resistance to relationality that can be found in soils everywhere. Soil refusal is not a type of soil or an exceptional condition, but an attunement to that otherness always present as soils engage with animals, minerals, and vegetables. Soil refusal is an analytical gesture toward the visibility of that non-reducible excess of soils, that radical difference that at some point always emerges in our relationship with soil ecologies.

As I have tried to suggest, soil refusal is not the rejection of relations with and within soils. It is rather speculating about the possibility of implicating non-relationality in relationality—or to think soils as both being part of relations and resisting them. Inspired by feminist geophilosophies, soil refusal attempts to situate soil–human relations in the context of soil's inhumanness: matter always preserving a part that has not been and cannot be counted—a part withdrawn from engagement, a negative prehension, as A.N. Whitehead (1929) would have it.

To clarify, this does not mean that soils in refusal are outside relations. It means that "relationality" might be just one form of beings-in-proximity. Actually, my encounters with soils' resistances abounded in intensities, emotions, and chemical reactions. The question, hence, is not whether the soils I encountered rendered possible a relation between them and my body, or which soils allow for more relations or less. Rather, my question is to what extent "life" sometimes presents itself in a form different to the imaginary of thrive-ness and continual entanglement. My exploration is about how to think soil relationality accounting for those moments in which soil resists the relational gesture and emerges as radical alterity. And my argument is that soils in refusal modify the parameters of what "relation" means, and for whom. They point to moments in which soil–human energetic exchanges are painful, fragmented, or even deadly—that is, outside the usual grammar of friendship and solidarity. Elsewhere I have referred to these energetic implications with inhuman matter as *geo-affect* (Tironi 2019). Here I have borrowed from Latimer (2013) the notion of alongsideness to think about these reverberances without resorting to images of unity and co-becoming that may occlude the radical alterity at play. The alterity of soils demands, I have argued, another mode of togetherness, one that does not imply embroilment or communion. It demands being in extension, being at unison, in proximity, exchanging intensities without any further commitment, without an ethical project other than being together in divergence.

The pragmatic and theoretical program behind soil refusal is critical, I suggest, in a time of enhanced ecological sensitivity. Modern enlightenment has accounted for critters, landscapes, and the elements only insofar as they are introduced into the dramaturgy of the human. They are brought into sharp relief when they need to be mobilized for industrial development or capitalist expansion, or when they are called upon for our enjoyment in gardens and "conservation areas," or when they get mixed up in our political disputes, or when they need to stand as bearers of our identities, imaginations, and anxieties. But on their own, mountains, rivers, trees, polar bears, and rocks are little more than the setting of History, secondary actors trapped in a plot whose arc is indifferent to their proclivities and needs. The Other shines only under the spotlight of the One.[2]

This modern contract is at the root of our current ecological crisis, and the recognition of nonhuman Others *as such* is, many have asserted, a critical condition for resisting planetary catastrophe (Hird 2009; Ginn et al. 2014; Van Dooren 2014). For all its complexities and limitations, the so-called "Anthropocene" has summoned the need for a new pact of conviviality with earthly things and processes, and critical thinkers have stressed that this call will be futile if it does not involve a serious and profound attempt at thinking *with* nonhumans, and not only for them.

Soil refusal is an attempt at taking this call seriously. What does it mean to account for soils *as such*? Recently, Anna Krzywoszynska (2019) has invoked the relevance of *attentiveness* for generating more ethical relations with soils and nonhumans at large. I heed this call, while adding that attentiveness can only be fully attentive to the existence of more-than-human entities if human modes of attention are not imposed onto them. The relational program needs to be expanded to include non-relationality as one of the terms that need to be included, with the consequent risk of transforming "relationality" into a floating signifier—but gaining the possibility of including soils, rocks, air, rivers, and biota into relational experiments in their full ontological capacities.

Notes

1 I thank Anna Krzywoszynska for pointing out this connection.
2 Viveiros de Castro's discussion on native epistemologies and equivocal relationality
   provides apt reflection for this discussion. As in the challenge posed by Viveiros de
   Castro (2014), the problem is not how to account for the Other but to what extent
   the Other is able to define what Otherness means.

References

Abrahamsson, S. and F. Bertoni (2014), "Compost Politics: Experimenting with
   Togetherness in Vermicomposting," *Environmental Humanities*, 4 (1): 125–48.
Bingham, N. (2006), "Bees, Butterflies, and Bacteria: Biotechnology and the Politics of
   Nonhuman Friendship," *Environment and Planning A*, 38 (3): 483–98.
Blaser, M. and M. de la Cadena (2009), "Introducción," *RAM-WAN*, 4: 3–9.
Bosworth, K. (forthcoming), "The Crack in the Earth," in P. Kingsbury and A. Secor (eds.),
   A Place More Void, Omaha, NB: Nebraska University Press.
Clark, N. (2010), *Inhuman Nature: Sociable Life on a Dynamic Planet*, London: Sage.
Cohen, J. J. (2015), *Stone: An Ecology of the Inhuman*, Minneapolis, MN: University of
   Minnesota Press.
Frodeman, R. (2003), *Geo-logic: Breaking Ground between Philosophy and the Earth
   Sciences*, Albany, NY: State University of New York Press.
Ginn, F., U. Beisel, and M. Barua (2014), "Flourishing with Awkward Creatures:
   Togetherness, Vulnerability, Killing," *Environmental Humanities*, 4 (1): 113–23.
Ginocchio, R. (2000), "Effects of a Copper Smelter on a Grassland Community in the
   Puchuncaví Valley, Chile," *Chemosphere*, 41 (1/2): 15–23.
Ginocchio, R., G. Carvallo, I. Toro, E. Bustamante, Y. Silva, and N. Sepúlveda (2004),
   "Micro-spatial Variation of Soil Metal Pollution and Plant Recruitment Near a Copper
   Smelter in Central Chile," *Environmental Pollution*, 127 (3): 343–52.
Haraway, D. (2016), *Staying with the Trouble: Making Kin in the Chthulucene*, Durham,
   NC: Duke University Press.
Harman, G. (2010), *Towards Speculative Realism: Essays and Lectures*, London: Zero
   Books.
Helmreich, S. (2016), *Sounding the Limits of Life: Essays in the Anthropology of Biology and
   Beyond*, Princeton, NJ: Princeton University Press.
Hinchliffe, S. and S. Whatmore (2006), "Living Cities: Towards a Politics of Conviviality,"
   Science as Culture, 15 (2): 123–38.
Hird, M. J. (2009), *The Origins of Sociable Life: Evolution after Science Studies*, Basingstoke:
   Palgrave.
Hird, M. J. (2010), "Indifferent Globality," *Theory, Culture & Society*, 27 (2/3): 54–72.
Ingold, T. (2000), *The Perception of the Environment: Essays on Livelihood, Dwelling and
   Skill*, London: Routledge.
Kozlov, M. (2005), "Pollution Resistance of Mountain Birch, *Betula pubescens* subps.
   czerepanovii, Near the Copper–Nickel Smelter: Natural Selection or Phenotypic
   Acclimation?" *Chemosphere*, 59 (2): 189–197.
Kozlov, M. and E. Zvereva (2007), "Industrial Barrens: Extreme Habitats Created by
   Non-ferrous Metallurgy," *Reviews in Environmental Science and Bio/Technology*,
   6 (1/3): 231–59.

Krzywoszynska, A. (2019), "Caring for Soil Life in the Anthropocene: The Role of Attentiveness in More-than-Human Ethics," *Transactions of the Institute of British Geographers*, 44 (4): 661–75.

Latimer, J. (2013), "Being Alongside: Rethinking Relations amongst Different Kinds," *Theory, Culture & Society*, 30 (7/8): 77–104.

Latour, B. (1999), *Pandora's Hope: Essays on the Reality of Science Studies*, Cambridge, MA: Harvard University Press.

Law, J. (2004), *After Method: Mess in Social Science Research*, London: Routledge.

Levinas, E. (1969), *Totality and Infinity: An Essay on Exteriority*, Pittsburgh, PA: Duquesne University Press.

Lynes, K. G. and K. Symes (2016), "Cyborgs and Virtual Bodies," in L. Disch and M. Hawkesworth (eds.), *The Oxford Handbook of Feminist Theory*, 122–42, Oxford: Oxford University Press.

Lyons, K. (2014), "Soil Science, Development, and the 'Elusive Nature' of Colombia's Amazonian Plains," *Journal of Latin American and Caribbean Anthropology*, 19 (2): 212–36.

McCall, J., J. Gunn, and H. Struik (1995), "Photo Interpretive Study of Recovery of Damaged Lands Near the Metal Smelters of Sudbury, Canada," *Water, Air, & Soil Pollution*, 85 (2): 847–52.

Mol, A. (1999), "Ontological Politics. A Word and Some Questions," *Sociological Review*, 47 (suppl. 1): 74–89.

Myers, N. (2018), "From Edenic Apocalypse to Gardens against Eden: Plants and People in and After the Anthropocene," in K. Hetherington (ed.), *Infrastructure, Environment, and Life in the Anthropocene*, 115–48, Durham, NC: Duke University Press.

Povinelli, E. A. (2016), *Geontologies: A Requiem to Late Liberalism*, Durham, NC: Duke University Press.

Puig de la Bellacasa, M. (2014), "Encountering Bioinfrastructure: Ecological Struggles and the Sciences of Soil," *Social Epistemology*, 28 (1): 26–40.

Puig de la Bellacasa, M. (2015), "Making Time for Soil: Technoscientific Futurity and the Pace of Care," *Social Studies of Science*, 45 (5): 691–716.

Shiva, V. ([1999] 2016), *Earth Democracy: Justice, Sustainability, and Peace*, London: Zed Books.

Tironi, M. (2014), "Hacia una política atmosférica: Químicos, afectos y cuidado en Puchuncaví," *Pléyade*, 14: 165–89.

Tironi, M. (2018), "Hypo-interventions: Intimate Activism in Toxic Environments," *Social Studies of Science*, 48 (3): 438–55.

Tironi, M. (2019), "Lithic Abstractions: Geophysical Operations against the Anthropocene," *Distinktion: Journal of Social Theory*, 20 (3): 284–300.

Tironi, M., M. J. Hird, C. Simonetti, P. Forman, and N. Freiburger (2018), "Inorganic Becomings: Situating the Anthropocene in Puchuncaví," *Environmental Humanities*, 10 (1): 187–212.

Van Dooren, T. (2014), *Flight Ways: Life and Loss at the Edge of Extinction*, New York: Columbia University Press.

Viveiros de Castro, E. (2014), *Cannibal Metaphysics*. Minneapolis, MN: Univocal Publishing.

Whitehead, A. N. (1929), *Process and Reality*, New York: Free Press.

Winterhalder, K., W. E. Lautenbach, and P. Beckett (2001), "The Sudbury Regional Land Reclamation Program: A Case Study," in J. B. Burley (ed.), *Environmental Design for Reclaiming Surface Mines*, 286–94, Lewiston, NY: Edwin Mellen Press.

Yusoff, K. (2012), "Aesthetics of Loss: Biodiversity, Banal Violence and Biotic Subjects," *Transactions of the Institute of British Geographers*, 37 (4): 578–92.

Yusoff, K. (2013), "Insensible Worlds: Postrelational Ethics, Indeterminacy and the (K)nots of Relating," *Environment and Planning D*, 31 (2): 208–26.

Yusoff, K. (2015), "Queer Coal: Genealogies in/of the Blood," *philoSOPHIA*, 5 (2): 203–29.

12

Geophagiac: Art, Food, Dirt

Lindsay Kelley

What is Geophagy? What is Food?

Everybody eats dirt. Every day people unknowingly ingest small amounts of dust and earth. "Geophagy" refers to knowingly and intentionally ingesting soil, clay, or earth. Immunologist Gerald Callahan's research on geophagy considers supplemental geophagy—soil or clay as vitamin—focusing on pregnant women and children: "because of their rapid growth, [children] have special nutritional needs and surface soils may serve as supplemental nutrients" (2003: 1018). An interview with his 2-year-old daughter is inconclusive:

> Eating dirt appears nearly universal among children under 2 years of age. When I asked my 2-year-old daughter why she ate dirt, she just stared at me, her eyes wide open, a thick moustache of loam lining her lips. She must have decided that either what I had asked was unfathomably abstract or her answer would be far beyond my comprehension.
>
> 2003: 1018

Callahan's interpretation of his daughter's regard touches on three tensions that pull at geophagy scholarship. First, defining geophagy can be difficult. Although we intentionally if naively eat dirt as children and unintentionally inhale and ingest small amounts of dirt as adults, neither of those scenarios qualifies as geophagy. Second, as Callahan's interaction with his daughter indicates, struggles to comprehend the practice animate many analyses of geophagy. Studies of geophagy are rarely, if ever, written or conducted by scholars who share the practices they investigate. Callahan implies that he abstains from his daughter's feast of soil. Third, studies of geophagy struggle with the ways in which geophagy has become a pathologized practice. Callahan's earnest questioning is not a typical parent's response to a child eating dirt. Pathologizing geophagy begins by admonishing: no, don't eat dirt.

Definitions of geophagy emerge from the colonial capitalist logics of slavery, where cultures of the enslaved are assumed to be problematic, even diseased, perverted, and contagious. Geophagy's first uses in English referenced enslaved people in the American South, naming "a diseased appetite" (1850), "a perverted appetite" (1897), and in 1961, "a disease brought over from Africa" (all quoted in the *Oxford English Dictionary*'s "Geophagy" entry). Below I consider alternatives to pathologizing geophagy and "pica," which refers to ingesting substances not regarded as food. Scholars engage geophagy through familiar frameworks of supplementation attached to conditions including anemia, vitamin deficiency, pregnancy, and "gastrointestinal distress" broadly conceived (Vermeer 1966; Geissler et al. 1998; Abrahams et al. 2006; Kawai et al. 2009; Young et al. 2010). To combat inherited imperial prejudice, medical frameworks might make space for cultural aspects of geophagy.

Words ending with the suffix *-phagia* refer to "conditions related to eating or ingestion" (*Oxford English Dictionary*) and pathologize ingestions by frequency (adephagia: insatiable appetite; polyphagia: excessive appetite) or substance (trichophagia: eating hair, wool, and other fibers; mucophagia: eating mucus; onychophagia: nail biting; and dozens more). Complicating the conditional clinical gaze that pathologizes geophagy demands questioning and dismantling the racist colonial structures that, in Kathryn Yusoff's words, "have been ending worlds as long as they have been in existence" (2018: xiii). Tasting soil activates intangible aspects of cultural identity and memory capable of ameliorating, in Linda Tuhiwai Smith's words, "the reach of imperialism 'into our heads'" (2012: 24), and, I would argue, into our stomachs.

Clay and soil appear in diets regularly despite this persistent pathologized regard for geophagy. Beside Callahan's daughter, many begin their culinary experiments with soil and earth as infants. In adulthood, geophagy becomes a familiar practice for anyone who has ever swallowed a dose of the anti-diarrhea medication Kaopectate. Historically, Kaopectate bound and solidified excrement with kaolinite, or white clay, and pectin (hence the name). In the United States, Kaopectate now follows Pepto-Bismol in using bismuth subsalicylate as an antacid, but elsewhere, attapulgite, a clay found and eaten in the US South and more similar to kaolin than bismuth subsalicylate, continues to act as its active ingredient (Kim-Jung et al. 2004). Clay blocks toxins from entering the bloodstream and coats the esophagus and stomach to aid digestion (Rowland 2002; MacGregor 2013).

Medical geology, or the study of place-related health concerns, joins immunology, nutrition, anthropology, ethology, and more to position geophagy across many fields of study. Within the fields that contain studies of geophagy and pica, scholars agree that eating dirt is eating, and need not be understood primarily through the lens of pathology. Geophagy should "be considered within the normal range of human behavior" because "there are perfectly sensible reasons as to why certain people deliberately eat soil, and the consumer can benefit from indulging in geophagy in a number of ways" (Abrahams 2013: 433). (Another inflection on this invitation to consider geophagy as "indulgence" emerges with *tierra bendita* below.) Sera Young, Paul Sherman, Julius Lucks, and Gretel Pelto conducted a data-driven analysis of the geophagy literature, and conclude "that it is time to stop regarding geophagy as a bizarre, non-adaptive gustatory mistake. Our data indicate clearly that geophagy is a widespread behavior in humans and other vertebrates that occurs during both vulnerable life stages and when facing ecological conditions that require protection" (2011: 115).

Work on geophagy often considers foodways of both people and animals. A more-than-human approach to soil and the body contributes to what Stefan Helmreich calls the "erosion of human organismic integrity" (2016: 71). When Callahan asserts that "other than water, what little stuff we humans have inside us is largely dirt" (2003: 1016), he contributes to Helmreich's collection of "ecologically minded folklore" of the body (2016: 62), including references to bodies as mostly water and mostly microbes. Far from inert or hidden beneath our feet, soil and earth walk around inside the digestive organs of vertebrate bodies. Dirt bodies, similar to microbe bodies and bodies of water, recall Astrida Neimanis's argument that figuring elemental bodies allow for a shift in perspective, evoking "planetary species" (2017: 170) held in tension with Leslie Head's "species error," the undifferentiated human evoked in Anthropocene discourse (quoted in Neimanis 2017: 163).

The question of vulnerable lives and ecologies invokes connections between geology, earth materials, and work in the arts and humanities advancing under the banner of the Anthropocene. Remembering that this banner was crafted by geologists, Anthropocene discourse prompts settler populations to acknowledge environmental conditions that have long been the apocalyptic daily reality in occupied territories and for enslaved and colonized peoples all over the world. Yusoff's "billion Black Anthropocenes" refers in part to "the presumed absorbent qualities of black and brown bodies to take up the body burdens of exposure to toxicities and to buffer the violence of the earth" (2018: xii). This evocative encapsulation of environmental racism and the extractivist and racist politics of "White Geology" (Yusoff 2018: xii) suggest the need for a deeper understanding of the "absorbent." Many eat clay for its "alexipharmic" qualities, that is, its capacity to absorb, adsorb, or ameliorate the effects of toxins. Yusoff's bodies of "absorption" suggests the alexipharmic capacities of clay bodies, people who eat clay, and bodies forced into alexipharmic roles at metaphoric and material levels. A non-pathologized acceptance of geophagy may yield as-yet-unknown benefits for "planetary species" that are vulnerable and require protection.

Geophagy need not become another site of human exceptionalism, nor need its multispecies reach stigmatize people who eat earth. Geophagy freed of pathology becomes an avenue for solidarity with nonhuman animals, for many vertebrates eat dirt to thrive. The practice may be read as socioculturally meaningful in multiple ways, with soil ingested as food, as miracle and medicine, and as protest.

Art, Speaking Back, Unexpected Knowledge

Arts-led research resists frameworks of pathology when addressing practices such as geophagy and pica. Writing about how collaborative "biomedical art" projects render patients and doctors interdependent rather than oppositional, curator-scholar Rebecca Dean agrees that art has the capacity to both educate and resist stigma: "artists speak back to the medical gaze and the scientific gaze with lively material complexity" (2019: 117). This "speaking back" indicates art's capacity to open up social and political positions for audiences and participants. I am not describing the process of experiencing, "taking in," or viewing an art object. Instead, I refer to the ways in which art projects invite unexpected knowledge that then transfers and extends outside the art context into actions and reflections that impact social and cultural worlds.

This distinction describes the difference between regarding art as commodity versus regarding art as relation, or social exchange. Histories of Fluxus and feminist art practices from the 1960s onward have attended to art's world-changing capacities, and histories of social change read alongside these projects indicate productive correspondences.

Drawing art and medical contexts together, Amelie Hastie (2013) argues that using embodied language to name pathologies and symptoms extends the agency of patients. Reading cookbooks, literature, and memoirs, Hastie proposes that she is not simply anosmic (one who is not able to smell), she is an anosmiac: the -*iac* "offers a maniacal quality to my new identity" (2013: 64). I follow Hastie by developing the dysphagiac, from dysphagia, the inability to swallow, in a series of tastings and performances created in relation to a speculative kitchen appliance designed to bring the dysphagiac back into the social heart of the kitchen (Kelley 2016: 170–78). This chapter expands our maniacal contingent by introducing the "geophagiac." Adding embodied agential "mania" to geophagy contributes to an interdisciplinary project of taking arts-led research as a basis for interrupting a medical establishment quick to label behaviors as pathologies.

My experiments with dysphagia and geophagy in art and performance began in 2006, with *Starvation Seeds*, a series of recipe development experiments and public tasting engagements. This chapter traverses the research I undertook to support my sculptures, performances, and installations and extends beyond my practice to argue for art's capacity to socialize uncommon ingestions. Geophagiac, like dysphagiac and anosmiac, brings maniacal intensity and agency to clinical contexts that sometimes regard patients as objects. I coin these awkward transitional constructions anticipating that "dysphagiac" and "geophagiac" will be overwritten by "eater," "diner," or even "gourmet."

I find parallels between the methodologies of artists and science and technology studies (STS) scholars. Helmreich and Jones write about how arts-led research shares STS scholarship's "analogous" claims "that technoscience must be known not only with respect to its theoretical frameworks, but as socially located discourse and practice" (2018: 98). Taking geophagy as a nexus of medical, artistic, and science studies approaches to the lived reality of eating, this chapter considers how arts-led research interrupts and opens up avenues of comprehension by implicating audiences and analysts in the lived realities of the geophagiac. In participatory art worlds, scholarly distance becomes difficult to maintain. Writing about Diane Borsanto's multispecies ecological art projects, Stephanie Springgay finds that socially and scientifically engaged art practices "transform pedagogy from learning 'about' to the mobility of *thinking-doing,* which demands that the boundaries between human and non-human become viscous" (2016: 2). Helmreich and Jones find mobility through the conventions of anthropology. Being an artist, I will consider art on its own terms, asking how participatory methods produce new attentions and subject positions through activities of tasting and eating. The ways in which these attentions and positions affect or reflect back on anthropological and clinical approaches to geophagy remain to be seen.

Participatory art practices often include food both as motivation for participation as well as a tool for generating intercultural knowledge exchange. For example, drawing from artists brought together in the 2012 exhibition *Feast: Radical Hospitality in Contemporary Art*, Ana Prvački's *The Greeting Committee* (2011–12) offers a taste of Serbian *slatko* as a way to uncover cultural assumptions about the "sweet tongue" (Smith 2013: 278–85). Alison Knowles (2015) has been performing *Make A Salad* since 1962. Her salads range from intimate to industrial in scale and are prepared and consumed as an art of everyday life. Rirkrit Tiravanija's large-scale *pad thai* preparation performances (1992, ongoing) and cookbooks evoke an "art-as-everyday-life" framework with precedent in feminist art and Fluxus, which Nicolas Bourriaud (1998) rebranded as "relational aesthetics" (Smith 2013: 334–45). Since 2006, Michael Rakowitz's *Enemy Kitchen* appears to be a food truck but is actually a participatory art event designed to involve American veterans and eaters in Iraqi cuisine (Smith 2013: 294–305). In these examples and in the soil-focused works I discuss below, food operates within participatory art as material object, as active agent or subject, and/or as reward for participation. As Dean (2019) argues regarding the ways in which art practice interrupts the label "patient," arts-led research challenges assumptions and dichotomies in health and medical discourse. In my experiments and in this chapter, food, art, and eating bodies are positioned through acts of tasting and eating soil, earth, and dirt. My current art practice continues these lines of enquiry, working through tasting and eating as methodological approaches to understanding the intersection of food, taste, and culture.

I read geophagy through contemporary art practices with an eye on how arts-led research creates space for an embodied geophagiac who resists pathology. This reading progresses through three textures. First, I consider soil as material with Laura Parker's *Taste of Place* (2008–11). Parker's soils are loamy, sometimes lush, and agriculturally viable. Next, from agriculture to amulet, I turn to *tierra bendita*, holy earth, as consumed in New Mexico and Guatemala. Drier and sandier, with more clay content, *tierra bendita* is ingested by the spoonful as well as in small packets and dried loaves. The visual cultures of the Santuario de Chimayó sit beside Jennifer Teets and Lorenzo Cirrincione's *Elusive Earths* research initiative and exhibition series (2014–16). Finally, I attend to the practice of eating soil and clay as both a starvation food and a form of resistance by following the Haitian trade in *terre* alongside Fabrice Monteiro's photo series *Marrons* (2011) and Tania Bruguera's performance *The Burden of Guilt* (*El Peso de la Culpa*) (1997–99). These wet muddy clays are the smooth slippery texture of resistance across oceans.

Terroir and Laura Parker's *Taste of Place*

California-based artist Laura Parker created a body of work designed to reveal connections between agriculture and art. With *Palette* (2001), Parker draws out a metaphoric relationship between artists and farmers. Representing soil as the material language of agriculture in the way that the painter's palette establishes a materiality of a painting, a collection of soil samples sit in a four-by-five grid of round containers accompanied by handwritten annotations. When first exhibited, *Palette* inspired a performance that prototyped her subsequent *Taste of Place* series. Parker "glamorized the experience of soil quality by setting small portions of damp soil in wine glasses for people to test its aroma" (Cohn 2004: 71). Wine is perhaps most closely associated with *terroir*, a word that encompasses all factors specific to an agricultural site that might influence or produce certain flavors. Although anything edible made or grown in relation to specific environmental conditions—vegetables, fruits, even cheese—can be interpreted through an articulation of *terroir*, wine dominates most people's associations with *terroir*. Pouring soil into wine glasses suggests applying the actions undertaken in a wine tasting: swirling, smelling, looking, and tasting. With the wine glass presentation, Parker demands that participants bring expanded sensory engagement to the soil that nurtures grapes, dairy cows, fruits, and vegetables.

Writing about how *terroir* contributes to nationalist identity for the stateless nation of Catalonia, Robert Davidson (2007) argues that "taste has become the new 'space,'" for the concept of *terroir* allows a given food or wine produced in a given soil to be portable and localized at once. Mindful of the expertise and subjectivity required for interpreting *terroir*, Davidson attends to the ways in which specific agricultural regions have been leveraged to produce Catalan nationalism through bureaucratic regulation and promotional materials. Considering Davidson's argument about the cultural factors behind taste becoming space through *terroir*, Parker's *Taste of Place* becomes a pedagogical platform for understanding food as emplaced. Terri Cohn situates Parker's practice in a lineage of land and environmental artists committed to disrupting boundaries between nature and culture, writing that "such work creates a somewhat unsettling metaphor for the human ability to sustain and dislocate natural processes" (2004: 73). This language describes the tension between taste and place in Davidson's *terroir*. Parker names and shares specific soils through sensory encounter, storytelling, and an implied, imaginary form of geophagy.

Taste of Place finds audiences joining Parker in a performance that engages soil, dialogue, and materiality across art and agriculture. I witnessed the performance in 2008 at the international festival and conference *Intervene! Interrupt! Rethinking Art as Social Practice* at the University of California Santa Cruz.[1] Parker manages expectations with a short question-and-answer page on the project's website. She writes:

> Am I expected to eat dirt?
> No, you will smell the soil and taste the food grown in it. Through this experience you will taste the soil.
> . . .
> What do I do?
> 1. smell the soil, develop impressions
> 2. taste food grown in the same soil and reflect on each, exploring the relationships
> Parker, n.d.

The process described above suggests that all eating is geophagy. Eating a given fruit or vegetable means that dirt is being eaten, even without directly ingesting the soil samples on offer. Parker's shift from "dirt" to "soil" would suggest that dirt remains, with Mary Douglas (1966), "matter out of place," while "soil" does have a place, and belongs at the table. "Terroir" and "earthiness" do enter food vocabularies, but chalky, dusty, and muddy are not typically desirable attributes for a taste experience. Parker shows how literal or attitudinal geophagiacs are well positioned to consider how food systems create culture, and how the fringes or outsides of systems shift perceptions of everyday meals.

Taste of Place challenges the compulsion to view crops and food products only in terms of their monetary value. Maria Puig de la Bellacasa declares her investment in "conceptual and practical reorientations in soil science that could question … a productionist ethos that subjects soil care, and, more generally, human–soil relations, to the extraction of future economic value" (2015: 698). When artists take up food as a motivator, reward, or pedagogical tool, notions of economic value and temporal dislocation are unmoored from systems of capital. With Parker's work, solidarity produced between the work of artists and the work of farmers questions, with Puig de la Bellacasa, economic futurity as the only motivation for participation. Even as participants are reassured they will not be expected to eat dirt, the performance conveys that we are eating dirt all the time, having smelled, observed, and tasted connections between soil and the foods it acts upon and influences. Without explicitly invoking geophagy as pathology, Parker's soil tastings socialize the idea that everyone is a geophagiac.

Tierra bendita, Tierra santa, and Jennifer Teets and Lorenzo Cirrincione's *Elusive Earths*

This section finds the geophagiac ingesting holy earth. This practice cannot be explained by vitamin deficiency. As with Parker's performance, links between place, taste, and a "productionist ethos" are together troubled by, in this case, the literal rather than conceptual ingestion of clay and earth.

In New Mexico, El Santuario de Chimayó is a pilgrimage destination. Pilgrims enter assisted by crutches and canes, pray to El Niño de Atocha, the pilgrim Christ child who lives there, and eat a spoonful of the dirt from a hole in the ground, called the *posito*. They then leave their crutches behind and walk out healed. Callahan introduces "Eating Dirt," his article about geophagy, with a vivid description of *tierra bendita* at Chimayó (2003: 1016). Pilgrims arriving at El Santuario de Chimayó enter "a low-ceilinged room off the main entrance. There, a hole (the *posito*), half a meter across, pierces the floor. Beside it, someone has left a plastic spoon to aid the faithful. Beyond the spoon, beneath the opening, lies only dirt, only the deep-red dirt of Chimayó" (2003: 1016). Callahan does not mention the earth-moving vehicles that have been in use just outside El Santuario during several of my visits—Chimayó's soil moves around and is rearranged on a regular basis. Undertaking an investigation for the Center for Skeptical Inquiry, Joe Nickell (2013) refutes local legends that the *posito* is refilled without human intervention by locating and photographing "the storage area where five-gallon containers of the reddish soil are stored." A stack of earth-filled buckets sit beside a handcart, a bag of ice melt, and the long-handled wicker collection baskets passed up and down the pews during mass.

Chimayó is a challenging place to live: the Española Valley faces crises of addiction and drug trafficking that arise in many small towns in the United States (La Luz Baez

Figure 12.1 The *posito* can be seen in the back of the room through the doorway to the right. The walls are lined with crutches cast off by pilgrims. El Niño lives in the small enclosure to the left beside the crutches in the foreground. 'Santuario de Chimayó Prayer Room With Discarded Crutches and Testimonials' by Marshall Henrie, 2004. Available online: https://commons.wikimedia.org/wiki/File:Santuario_de_Chimayo_Prayer_Room_with_discarded_crutches_and_tesminonials.JPG (accessed 15 June, 2019). Licensed under CC-BY-SA 3.0 (https://creativecommons.org/licenses/by-sa/3.0/deed.en).

2010). The miracles that take place in the chapel relate to opioid addiction—crutches and casts signal pain managed through "mass pharmaceutical regimes" and "maximum treatment" (Dumit 2012: 210, 215). I have visited Chimayó many times, sometimes to buy a rug at Trujillo's or chiles from the Holy Chile cart outside the *Santuario*. Most memorably, after five breaks across both feet, I went to Chimayó as a pilgrim instead of a tourist. The piles of braces and crutches left for El Niño provided material evidence that *tierra bendita* might help my feet. (Almost twenty years later, I have not had another break.) The plastic spoon makes a hole in the ground into medicine, suggesting that a complex process not unlike transubstantiation occurs when a pilgrim visits El Niño and consumes Chimayó's red earth. The priests' activity refilling the *posito* does not contradict local legends that the *posito* fills itself, a workflow that supports a logic of transubstantiation.

In eastern Guatemala, clay is sieved, molded or stamped with a holy image, and sun-dried. The resulting tablets are known as *pan del Señor* or *tierra santa*. Abrahams notes the commercial trade in *tierra santa* tablets, and observes that "the soil is used as a pharmaceutical, and with its religious associations it provides psychological comfort" (2013: 446). Captioning an image of a young woman wearing a red-and-white checked frilly apron, Abrahams explains that she "is daubing candy makers' red dye onto the tablets to simulate the blood of Jesus" (ibid.). Her basket and the pile of baskets behind her suggest that she will be selling the tablets, which are pale gray in color, similar to the bentonite clay sold as supplements. The food dye contrasts with the pale gray clay body. In Chimayó, the already-red earth does not require supplemental coloring to evoke blood.

Similar to the recipes, process, and purpose of *pan del Señor* or *tierra santa*, *terra sigillata*, Lemnos bread, or sealed earth has been excavated from ancient sites in Greece. Writing in a volume devoted to *A History of Geology and Medicine*, Arthur MacGregor defines these medicinal not-quite-foodways as "clays with perceived medicinal or alexipharmic properties" (2013: 113). Lemnos bread is a living practice linked to contemporary ingestions. Kaopectate could be considered alexipharmic—an adsorbent antidote to an obvious ailment. Kaopectate could be read as adaptive and protective, helping to stabilize the gut by coating, an amulet against loose stool. Many species have been eating clay in order to eat other things for tens of thousands of years. Archaeologist Michael Rowland (2002) theorizes that people adapted to poisonous plants by selectively ingesting clays and charcoals capable of adsorbing toxins. Rowland counters "a residual distrust of [Indigenous] knowledge" by shifting an understanding of geophagy from "aberrant or pathological" to "the most fundamental human plant-processing detoxification technique, with behavioural antecedents in a wide range of other species" (2002: 59–60). By coating their insides with clay, ancient geophagiacs were able to process poisons. Clays and charcoals buffer by coating and bind any extra liquid produced through the body's efforts to flush out whatever is irritating the digestive tract.

Lemnos bread inspired curator Jennifer Teets to collaborate with artist Lorenzo Cirrincione and develop an ongoing research project and exhibition series called *Elusive Earths*. A series of exhibitions have commissioned new works and restaged existing works created by artists who engage earth, clay, and soil (Preston 2014; Córdova 2016). Dedicated to geophagy as cultural practice, *Elusive Earths* works "to take further inventory of ingestible clays and the imaginaries created around them; to look further at our vested belief in their truth, so as to ruminate on potent pharmacological convictions in an effort to expose a point of vulnerability within an economy seeking to commodify the longing for a cure" (*documenta 14*, 2017). Interested in how geophagy adds a moral and political element to digestion, given the commodification, trade, and counterfeit of Lemnos bread (Abrahams 2013: 444), Teets and Cirrincione follow geophagy from Ancient Greece to Guatemala and Oaxaca.

Works included across the exhibition series involve artists with materials and concepts drawn from the geophagy imaginary. For example, Laura Preston (2014) describes Anicka Yi's contribution to the Brussels iteration as "boiling buckets of inorganic and organic materials, *Convox Dialer Double Distance Of A Shining Path, Diamond Age, Cobweb* (2011–14), bubbling up from the basement." Yi presents a visceral work of conceptual recipe art, appending an ingredients list to her buckets that includes "Korean thermal clay," "three pumice stones," "hate crimes," "female sweat," "bat virus," and "large chicken ribcage bones" (Preston 2014). Jean-Marie Appriou built a ceramic environment to host "sculptures of various types of sticky, oozing or burnt matter," which included soil from Lemnos (ibid.). Ajay Kurian's *How many faces does a coin have? (parts and wholes) 1* (2014) chars rounds of bread until indium placed atop each loaf melts to form abstract metallic insignia that evoke the stamps imprinted on *pan de tierra bendita* (Ross 2014).

Elusive Earths maps onto scholarly research into geophagy, including Abrahams's medical geology survey article and Callahan's lively and personal investigation. Cirrincione created a documentary video (2016) about the process of creating *pan de tierra bendita*, following an unnamed woman through the process of kneading, shaping, and stamping "loaves" of clay. Cirrincione asks occasional questions about her methods and the process. This video could be read alongside Abrahams's photos of geophagiacs at work in Tanzanian salt licks (2013: 438) and John Hunter's photo of a *tierra santa* vendor (2013: 446). The video documents a practice in the same straightforward way as the photos reproduced in medical journals. Yet, the *Elusive Earths* exhibitions are different from science and different again from ethnography. Teets and Cirrincione's research into a single family lineage carrying geophagy recipes from Guatemala to Oaxaca shows how art and curatorial processes invite inclusive consideration of geophagiacs. As with Parker's *Taste of Place*, when confronted with material sensory encounter, participants cannot stand outside of the lived reality of eating soil, earth, and clay.

Teets (2014) writes that "this research regards what I call the naked rudeness of a moral economy of the land—what it is like to devour the earth's problems and contents in one whole and spit them out again." Perhaps the small-scale excavation of clays used in *pan de tierra bendita* and the earth-moving vehicles combing the land and filling the buckets at El Santuario de Chimayó could be viewed as tiny extraction economies. Teets imagines that *terra sigillata* would be spat out, rejected, or refused, rather than swallowed. This rejection would imply a political or moral position on land more broadly. This brief reference to spitting out highlights the bodily processes *tierra bendita* depends on for legibility. If *tierra bendita* functions as protection, an edible amulet for the gut, then geophagiacs are much more likely to shit out rather than spit out "the earth's problems and contents" (Teets 2014). "Becoming geological" hinges on incorporation, not doubly extractive rejection.

Recalling Henri Cartier Bresson's objection to Ansel Adams and Edward Weston's "photographing rocks" in the face of social crisis, the "world going to pieces," Heather Davis and Etienne Turpin ask, "If art is now a practice condemned to a *homolithic earth*—that is, to a world 'going to pieces' as the literal sediment of human activity—how can aesthetic practices address the social and political spheres that are being set in stone? Becoming-geological undoes aesthetic sensibilities and ungrounds political commitments" (2015: 3). Elsewhere in Davis and Turpin's anthology *Art in the Anthropocene* (2015), Bruno Latour observes a shift from "artists capturing some sort of aesthetic aspect of science" to a "common articulation of the Anthropocene," a formulation that reinforces the move from object-observed to social practice relations (2015: 47).[2] Becoming-geological has unanticipated aesthetic and political effects and agencies when one becomes geological by way of ingestion. Arguments about the geological record rarely consider its taste and edibility. *Elusive Earths* and Parker's *Taste of Place* mobilize aesthetics as grounded politics through supposedly inert clay and sediment. Art tangibly demonstrates some of the key commitments of science and technology studies by convincing publics that science has politics, and political force.

Geophagiac Life and Death: Fabrice Monteiro's *Marrons*, Tania Bruguera's *The Burden of Guilt* (*El Peso de la Culpa*)

The tradition of *tierra bendita* might be practiced by a range of people, some hungry, some well-fed, but the geophagiac pilgrims who ingest Chimayó's holy earth do this as a supplementary activity of religious devotion. *Tierra bendita* is neither a meal replacement nor a protest. This section focuses on the Caribbean and its diasporas, another cultural context for geophagiac belonging, finding geophagy in performance and as reenactment in the work of photographer Fabrice Monteiro and performance artist Tania Bruguera.

Haiti's food economy regularly appears in the media. "Mud cookies" are described as a direct consequence of the country's food shortages. They appear to have a high clay content, although I cannot tell from photographs if the clay has the almost spongy absorbent properties of bentonite. They are formed by hand in the same manner as one might work to form plates and bowls with a wet clay, almost a slip, on a dry surface, then are sunbaked into crunchy plates. With headlines such as "Haiti's poor resort to eating mud as prices rise," "Dirt Poor Haitians Eat Mud Cookies To Survive," and "Desperate Haitians Survive On Mud Cookies," media reports tell a story about Haitian geophagiacs resorting to the practice because of economic hardship, deforestation, famine, and scarcity.[3]

Haiti imports most of its increasingly expensive food supply, but scarcity did not produce geophagy: pregnant women and children have eaten the mountain clay used in *terre* (which US media translate as "mud cookies") for a very long time, and will likely continue to do so even if Haiti's food shortages become surpluses. Martin Munro and Elizabeth Walcott-Hackshaw ask, "Is this the ultimate irony: a people long fed myths of land and authenticity by Haitian culture finally, literally, living on, consuming, and receiving the meager nourishment of the dried-out land? Who said a people cannot survive on its myths?" (2005: xi). Munro and Walcott-Hackshaw are careful to caution that it is "almost impossible to avoid clichés when thinking about 'the first black republic in the New World' or 'the poorest country in the Western Hemisphere,'" especially in an arts context (ibid.).

Consumers of *terre* know the biscuits are not the most nutritious possible foodstuff. Marie Noel sells and eats the biscuits. She reports, "I'm hoping one day I'll have enough food to eat, so I can stop eating these. I know it's not good for me" (Katz 2008). Marie Noel understands that *terre* meals are not good for her because she understands the difference between eating clay as a substitute for food and eating clay as one food of many. Although unreported in stories focused on *terre*'s role in famine conditions, if asked, Noel likely would have explained that there are appropriate times for supplementing with geophagy, for example during pregnancy. Given Haiti's connection

Figure 12.2 Shaping *terre* before drying in the sun. The process of flattening the portions of mixture shows the dough's soft and wet texture. "Haitian Dirt Biscuits" by Feed My Starving Children, 2011. Available online: https://commons.wikimedia.org/wiki/File:Haitian_Dirt_Biscuits.jpg (accessed June 15, 2019). Licensed under CC-BY 2.0 (https://creativecommons.org/licenses/by/2.0/deed.en).

to West African culture through the Middle Passage and the presence of appropriate clays nearby, this knowledge would be circulating in a culture of geophagiacs.

Supporting the findings of researchers from medical geology and medicine more broadly, anthropologists Andrew Wiley and Solomon Katz (1998) argue that geophagy during pregnancy and early childhood has nutritional value and should not be pathologized. They attribute geophagy in the US South to "the persistence of a tradition with African origins" and call for more ethnographic analysis of geophagy in the US South and around the world, citing the role that ethnographic and anthropological study could play in "overcom[ing] the widespread bias against this practice" (Wiley and Katz 1998: 534, 543). The women in Wiley and Katz's study treat geophagy as a supplemental "snack food," consumed only during pregnancy, and with a medicinal intent. Marie Noel, her children, and other Haitians (including men) share diasporic knowledge formations about geophagy with the women Wiley and Katz studied; however, they make, sell, and eat *terre* outside of these traditions because of famine conditions.

Fabrice Monteiro produced *Marrons* in 2011. Drawing on archival research, Monteiro recreated shackles, collars, and other disciplinary devices from the height of the trans-Atlantic slave trade. He then staged collaborative performance portraits incorporating the devices with men living in Benin, where slavery decimated the population and transported people, foods, and culture, including the Vodun religion, elsewhere, including to Haiti. The portrait series features two masks. One would limit the senses, with heavy metal eyelids acting as blinders and a curved shape covering the face and blocking peripheral vision. The other restricts the ears and nose, but allows vision. A rough sieve fits over the mouth, which the mask muzzles, blocking the person wearing it from eating anything that would not pass through the holes. As if he had attempted to drink, rivulets of water spill across his chest.

In their comprehensive *What the Slaves Ate: Recollections of African American Foods and Foodways from the Slave Narratives* (2009), Herbert Covey and Dwight Eisnach analyze historical records to find that despite its Ancient Greek origins, Southern whites "perceived the West African-based cultural practice of eating or chewing clay or soil as a disease peculiar to slaves" (2009: 17).[4] The pathology of geophagy becomes bound to white supremacist ideologies. Enslaved geophagiacs were punished in countless ways, "including using mild purgatives, threats, punishments, or iron masks or gags, [and] cutting off the heads of those dying from the practice" (Covey and Eisnach 2009: 17). Writing about Monteiro's *Marrons*, anthropologist Mark Auslander offers that "Such devices were used to punish slaves who attempted to eat fruit or sugar cane in the fields; the contraption allowed them to drink with difficulty, but not to eat or speak" (2016: 64). Recalling Mary Douglas and "matter out of place," these masks embody the ways in which food and dirt "patterns" can be violently enforced, even weaponized.

Covey and Eisnach (2009: 17) conclude that enslaved people likely ate clay due at least in part to malnutrition. Masks in both *Marrons* and in the archive could be interpreted as punishment for seeking adequate nutrition. The masks act as insurance: enslaved people became sick from eating dirt combined with malnutrition, and because eating dirt was seen as a path to suicide, the mask protected the slave owner's investment. "*Marrons*," "maroons," or in Haitian "*mawons*," identifies enslaved people who have escaped and are living freely, often in remote areas. Titling the series *Marrons* implies a narrative trajectory which suggests that eating dirt may have been a successful act of resistance that facilitated escape. Haitian *terre* and Munro and Walcott-Hackshaw's connection between eating earth and eating myth connect back to the ways in which resistance to enslavement precipitates a return to myth and the earth by ingestion.

Geophagiac resistance inspired performance artist Tania Bruguera to create *The Burden of Guilt* (*El Peso de la Culpa*) (1997–99). Monteiro and Bruguera share a methodological commitment to archival research and reenactment—while Monteiro recreates the disciplinary tools of slavery, responding to the spontaneous embodied responses of his subjects, Bruguera reenacts the geophagia that precipitated a mass suicide of Indigenous people under Spanish occupation in Cuba. Reading Jamaican writer and philosopher Sylvia Wynter's unpublished manuscript "Black Metamorphosis," Yusoff considers how slavery and revolt co-constitute one another and draw strength from an allegiance with soil: "Kissing the earth before rebellions was an oath-act that maintained a social contract with the earth often to the point of death" (2018: 37). This protest, a kiss too deep, resonates across time and social space centuries later. Barred from performing at the Sixth Havana Biennial, Bruguera staged the performance's first iteration outside her house. Burdened by a headless lamb carcass around her neck, Bruguera mixed Cuban earth with water and salt and consumed the result for about an hour.

The Cuban expression "*comer tierra*" (eat dirt) refers to this specific mass suicide and through that association has come to mean "to suffer strong hardship" (Mosquera 2010). José Esteban Muñoz situates the performance in a "politics of introjection" (2008: 259–63), where "guilt over colonial brutality … organizes and forms this particular origin narrative of Cuban consciousness" (2008: 254). Beside the masks of *Marrons*, Bruguera's politics of introjection, "holding guilt," in Muñoz's words, recalls the ways in which soil and earth contain identity, resistance, and autonomy over the body and life force. "Holding" evokes the intestinal activity desired by geophagiacs who ingest clay to stabilize their stool. "Holding" suggests the health complications that would arise if geophagiacs overindulge. (Rowland cites a study where nearly half of a group of geophagiacs in the Kimberly became ill due to obstruction of the colon [2002: 56].) Holding evokes responsibility, oaths, and promises: "I'm holding you to that." By resuscitating and embodying geophagiac actions across history and life/ death barriers, Bruguera and Monteiro locate an unconscious "archive of feeling" (Cvetkovich 2003) in soils both in the ground and walking around, ingested by, passing through, and stilling bodies. Soil becomes a material substance of introjection, a tangible location for unconscious actions made conscious through performance and reenactment.

Conclusion

This chapter figures the geophagiac, shaped and embodied by contemporary art practices that insist on sensory participation and imagination in order to resist pathology and stigma. Geophagiacs are poor, rich, young, old, sick, healthy. We eat dirt in uneasy, complex ways, knowingly, unknowingly, consciously, unconsciously. There are no simple connections to be made between *terre*-eating Haitians, *terroir*-sniffing Californians, reenactors of suicidal protests against genocide, two-year-olds in the garden, Kaopectate drinkers, and New Age bentonite-eaters. This chapter's textural progression moves from fertile loam to sacred soil to muddy resistance and oath-acts in order to reflect on how contemporary artists ingesting soil and clay take up geophagy to ask serious questions about agriculture, spirituality, health, and resistance. These approaches dismantle a pathologized orientation to geophagy by presenting a depth of struggle and knowledge that cannot be contained by the racist logics that coined the word in the nineteenth century.

Texture presented a significant challenge when I engaged geophagy in my art practice. With many visits to Chimayó under my belt and in my stomach, I started researching Haitian *terre* to supplement *Starvation Seeds*, an arts-led research initiative that started with humanitarian aid and famine food and grew to include three case studies in fringe foods and alternative modes of ingestion. Between 2007 and 2009, I made several attempts at mud cookies, with varying success. My earliest effort used garden soil from Los Gatos, California, beginning close to home. Loamy garden soil, as I anticipated, was not a successful biscuit base: the dough could not hold its shape, and it ended up back in my garden enriched with sugar, salt, and oil. My second attempt combined finely processed commercially available edible bentonite powder with water, sugar, and oil. This yielded a sweet, gummy paste that baked into sticky biscuits that were compellingly gray in color and crunchy in texture, and left particles between the teeth, which added an unexpected finish to their mouth feel. In my third attempt, I sought out a recipe from a commercial bentonite vendor and, following their advice, used flour and grains. Doubling the amount of bentonite specified in the vendor's About Clay website's recipe archive,[5] I made oatmeal biscuits that baked and ate like wheat-based biscuits but left a gritty after texture. About Clay addresses the challenge of destigmatizing and depathologizing geophagy and pica by appealing to New-Age and health-conscious consumers with its mandate to "get more clay into your diet." Although the bentonite-only biscuits were edible, the oatmeal biscuits were more conventionally palatable, if particulate. These biscuits were easy to socialize. They resembled shapes and textures that go into the mouth every day, and audiences were comfortable enough to try a bite.

I worked with the biscuits in performance in two contexts. First, I trialed them at research seminars. My presentation included a tasting. The seminar table evokes a dining table; most people want to eat in the middle of a seminar, and peer pressure compels participation. Second, I walked around with a tray of biscuits at a museum opening. This, too, is a social space where people want to eat, especially off of trays— but I found that of the various foods I have presented with the comfortable trappings of catering, audiences were least convinced by these grey, vaguely slimy biscuits.

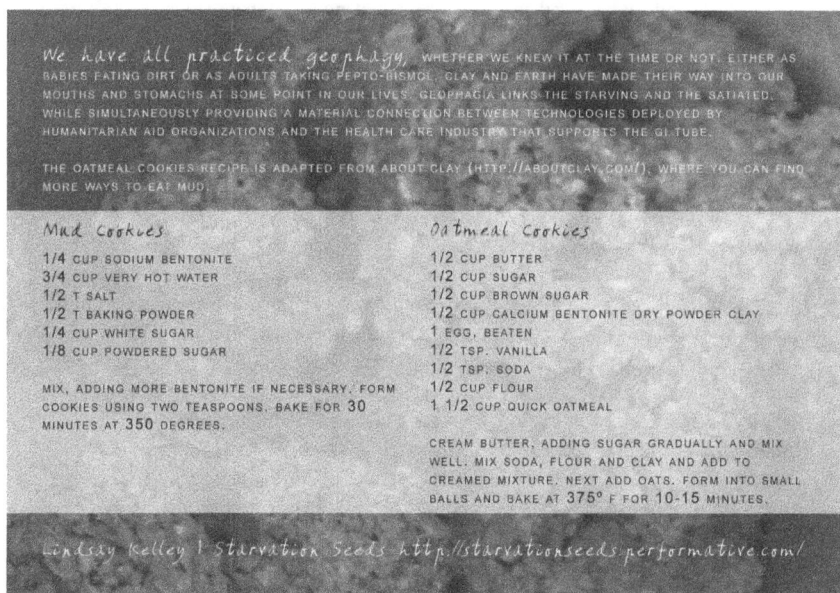

We have all practiced geophagy, WHETHER WE KNEW IT AT THE TIME OR NOT. EITHER AS BABIES EATING DIRT OR AS ADULTS TAKING PEPTO-BISMOL, CLAY AND EARTH HAVE MADE THEIR WAY INTO OUR MOUTHS AND STOMACHS AT SOME POINT IN OUR LIVES. GEOPHAGIA LINKS THE STARVING AND THE SATIATED, WHILE SIMULTANEOUSLY PROVIDING A MATERIAL CONNECTION BETWEEN TECHNOLOGIES DEPLOYED BY HUMANITARIAN AID ORGANIZATIONS AND THE HEALTH CARE INDUSTRY THAT SUPPORTS THE GI TUBE.

THE OATMEAL COOKIES RECIPE IS ADAPTED FROM ABOUT CLAY (HTTP://ABOUTCLAY.COM/), WHERE YOU CAN FIND MORE WAYS TO EAT MUD.

Mud Cookies

1/4 CUP SODIUM BENTONITE
3/4 CUP VERY HOT WATER
1/2 T SALT
1/2 T BAKING POWDER
1/4 CUP WHITE SUGAR
1/8 CUP POWDERED SUGAR

MIX, ADDING MORE BENTONITE IF NECESSARY. FORM COOKIES USING TWO TEASPOONS. BAKE FOR 30 MINUTES AT 350 DEGREES.

Oatmeal Cookies

1/2 CUP BUTTER
1/2 CUP SUGAR
1/2 CUP BROWN SUGAR
1/2 CUP CALCIUM BENTONITE DRY POWDER CLAY
1 EGG, BEATEN
1/2 TSP. VANILLA
1/2 TSP. SODA
1/2 CUP FLOUR
1 1/2 CUP QUICK OATMEAL

CREAM BUTTER, ADDING SUGAR GRADUALLY AND MIX WELL. MIX SODA, FLOUR AND CLAY AND ADD TO CREAMED MIXTURE. NEXT ADD OATS. FORM INTO SMALL BALLS AND BAKE AT 375° F FOR 10-15 MINUTES.

Lindsay Kelley | Starvation Seeds http://starvationseeds.performative.com/

Figure 12.3 Lindsay Kelley, recipe card produced for *Starvation Seeds* (2008). Reproduced with permission of the artist.

These concluding anecdotes about baking with clay and offering the results to well-fed museum-goers offer another perspective on how arts-led research intervenes in the literatures of geophagy—medical geology, medicine more broadly, anthropology, archaeology, and more. As articulated throughout this chapter, participatory and performance art projects that use quotidian eating experiences as frameworks for advancing aesthetic and cultural engagement have the capacity to destigmatize and normalize such practices. With geophagy scholars agreeing that the practice should not be perceived as a pathology while lamenting the societal structures that position geophagy as a pathology, including enduring colonial violence and racism, the question becomes, what actions and affects will produce change? For Springgay, an art of interdisciplinary participatory action has the capacity to "push us beyond the experience of art, where experience is understood as resemblance, towards an affective pedagogy of movement" (2016: 2). By considering arts-led research in interdisciplinary analyses of geophagy, untold stories and expanded subject positions for audiences yield a self-reflexive research praxis that learns movement, of both the social body and its bowels.

Notes

1   Full disclosure that I was paid coordinator of the festival.
2   Of course artists have been contributing more than aesthetic interpretation all along. For example, the Harrisons were making work more than thirty years ago that produced scientific findings. Terri Cohn's genealogy of earth artists produced results beyond interpretation as well, in some cases creating long-term experimental sites that continue to generate data across disciplines.
3   Examples of headlines include: Associated Press, "Haiti's poor resort to eating mud as prices rise," available from http://www.msnbc.msn.com/id/22902512/; Benno Schmidt, "Dirt Poor Haitians Eat Mud Cookies To Survive," available from http://www.huffingtonpost.com/2009/02/19/dirt-poor-haitians-eat-mu_n_168339.html; and Associated Press, "Desperate Haitians Survive On Mud Cookies," available from http://www.cbsnews.com/stories/2008/01/30/world/main3768430.shtml?source=RSSattr=H OME_3768430. (The first and third articles are the same AP story with different headlines from MSNBC and CBS.) All links were accessed in 2007 and most no longer work, but I include them to show media outlet attribution for each headline.
4   The *OED*'s etymology of "geophagia" includes the previously mentioned "diseased appetite" early usage penned by geographer Charles Lyell (1850), who observed geophagy among enslaved people in his *A Second Visit to the United States of North America*. Lyell becomes one of the key case studies in Yusoff's *A Billion Black Anthropocenes or None* (2018), epitomizing "White Geology" (74–82).
5   The About Clay recipe archive I consulted in 2007 no longer exists, but the recipe remains in the form of a recipe card I published alongside my performances. I found the Earth's Natural Clay website, which carries the same general ethos as the one I consulted in 2007, seeking to "get more clay into your diet" by "boosting the health aspects" of otherwise conventional biscuits (Earth's Natural Clay, "Vegan Bentonite Clay Breakfast Cookie," https://www.earthsnaturalclay.com/blogs/blog/87079495-vegan-bentonite-clay-breakfast-cookie; accessed March 19, 2019).

References

Abrahams, P. (2013), "Geophagy and the Involuntary Ingestion of Soil," in O. Selinus (ed.), *Essentials of Medical Geology: Revised Edition*, 433–54, Dordrecht: Springer.

Abrahams, P., M. Follansbee, A. Hunt, B. Smith, and J. Wragg (2006), "Iron Nutrition and Possible Lead Toxicity: An Appraisal of Geophagy Undertaken by Pregnant Women of UK Asian Communities," *Applied Geochemistry*, 21(1): 98–108.

Auslander, M. (2016), "By Iron Possessed: Fabrice Monteiro's *Maroons: The Fugitive Slaves*," *African Arts*, 49 (3): 62–67.

Bourriaud, N. (1998), *Esthétique relationnelle/Relational Aesthetics*, Dijon: Les Presses du Réel.

Callahan, G. (2003), "Eating Dirt," *Emerging Infectious Diseases*, 9 (8): 1016–21.

Cirrincione, L. (2016), "Pan de tierra bendita: sealed earth and clay eating in Oaxaca (Elusive Earths III)," *YouTube*, posted by user "Lorenzo Cirrincione," May 7 [https://www.youtube.com/watch?v=BuWGxIv_uKo; accessed March 20, 2019].

Cohn, T. (2004), "How Far Are You From the Farm: A Mile or a Generation? The Agricultural Art of Laura Parker," *Places*, 16 (3): 70–73.

Córdova, K. (2016), "Elusive Earths III," *Art Agenda*, June 7 [https://www.art-agenda.com/features/238850/elusive-earths-iii; accessed March 20, 2019].

Covey, H. and D. Eisnach (2009), *What the Slaves Ate: Recollections of African American Foods and Foodways from the Slave Narratives*, Santa Barbara, CA: Greenwood Press.

Cvetkovich, A. (2003), *An Archive of Feelings: Trauma, Sexuality, and Lesbian Public Cultures*, Durham, NC: Duke University Press.

Davidson, R. (2007), "*Terroir* and Catalonia," *Journal of Catalan Studies*, 10: 39–53.

Davis, H. and E. Turpin, eds. (2015), *Art in the Anthropocene: Encounters Among Aesthetics, Politics, Environments and Epistemologies*, London: Open Humanities Press.

Dean, R. (2019), "The Patient: Biomedical Art and Curatorial Care," doctoral thesis, University of New South Wales, Sydney.

documenta 14 (2017), "*Elusive Earths* at Otobong Nkanga's *Carved to Flow* with Lorenzo Cirrincione and Jennifer Teets," June 16 [https://www.documenta14.de/en/calendar/23037/elusive-earths; accessed March 20, 2019].

Douglas, M. (1966), *Purity and Danger*, London: Routledge.

Dumit, J. (2012), *Drugs for Life: How Pharmaceutical Companies Define Our Health*, Durham, NC: Duke University Press.

Geissler, P. W., C. E. Shulman, R. J. Prince, W. Mutemi, C. Mnazi, H. Friis et al. (1998), "Geophagy, Iron Status and Anaemia Among Pregnant Women on the Coast of Kenya," *Transactions of the Royal Society of Tropical Medicine and Hygiene*, 92 (5): 549–53.

"Geophagy, n.," *OED Online*, Oxford University Press [https://www.oed.com/view/Entry/77799?redirectedFrom=geophagy; accessed June 9, 2019].

Hastie, A. (2013), "Senseless Eating," *parallax*, 19 (1): 64–73.

Helmreich, S. (2016), *Sounding the Limits of Life: Essays in the Anthropology of Biology and Beyond*, Princeton, NJ: Princeton University Press.

Helmreich, S. and C. A. Jones (2018), "Science/Art/Culture Through an Oceanic Lens," *Annual Review of Anthropology*, 47: 97–115.

Katz, J. (2008), "Poor Haitians Resort to Eating Dirt," *Associated Press*, January 29, archived in *Free Republic* [http://www.freerepublic.com/focus/f-news/1971507/posts; accessed March 20, 2019].

Kawai, K., E. Saathoff, G. Antelman, G. Msamanga, and W. Fawzi (2009), "Geophagy (Soil-eating) in Relation to Anemia and Helminth Infection Among HIV-Infected

Pregnant Women in Tanzania," *American Journal of Tropical Medicine and Hygiene*, 80 (1): 36–43.

Kelley, L. (2016), *Bioart Kitchen: Art, Feminism and Technoscience*, London: I. B. Tauris.

Kim-Jung, L., C. Holquist, and J. Phillips (2004), "Kaopectate Reformulation and Upcoming Labeling Changes," *Drug Topics*, April 19: 58–60.

Knowles, A. (2015), "Make A Salad," interview with J. Sherman, *Lucky Peach*, Summer.

La Luz Baez, W. A. (2010), *Hispanos in the Valley of Death: Street-Level Trauma, Cultural-Post Traumatic Stress Disorder, Overdoses, and Suicides in North Central New Mexico*, Albuquerque: University of New Mexico [https://digitalrepository.unm.edu/soc_etds/25; accessed March 20, 2019].

Lyell, C. (1850), *A Second Visit to the United States of North America*, vol. 2, London: John Murray.

MacGregor, A. (2013), "Medicinal *Terra Sigillata*: A Historical, Geographical and Typological Review," in C. J. Duffin, R. T. J. Moody, and C. Gardner-Thorpe (eds.), *A History of Geology and Medicine*, 113–36, London: Geological Society of London.

Mosquera, G. (2010), "Cuba in Tania Bruguera's work: The Body Is the Social Body," in H. Posner, G. Mosquera, and C. Lambert-Beatty, *Tania Bruguera: On the Political Imaginary*, 23–35, Milan: Charta.

Muñoz, J. (2008), "Performing Greater Cuba: Tania Bruguera and the Burden of Guilt," *Women & Performance: A Journal of Feminist Theory*, 11 (2): 251–65.

Munro, M. and E. Walcott-Hackshaw (2005), "Introduction: Reinterpreting the Haitian Revolution and Its Cultural Aftershocks," *Small Axe*, 9 (2): viii–xiii.

Neimanis, A. (2017), *Bodies of Water: Posthuman Feminist Phenomenology*, London: Bloomsbury Academic.

Nickell, J. (2013), "Investigative Files: Miracle Dirt of Chimayó," *Skeptical Inquirer*, 37 (1), January/February [https://www.csicop.org/si/show/miracle_dirt_of_chimayo; accessed March 20, 2019].

Parker, L. (n.d.), *Taste of Place: An Installation by Laura Parker* [http://www.lauraparkerstudio.com/taste/; accessed August 3, 2019].

Preston, J. (2014), "Elusive Earths: Établissement d'en face projects, Brussels, Belgium," *Frieze*, December 15 [https://frieze.com/article/elusive-earths; accessed March 20, 2019].

Puig de la Bellacasa, M. (2015), "Making Time for Soil: Technospecific Futurity and the Pace of Care," *Social Studies of Science*, 45 (5): 691–716.

Ross, A. (2014), "Flet," *SpazioA*, November 15 [http://www.spazioa.it/index.php/flet/; accessed March 20, 2019].

Rowland, M. (2002), "Geophagy: An Assessment of Implications for the Development of Australian Indigenous Plant Processing Technologies," *Australian Aboriginal Studies*, 1: 50–65.

Smith, L. (2012), *Decolonizing Methodologies: Research and Indigenous Peoples*, 2nd edition, London: Zed Books.

Smith, S. (2013), *Feast: Radical Hospitality in Contemporary Art*, Chicago, IL: University of Chicago Press.

Springgay, S. (2016), "Learning to be Affected in Contemporary Art," *PORTAL Journal of Multidisciplinary International Studies*, 13 (1): 1–6.

Teets, J. (2014), "Jean-Marie Appriou, Piotr Bosacki, Lorenzo Cirrincione, Ajay Kurian, Anna Maria Maiolino, Robertas Narkus, Georgia Sagri, Anicka Yi: *Elusive Earths* Curated by Jannifer Teets," *Établissement d'en face* [http://www.etablissementdenface.com/in-the-past/jennifer-teets-elusive-earths; accessed March 20, 2019].

Vermeer, D. (1966), "Geophagy Among the Tiv of Nigeria," *Annals of the Association of American Geographers*, 56 (2): 197–204.

Wiley, A. and S. Katz (1998), "Geophagy in Pregnancy: A Test of a Hypothesis," *Current Anthropology*, 39 (4): 532–45.

Young, S., S. Khalfan, T. Farag, J. Kavle, S. Ali, H. Hajji et al. (2010), "Association of Pica with Anemia and Gastrointestinal Distress among Pregnant Women in Zanzibar, Tanzania," *American Journal of Tropical Medicine and Hygiene*, 83 (1): 144–51.

Young, S., P. Sherman, J. Lucks, and G. Pelto (2011), "Why On Earth? Evaluating Hypotheses about the Physiological Functions of Human Geophagy," *Quarterly Review of Biology*, 86 (2): 97–120.

Yusoff, K. (2018), *A Billion Black Anthropocenes or None*, Minneapolis, MN: Minnesota University Press.

Index

Page numbers in **bold** refer to figures.